The MOST asked
prophecy
questions

By Dr. John Ankerberg & Dr. Renald Showers
with Cathy Sims

ATRI
PUBLISHING

Edited by Cathy Sims

Layout by Beth Lamberson and Amy Dean

Cover Design by Amy Dean, ATRI Publishing, Chattanooga, Tennessee

ISBN 9781941135143

Printed in the United States of America

Table of Contents

Introduction 9

Question #1 11
    Why has God scheduled future events for planet earth?

Question #2 23
    What is the setting of the sealed scroll in Revelation 5?

Question #3 30
    Will Christ return to earth as a victorious conqueror?

Question #4 33
    Will God restore theocratic kingdom rule?

Question #5 38
    Who are the citizens of the Millennium?

Question #6 42
    Who are the "great multitude" that John saw in Revelation 7?

Question #7 45
    What is God's promise to Satan?

Question #8 53
    What do the dry bones in Ezekiel 37 represent?

Question #9 56
    What is God's eternal plan for the Jews?

Question #10 62
    Why will Russia lead the attack against Israel?

Question #11 64
    When will the Battle of Gog and Magog occur?

Question #12 66
    Is the Battle of Gog and Magog prophesied in Ezekiel 38-39
    the same as the one in Revelation 20:7-10?

Question #13 68
    What was Daniel's vision of the future?

Question #14 91
    What if you have not trusted Jesus Christ as your Savior before
    the Tribulation?

Question #15 93
Who are the 144,000 in Revelation?
Question #16 95
Will there be a new Temple built in Jerusalem, and what
preparations are being made for it?
Question #17 104
When does the Rapture take place?
Question #18 109
What is a mystery?
Question #19 111
Why is Jesus' teaching in John 14 an analogy of a Jewish
wedding which infers a Pre-Tribulation Rapture of the Church?
Question #20 117
Could Jesus return at any moment? Is Christ's return imminent?
Question #21 123
Where is the imminent return of Christ taught in the book
of James?
Question #22 126
What will your future be if you do not trust Jesus as your Savior?
Question #23 129
What is meant by "the Day of the Lord"?
Question #24 132
Will Christians escape God's wrath in the time period called "the
Day of the Lord "?
Question #25 137
When will the Lord come "as a thief in the night"?
Question #26 141
When will that future Day of the Lord begin?
Question #27 149
What is the mark of the beast?
Question #28 152
Will Christians go through the Tribulation? What does the phrase
"the hour of temptation" mean?
Question #29 154
Does the Bible teach two separate comings of the Lord?
Question #30 156
At the Rapture, and at the Second Coming, who will be taken
to Heaven, who will be left on earth?

Question #31 159

What does the Parable of the Dragnet tell us about the order of events during the Second Coming?

Question #32 161

In Matthew 24, is Jesus referring to the Rapture or His Second Coming?

Question #33 164

Who are "the elect" referred to in Matthew 24:31?

Question #34 168

In Matthew 24, is Jesus referring to believers or unbelievers?

Question #35 172

Are the Rapture and the Second Coming two different events?

Question #36 180

How do we know the Tribulation will last for seven years?

Question #37 184

Why does it matter to us that certain Hebrew words were translated a certain way in the Greek Septuagint?

Question #38 187

Will the Rapture begin the seven-year Tribulation period?

Question #39 189

What do Daniel 9:27 and 2 Thessalonians 2 tell us about the Antichrist?

Question #40 192

When will the Tribulation time period begin?

Question #41 194

What did Jesus teach about the seventieth week of Daniel and the abomination of desolation?

Question #42 196

What period of time do the words "birth pangs" refer to?

Question #43 198
Does the Book of Revelation teach that the Rapture will take place before the Tribulation?

Question #44 203
Do the first four seals teach that this is God's wrath upon the world or man's wrath?

Question #45 205
Is Christ the One who unleashes the Antichrist upon the world in Revelation 6:7?

Question #46 207
Are there Old Testament passages that predict God will bring wrath upon the nations by raising up the Antichrist?

Question #47 209
Is warfare upon the face of the earth an expression of God's wrath on the nations?

Question #48 211
Would God ever use famine as an instrument of His wrath upon the world?

Question #49 214
Who is the One that breaks the seals in Revelation 5 and 6?

Question #50 216
Does "the great day of God's wrath" begin at the breaking of the sixth seal, or before that?

Question #51 220
Does the dreadful Day of the Lord come after the beginning of the seventieth week of Daniel?

Question #52 222
Who are the two witnesses in Revelation 11?

Question #53 224
Does the Bible teach that there is a "broad" and "narrow" sense of the Day of the Lord?

Question #54 227
Where does the Bible teach that there is going to be a "narrow" Day of the Lord and is that the "Second Coming" of Christ?

Question #55 233
Doesn't the Day of the Lord have to begin in conjunction with Christ's Second Coming?

Question #56 236
Is the trumpet that sounds at the Rapture in 1 Thessalonians 4
the same as "the last trump" in Matthew 24?

Question #57 241
Is the trumpet at the Rapture the same as the trumpet at the
Second Coming of Christ after the Tribulation Period?

Question #58 243
Is the trumpet of the Rapture in 1 Thessalonians 4 one of the
seven trumpets mentioned in the Book of Revelation?

Question #59 245
The Rapture: which position is right and which is wong?

Question #60 252
When are the Marriage Supper of the Lamb and the Judgment
Seat of Christ?

Question #61 254
Why is the Pre-tribulation Rapture view the only view fully
consistent with the concept of imminency?

Question #62 256
What are some of the basic teachings of the Pre-wrath Rapture
view and the problems with those teachings?

Question #63 264
Where does the Bible teach that Christians will be removed
from the earth before the Day of the Lord ever begins?

Question #64 268
When will the Antichrist be revealed? When will the "man of sin"
be revealed?

Question #65 271
What is the sequence of future prophetic events as spelled
out in the Word of God?

Question #66 275
What is the order of the different resurrections mentioned in the
Bible?

Question #67 277
When will Old Testament saints be raised from the dead?

Question #68 279
Who is in the first resurrection in Revelation 20?

Question #69 281
Who are the parties of the New Covenant according to the
Old Testament?

Question #70 295
Why does the Bible forbid the setting of dates for the Lord's
return?

Question #71 297
Will Israel be invaded by a six nation confederation led by Russia?

Question #72 299
What will happen to Israel in the future when the six nation
confederation comes against them?

Question #73 301
What will take place at Armageddon?

Question #74 303
What are the different millennial views?

Appendix A: 338
What is the significance of the four blood moons?

Appendix B: 340
What is the Judgment of the Sheep and the Goats?

Appendix C: 346
What happens when a person dies?

Appendix D: 349
Does our soul sleep when we die?

Appendix E: 351
What is the purpose of The Judgment Seat of Christ?

Appendix F: 355
What can we expect at the Judgment Seat of Christ?

Appendix G: 358
What are some of the rewards Christians can gain or lose?

Appendix H: 367
What was the length of a year in Daniel 9?

Notes 370
About the Authors 378
How to Begin a Personal Relationship with God 379

Introduction

WITH THE EVENTS that are unfolding in our world today, people want to know more about biblical prophecy, especially the sequence of the many important events which the Bible says will occur during the end times.

Did you know that approximately 27 percent of the entire Bible contains prophetic material? Half of that has already come true; half remains to be fulfilled. That means that of the Bible's 31,124 verses, 8,352 contain prophetic material. Also, did you know that 1,800 verses in the Bible deal with the Second Coming of Jesus Christ? In the New Testament, approximately one out of 25 verses refer to the Second Coming. Would anyone dare to say to God that what He wrote in Scripture is worthless, unimportant, and shouldn't be studied? In fact, God brags about His prophetic statements as being proof that He exists. In Isaiah 46:9-11 (NIV) He says, "*I am God and there is no other; I am God and there is none like me. I make known the end from the beginning, from ancient times what is still to come. I say, 'My purpose will stand and I will do all that I please.' ...What I have said, that I will bring about; what I have planned, that I will do.*" In Mark 13:23 (NIV) Jesus said, "*So be on your guard; I have told you everything ahead of time.*" Jesus said in John 13:19 (NIV), "*I am telling you now before it happens, so that when it does happen, you will believe that I am who I am [God].*"

So, prophetic statements in the Bible prove that God exists, prove that Jesus is God, and are there to warn those without Christ and to comfort those who have believed in Christ.

Question #1

Why has God scheduled future events for planet earth?

HY HAS GOD SCHEDULED future events for planet earth? Why will there be a seven-year period of Tribulation, followed by the Second Coming of the Lord Jesus back to this planet, and then His thousand-year reign over the earth? There has to be a reason for these future events because God never does anything without a purpose. But in order to understand why things will take place the way they will near the end of time, we have to go back to the beginning of time and see some significant things that transpired then. What will happen in the future is based squarely upon significant things that happened near the beginning of time.

Back in eternity past God determined to have a kingdom over which He could rule as a sovereign King. That kingdom was to be known as the Kingdom of God. And God determined to create two major kinds of personal subjects to serve Him in His kingdom.

First, He created an enormous host of beings that the Bible calls angels. The apostle John tells us in Revelation 5:11 that he saw literally hundreds and hundreds and hundreds of millions of holy angels surrounding the presence of God in Heaven, probably billions of these spirit beings, called angels, that God created to serve Him primarily in the heavenly realm of His universal kingdom.

It appears that God created the angels with different degrees of intelligence and power and established various ranks of angels on the basis of these differences. This is implied by the fact that the Bible applies various terms, such as cherubim (Ezek. 10:1-22), seraphim (Isa. 6:1-7), archangel (1 Thess. 4:16), prince (Dan. 10:13, 20, 21; 12:1), thrones, dominions, principalities and powers (Col. 1:16) to angels.

It also appears that God organized the angels according to rank similar to the way armed forces are organized. One indication of this is the fact that God is called "Lord of hosts" numerous times in the Old Testament (for example, see Psa. 84). The Hebrew word translated "hosts" means "armies"; thus, God is "Lord of armies" (John E. Hartley, "sebaoth," Theological Wordbook of the Old Testament, Vol. II, p. 750).

The Bible indicates that the holy angels constitute a powerful heavenly army or armies that carry out God's commands (1 Ki. 22:19; Psa. 103:20-21), serve as His chariots (Psa. 68:17), and are divided into legions (Matt. 26:53). In light of this, God's title "Lord of armies" indicates that He is the Commander in Chief of the angelic armies of Heaven. Another indication of holy angels arranged according to rank as an army is the fact that some angels are under the command of other angels. For example, the archangel Michael (Jude 9) has angels under his command for the purpose of waging angelic warfare (Rev. 12:7). After God brought the angels into existence

He made planet earth. Job 38:4-7 indicates that the angels (referred to as *"the morning stars"* and *"all the sons of God"*) were present to witness God's creation of the earth. (The book of Job refers to angels as "the sons of God" [Job 1:6; 2:1], thereby indicating that God was their source. He created them—Franz Delitzsch, *Biblical Commentary on the Book of Job*, Vol. I, p. 53.) They sang God's praises and shouted for joy when they saw God perform this mighty work.

After He created the earth, He brought into existence the second kind of personal subject to serve Him in His Kingdom, and that was man. God created the first two human beings, Adam and Eve, and He placed them in a perfect environment here on planet earth. And according to Genesis 1:26, when God created man, He gave man dominion over everything that God had created and placed here on this planet.

Now, the fact that God did that tells us what the original form of government was as ordained by God for planet earth. The original form of government is that which is called a *theocracy*. The term **democracy** literally means *"rule of the people;"* the word *"theocracy"* means *"rule of God."* And if you were to look up that term in a good English dictionary, you would find it defined something like this: *"A theocracy is a form of government in which the rule of God is administered by a representative."* It was God's intention that Adam be His representative, administering God's rule on His behalf over this earthly province of God's universal Kingdom.

In order to represent God to the rest of the earthly creation, Adam had to be in God's image. He had to be a personal being with the kind of intellect that could understand God's instruction concerning how His rule was to be administered, and that could make communication between him and God possible. In addition, Adam had to be a morally responsible being who would administer God's rule in accord with His moral nature and character. Once God had created and established man on earth, His universal kingdom was complete. *"God saw every thing that he had made,"* and His evaluation was that *"it was very good"* (Gen. 1:31). In other words, no part of His created kingdom had gone against Him yet. But tragically, it would not remain that way very long.

Some time after God completed the creation of His Kingdom, the most intelligent, most powerful, highest ranking angel whom God had made, an angel who according to Ezekiel 28 was the anointed cherub who covered the unique presence of God in Heaven, that exalted angel was lifted up in pride over how great he was. And in his pride, he determined that he wanted to be just like God. We're told this in Isaiah 14:12-14 where he said, *"I will make myself like the Most High."* This exalted angel saw that God was the ultimate sovereign One of the universe; he wanted to be the ultimate sovereign one of the universe. He saw that God had a kingdom over which He ruled as a sovereign King; he wanted to have a kingdom over which he could rule as a sovereign king. He saw that God had both angels and human subjects serving Him in His Kingdom; if he were to be like God, he, too, had to have both angels and human subjects serving him in his kingdom.

But this angel had a problem which God did not have, and that's the fact that since he was only a creature and not the Creator, he did not have the ability to create other angels and human beings. So the most he could hope for was to persuade God's angels and human beings to join him in his revolt against God.

When this exalted angel began his revolt against God, God changed his name to Satan, which means *"enemy"* or *"adversary,"* because that's exactly what this exalted angel had now become: the great enemy or adversary of God.

Satan made his approach, first, to the other angels. And the Scriptures make it quite clear that he was successful in persuading a sizeable amount of God's angels to join him in his rebellion against God. And so there was a fall of some of the angels away from God that took place. One of the ways we know that is the fact that several times the Bible refers to *"the devil and his angels."* For example, the Lord Jesus, in Matthew 25:41 talked about *"the lake of fire which has already been prepared for the devil and his angels."*

Now that Satan had angels in his kingdom, he decided to make his approach to man. And we have the record of this in Genesis 3. Angels have the ability to take upon themselves any shape or form or size that they need in order to carry out a task. And so Satan took upon himself the deceptive form of a serpent and he entered into man's perfect environment on earth and tragically was able to persuade Adam and Eve, the first man and woman, to join him in his rebellion against God. And so the fall of man away from God took place.

Now, if we are to understand the purpose of future events, we have to note several tragic consequences of man joining Satan's rebellion against God. **The first tragic consequence is the fact that the theocracy was lost from planet earth**. Remember, theocracy is a form of government in which the rule of God is administered by a representative. And now that Adam, God's representative, had made the fateful choice to join God's enemy [Satan] in his rebellion against God, God lost His representative; and therefore the theocracy was lost from planet earth altogether.

A second tragic consequence of man joining Satan's rebellion is the fact that Satan was now able to usurp the rule of the world system away from God and the Scriptures make it quite clear that Satan and his forces have been dominating and controlling the world system ever since. In fact, they're doing so even right now in the day and age in which we are living.

Several things in the Word of God make it very clear that Satan was able to usurp the rule of the world system away from God. For example, in Luke 4:5-6, where Luke records Satan tempting Jesus while Jesus was here in His first coming, we find that one form of the temptation was that he took Jesus to the top of a mountain. And this is what we read (verse 5): "*And the devil, taking Him up into an high mountain, showed unto Him all the kingdoms of the world in a moment of time*" (NKJV). Notice, Satan had the authority to cause all the kingdoms of the world system to pass before the Lord Jesus in visionary form. Then verse 6: "*And the devil said unto Him, 'All this power will I give thee and the glory of them: for that is delivered unto me,*'" literally, "*it has been handed over to me,*" "*and to whomsoever I will, I give it.*"

Please note: Satan said to the Lord Jesus, "*I have the authority to turn over the rule of the whole world system to whomever I wish,*" and he told Jesus why he had the authority: "*for it has been handed over to me.*" Who handed over the rule of the world system to God's enemy, Satan? Adam did; because Adam was the one to whom God originally gave that rule. And whether Adam recognized it or not, when he made that fateful choice to join Satan's rebellion against God, he was thereby handing over the rule of the whole world system to God's enemy, Satan.

This is why the Lord Jesus, on more than one occasion while He was here in His first coming, referred to Satan as *"the prince of this world,"* literally, *"the ruler of this world."* One place where Jesus made such a reference was in John 14:30. And this is why the apostle Paul in 2 Corinthians 4:4 referred to Satan as *"the god of this age"* (NKJV). He's the one who controls the whole spirit and temperament of the present age in which we are living.

This is also why John very literally said in 1 John 5:19, *"The whole world lies in the power of the evil one"* (NASB). And, by the way, this is why James warns Christians in James 4:4 that we had better not be a friend of the world system in which we live, because whoever makes himself the friend of the godless world system thereby becomes an enemy of God. The reason is because God's enemy is the one who is dominating and controlling that world system today. So the theocracy was lost and Satan was able to usurp the rule of the world system away from God.

But there was a third tragic consequence of man joining Satan's revolt against God there in the Garden of Eden, and that is the fact that all of nature was put under a curse. In Genesis 3, after Adam and Eve had fallen away from God, and God came down to the earth to confront Adam, Eve and Satan with their roles in the fall of man, this is what God said to Adam: *"Cursed is the ground for your sake. From now on, it will be by the sweat of your brow that you will till the ground to grow food to sustain life."* The implication seems to be that through the curse that was put upon the ground, the fertility level of the soil of planet earth was radically reduced from what it was when God originally created it. And as a result, it would be much more difficult for man to grow food or crops to sustain life here on planet earth. Even animal nature was radically changed from that curse. There are implications in the Bible to the effect that before the Fall of man, all animals were completely tame and were vegetarian in diet. But now that the curse of man's sin came upon them, animals became wild and many of them became carnivorous or flesh-eating, tearing at each other's flesh as a source of food. This is why the apostle Paul says in Romans 8 that "*all of creation was subjected to vanity, not of its own choosing.*" Nature didn't ask to be put under this curse, but it was subjected to it nonetheless. And Paul goes on to say that "*the whole of creation groans and travails in pain*" and can hardly wait until the ultimate day of redemption when the curse of man's sin will be lifted off of nature.

Well, now that Satan had both angels and humans as subjects within his kingdom, his kingdom was established and functioning. So now there were **two major spiritual kingdoms functioning in the universe: the kingdom of God** and **the kingdom of Satan.** And since Satan's goal was to become the ultimate sovereign one of the universe, and God was already that ultimate Sovereign One, and since there can only be one ultimate sovereign one, this meant there was going to be all-out war. And Satan, throughout the course of history, has been working to try to overthrow God as the Sovereign Lord of the universe and make himself that sovereign lord.

And that warfare which began back near the beginning of time has continued on down through the ages of time. It's going on around us in the world today, and as we shall see, it's going to go on into the future. It is that continuing warfare between the Kingdom of God and the kingdom of Satan that provides us with the key for understanding **the ultimate purpose of history.** Satan's purpose is to unseat God as the Sovereign Lord of the universe and make himself that sovereign lord in place of God. But **God's purpose for history, and therefore the ultimate purpose, is to glorify Himself by demonstrating the fact that He alone is the sovereign God of this universe.**

Now, the Scriptures indicate that in order for God to accomplish that purpose, there are **three significant things God must do before the history of this world comes to an end. Number one, God must crush His enemy Satan and get rid of him and his kingdom rule and his forces from this planet altogether.** Since this earth started out without Satan and his forces controlling the world system, but then Satan was able to usurp the rule of the world system away from God through the Fall of man, if God doesn't get rid of Satan and his rule from planet earth before the history of this earth comes to an end, then God ends up defeated by His enemy Satan within the scope of this earth's history. God must crush Satan and get rid of him and his kingdom rule from planet earth altogether.

The second thing God must do is this: after He does crush Satan, God must restore His theocracy back to this planet in which once again God will have a man, an Adam, as His representative administering His rule over this entire earth. And the Word of God makes it very clear that God has such a man. His name is Jesus Christ. And this is why the apostle Paul, in 1 Corinthians 15:45, calls Jesus *"the last Adam."* You see, the first Adam lost the theocracy for God by joining Satan's revolt against God. But Jesus Christ, in His glorious Second Coming back to planet earth after the seven-year Tribulation, will return as the last Adam to restore God's theocracy and then, as His representative, to administer God's rule over this entire earth for the last great age of world history that is called "The Millennium."

May I point out to you, this is one of the reasons, not the only one, but one of the major reasons why the incarnation of Jesus Christ was absolutely essential. One reason, obviously, was so that He could die as our substitute on the cross of Calvary to pay the penalty for our sins. But another reason is so that, in His Second Coming, He can return to planet earth as a man, as an Adam, to function as God's representative administering His rule. If you look in the Gospels at the places where Jesus referred to His Second Coming, almost invariably He calls Himself "the Son of man" at His Second Coming. He'll still be the Son of God, absolute deity, but He's emphasizing His humanity in His Second Coming because He's returning as the last Adam to restore God's theocracy.

But then the third thing God must do to fulfill His purpose for history is this: When He does restore that theocracy through His Son, Jesus Christ, God must lift the curse of man's sin off of nature and restore nature back to the way it was before the Fall of man took place.

Now, how will God accomplish these three things?

How will He accomplish the first thing, crushing Satan and getting rid of him and his kingdom rule from planet earth altogether? He'll accomplish the first thing through the combination of the seven-year Tribulation period and Second Coming of Jesus Christ to the earth. When you study Revelation chapters 6-18, which cover the major events of the future seven-year Tribulation period, you will find that throughout that seven-year span of time God will pour out three series of judgments here on planet earth.

First, there will be seven seal judgments; then, seven trumpet judgments; and finally, seven bowl or vial judgments. *Why is God pouring out these judgments upon the earth during the seven-year Tribulation period?* The reason is this: This is His means of beginning to systematically attack and tear down or crush Satan's kingdom rule here on planet earth.

It is very significant that the apostle John recorded for us by revelation of God in the Revelation 11:15. John is recording here a significant thing that will transpire when the seventh trumpet judgment will be unleashed on planet earth. Now, keep in mind again, there will have already been seven seal judgments and six trumpet judgments. So this is the last of the second series of judgments. And if we read beyond Revelation 11, we find that the seventh trumpet consists of (or contains within itself) the whole third and final series of judgments—the seven bowls or vials are wrapped up in the seventh trumpet. That's very significant because that means **when the seventh trumpet is sounded and that judgment unleashed upon the earth, that will begin the final series of judgments which will culminate with the Second Coming of Christ and the ending of Satan's rule on planet earth**.

In light of that, here's what John tells us in Revelation 11:15: "*Then the seventh angel blew his trumpet, and there were loud voices in heaven, saying, 'The kingdom of the world has become the kingdom of our Lord and of his Christ, and he shall reign forever and ever.'*" Does that sound familiar? This is Handel's *Messiah*. And it's from this particular passage that Handel derived that tremendous refrain. Do you realize what that is? That's a tremendous cry of victory! When God's creatures in heaven see God unleashing the last series of judgments, which will end His enemy Satan's rule on planet earth, they get so excited in anticipation of what this means that they can't hold in their excitement. And they cry forth that tremendous expression of victory: *"The kingdoms of this world are become the kingdoms of our Lord and of His Christ. And He shall reign forever and ever."* It's almost as they say, "Finally, after God in His sovereignty, for His own purposes that only He can understand, has allowed His enemy and His enemy's forces to dominate this world that God created for ages, God is finally bringing Satan's rule to an end. And God and His Messiah, His Christ, are going to take back the rule of the earth for the honor and the glory of God. So God, through the seven-year Tribulation period, will be systematically attacking and tearing down Satan's kingdom rule through these three series of judgments.

Question #2

What is the setting of the sealed scroll in Revelation 5?

I

N REVELATION 4 AND 5, where John began to be introduced to things that "*must*" take place in the future (4:1), the apostle saw Christ take a scroll from the hand of God the Father. The scroll was sealed with seven seals. Christ took the scroll so that He could break its seals, open it and read what was written inside (5:1-7). The identification of the scroll is critical to an understanding of the future events revealed in Revelation 6-20. To discern that identification, we must observe several things emphasized in Revelation 4 and 5.

First, Revelation 4:11 emphasizes that **God created "*all things*"** that have been created, and that He created these things for His own benefit or purpose.

Second, God's power or authority to rule all of creation is emphasized in two ways in chapters 4 and 5. First, God's throne is mentioned 17 times. The word for throne indicates dominion or sovereignty.[1]

In the second way, the doxologies in Revelation 4:11 and 5:13 use two words to ascribe great power to God. One of those words (*kratos*—5:13) sometimes "*is designed to stress the power of God which none can withstand and which is sovereign over all."* [2] *"It denotes the superior power of God to which the final victory will belong."* [3]

The other word (*dunamis*—4:11) was used in statements that express *"the hope and longing that God will demonstrate His power in a last great conflict, destroying His opponents and saving those who belong to Him. Thus, the righteous wait for God to reveal Himself in power and definitively to establish His dominion."* [4]

These two words portray a divine power that is active in history; a power that shapes and sets a goal for history in accordance with God's sovereign will and purpose. [5]

Third, Revelation 5:9, 12 portrays **Christ as the Redeemer**. It emphasizes His work of redemption through His death and shed blood, and that He alone is worthy to take the scroll from God's hand, break its seals, open and read it because of His work of redemption.

Fourth, Revelation 5:12-13 points out **Christ's worthiness as the Redeemer to exercise God's ruling power.** There the same power words for God's rule noted earlier are ascribed to Him. In fact, in 5:13 one of those words is used jointly for God and Christ. In light of these four things emphasized in the part of Revelation that introduces the sealed scroll, the following conclusion can be drawn: The identification of the sealed scroll must relate to the facts that God created all of creation for His own benefit and purpose, that He has the power or authority to rule all of creation, and that, as the Redeemer, Christ alone is worthy to take the scroll from God's hand, break its seals, open it and read it and to exercise God's ruling power.

The background of the sealed scroll

Bible teaches that, because God created the earth and everything in it, He is its owner and sovereign King (Ex. 19:5; 1 Chron. 29:11; Psa. 24:1-2; 47:2-3, 7-9). When God established His theocracy, He gave His earth to mankind to possess as an inheritance forever (Psa. 115:16; Gen. 1:26-28; Isa. 24:5 ["the everlasting covenant"]). Mankind, however, was not to regard themselves as sole owner and authority of the earth. Since God was the ultimate owner, mankind was responsible to serve as His representative, administering His rule over the earth for His benefit in accord with His sovereign purpose and in obedience to His commands (Gen. 2:15-17). God was the landlord; mankind was the tenant possessor.

Since God was the owner, and mankind was only His tenant possessor, mankind did not have the right or authority to forfeit tenant possession or administration of God's earth to anyone else (to a non-kinsman). Tragically, mankind did forfeit tenant possession of their earth inheritance to Satan (a non-kinsman of mankind) by following his lead to rebel against God (Gen. 3). Satan thereby usurped tenant possession of the earth from its original tenant (mankind) and, therefore, from God, and he has exercised administrative control of the world system against God ever since. Mankind's loss of tenant possession inheritance of the earth to Satan is temporary. This is so because God has established a program of redemption to prevent this loss from being permanent.

This program is based upon the work of a kinsman-redeemer (a relative of the same human kind as mankind). That Kinsman-Redeemer is the incarnate Jesus Christ. As the Kinsman-Redeemer, Christ had to pay a redemption price in order to redeem mankind and their forfeited inheritance. The redemption price He paid was the shedding of His blood (Eph. 1:7; Col. 1:14; 1 Pet. 1:18-19; Rev. 5:9).

Although Christ paid the redemption price, He will not return the administration of the whole earth to Adam, the man who forfeited mankind's inheritance. As the Kinsman-Redeemer and last Adam, Christ will keep the earth to administer it for God's purposes (Rev. 11:15). He "shall be king over all the earth; in that day there shall be one Lord" (Zech. 14:9).

Conclusion concerning identification of the sealed scroll

In light of the things emphasized in Revelation 4 and 5 and the background of the sealed scroll, the sealed scroll of Revelation 5 can be identified as the deed of purchase for mankind's tenant possession inheritance of the earth that was forfeited when mankind fell away from God. Just as scroll deeds of purchase were made when Jeremiah paid the redemption price to redeem his cousin's tenant possession of land (Jer. 32:6-12), so a scroll deed of purchase was made when Christ paid the redemption price to redeem mankind's tenant possession of the earth by shedding His blood. Alfred Jenour wrote, "*We regard it as a **covenant deed**, the book in which were registered the terms of man's redemption, and his restoration to the dominion of the earth and all those privileges which he had forfeited by transgression.*"[6]

Jeremiah's scrolls were legal evidence of his payment of the redemption price and, therefore, of his right of tenant possession of the land. The word translated "*evidence*" and "*book*" in Jeremiah 32:12 was used for important legal documents that were usually in scroll form.[7] In the same manner Christ's scroll deed is legal evidence of His payment of the redemption price and, therefore, of His right of tenant possession of the earth.

The need for the sealed scroll deed

One of Jeremiah's scroll deeds was sealed to prevent anyone from changing its contents (Jer. 32:10-11). That gave the scroll the nature of irrefutable legal evidence that Jeremiah was the kinsman-redeemer who had the right to take tenant possession of the land because he had redeemed it through the payment of the redemption price. Gottfried Fitzer wrote that "*The seal served as a legal protection and guarantee in many ways, especially in relation to property.*"[8] Parallel to this, the scroll deed of Revelation 5 is sealed with seven seals. That gave that deed the nature of irrefutable evidence that Christ is the Kinsman-Redeemer who has the right to take tenant possession of the earth because He has redeemed it through the payment of the redemption price, the shedding of His blood on the cross.

Jeremiah's scroll deeds were placed in a secure place where they could be preserved for a long period of time, since he did not take actual possession of the land immediately after paying the redemption price (Jer. 32:13-15). Circumstances removed him far from the land for many years. In like manner, Christ's scroll deed was placed in a secure place (God's right hand in Heaven—Rev. 5:1, 7) for a long period of time, because He did not take actual possession of the earth immediately after paying the redemption price at the cross. He removed to a location far from the earth (Heaven—Acts 1:9-11) for many years.

Just as squatters controlled the land of Israel (including the land Jeremiah had purchased) for many years while the Jews and Jeremiah were removed from it, so squatters (Satan and the human members of his kingdom) are controlling the world system during the years Christ is removed from the earth.

The two responsibilities of the kinsman-redeemer

Land redemption in Israel involved two responsibilities for a kinsman-redeemer. **First**, he had to **pay the redemption price** for the forfeited land and thereby obtain the right of tenant possession. Second, he then had to take actual possession of the land and exercise administrative rule over it. Sometimes this required him to evict squatters who had begun to exercise tenant possession of the land illegally.

In like manner, the redemption of the earth involves the same two responsibilities for Christ, mankind's Kinsman-Redeemer. **First, He had to pay the redemption price** for the earth and thereby obtain the right of tenant possession. **Second**, now that Christ has obtained that right, **He must take actual possession of the earth and exercise administrative rule over it**. This will require Him to evict the squatters, Satan and his forces, who have exercised illegal tenant possession of the earth since mankind's fall.

The significance of Christ's action with the sealed scroll

If illegal squatters challenged an Israelite kinsman-redeemer's right to take tenant possession of land, the redeemer had to produce legal evidence that he had paid the redemption price and, therefore, had the right to take possession. The sealed scroll deed of purchase was that legal evidence.

Christ will return to the earth to take tenant possession at His Second Coming after the end of the 70th week of Daniel (the seven-year Tribulation Period). By the end of that period Satan and his forces will have drawn the rulers and armies of the world into the land of Israel to fight against Christ (Psa. 2:1-3; Zech. 12-14; Rev. 16:12-16; 19:11- 21). This will be Satan's ultimate challenge to Christ's right to take tenant possession of the earth and to rule it.

This challenge will require Christ to provide irrefutable legal evidence of His right of tenant possession before he evicts the squatters and takes actual possession. His sealed scroll deed will be that evidence. At the beginning of the seven-year Tribulation Period, Christ will take that deed from God's hand and begin to break its seven seals one by one. He thereby will instigate three series of judgments that will devastate significant areas of Satan's earthly domain (Rev. 6-18) and demonstrate that He has the power necessary to evict Satan and his forces. As a result of having broken all seven seals during the Tribulation Period, Christ will have the scroll deed open by the time of His Second Coming. At that time He will read the contents of the scroll publicly as the conclusive legal evidence that He is the true Kinsman-Redeemer of mankind's forfeited inheritance and, therefore, has the right to evict Satan and his forces and to take tenant possession of the earth (Psa. 2:7-9). After presenting this evidence Christ will fully exercise that right by ridding the earth of Satan and his forces and taking the rule of the earth as the last Adam (Rev. 19:19-20:6).

Question #3

Will Christ return to earth as a victorious conqueror who crushes Satan?

So, IMMEDIATELY AFTER THE Tribulation, the Lord Jesus as the last Adam will come out of Heaven in His glorious Second Coming, this time down to planet earth to take back the rule of the earth on behalf of God. And so in Revelation 19, John records the Second Coming of the Lord Jesus and he sees heaven open and Jesus comes riding out of heaven on the back of a white horse. Now, in John's day, in that part of the world, a rider on a white horse symbolized a victorious conqueror. So when **Jesus will come out of heaven in His Second Coming on a white horse**, He's returning to the earth as God's victorious conqueror to finish the job of crushing Satan and getting rid of him and his kingdom rule from this planet altogether. John saw, down on planet earth, pitted against the Lord Jesus, Satan's ultimate man, the Antichrist, a false religious leader under Satan's direction, the false prophet, the rulers and the armies of all the world gathered together in the land of Israel. And they're gathered there for one purpose: to try to prevent the Second Coming of Jesus Christ from taking place here on planet earth. Satan realizes that if Jesus gets back here, it'll be all over for him. And so he's played a role in pulling all the armies and rulers of the nations of the world together to the land of Israel to try to prevent Christ from coming back.

He knows, according to Zechariah 14:2-3, that the first place that Jesus' feet will touch down on the earth will be on the Mount of Olives just outside of Jerusalem. So that's why Satan gathers the armies there into Israel around Jerusalem to try to prevent Christ from coming. And John indicates that the Lord Jesus will have the Antichrist and the false prophet removed from the earth, cast into the eternal lake of fire where they'll be tormented day and night under the judgment of God. And then he sees the Lord Jesus destroying the rulers and the armies of all these godless nations that are there. So there, Jesus crushes Satan's forces.

Then, in Revelation 20:1-3, John saw an angel come down from heaven, binding Satan with a chain. Satan is removed from the earth and is cast into the bottomless pit or the abyss where he will be confined or imprisoned by God for the next one thousand years.

In Isaiah 24, at the end of that chapter, Isaiah received revelation to the effect that at that same time all of the demons or evil angels will also be cast into that same pit and imprisoned. So you see that through this seven-year Tribulation period and the Second Coming of the Lord Jesus, Satan and all of his forces will be crushed and will be removed from planet earth altogether and will not have influence of any kind whatsoever on the earth throughout the last thousand-year period of world history, which is called "The Millennium."

So God will accomplish the first thing He must do to fulfill His purpose for history, namely, crushing Satan and getting rid of him and his kingdom rule from planet earth. God will accomplish that through the combination of the seven-year Tribulation period and the Second Coming of the Lord Jesus.

Question #4

Will God restore
theocratic kingdom rule?

EARLIER WE SURVEYED THE conflict of the ages between the kingdom of God and kingdom of Satan. We saw how Satan's goal for history is to overthrow God as the Sovereign Lord of the universe and replace God with himself as that sovereign lord. But we also noted how God's purpose for history, therefore the ultimate purpose, is to glorify Himself by demonstrating the fact that He alone is the Sovereign God of this universe. We noted that in order for God to accomplish that purpose, there are three things He must do before the history of this world ends. He must crush Satan and get rid of him and his kingdom rule from planet earth. We have thus far noted how God will accomplish that through the combination of the seven-year Tribulation Period plus the Second Coming of Jesus Christ back to planet earth.

But then we noted that a second thing God must do before the history of this world ends is this: He must restore His own theocratic kingdom rule to planet earth. When God created the earth and then placed man as His creature upon this planet, God gave man dominion over everything else that God had placed here. And we saw that was God's way of establishing a theocracy as the original form of government. A theocracy is a form of government in which the rule of God is administered by a representative. Adam was God's original representative administering God's rule over this earth. But Adam rebelled against God in Genesis 3; the Fall of man took place; and since God lost His representative, the theocracy was lost from planet earth. God must restore His theocracy to planet earth before the history of this world ends.

It's very interesting to note that in Revelation 20:4-6—which comes right after the record of how at the Second Coming, Satan and his forces will be crushed and removed from the earth and will be imprisoned in the abyss or bottomless pit for a thousand years—God indicates that after Satan is removed from the earth Christ and His saints will reign here on the earth for one thousand years. That is stated more than once in those verses; that Christ and His saints will reign on the earth for one thousand years. That's indicating that the theocracy will be restored to planet earth after Satan is removed from the earth; Jesus, as the last Adam, the Son of man, will restore that theocracy for God and as God's representative will administer God's rule together with God's saints over this planet for one thousand years.

Interestingly, in Zechariah 14, God foretold how, when Messiah will come in His Second Coming, that all the armies of the world will have the city of Jerusalem encircled, beginning to systematically destroy that city. And the Messiah or Christ will go to war; He will destroy those forces; graphically describing His destruction of them in Zechariah 14. But then in Zechariah 14:9 it states this: "*And the Lord will be King over all the earth,*" indicating that the Messiah, Jesus Christ, will rule the earth, the entire earth, on behalf of God when He returns to this earth in His glorious Second Coming. So, the theocracy will be reestablished here before the history of this world ends.

Now, theologians have called that thousand-year reign of Jesus and the saints "the Millennium." Maybe you've often wondered, "Where does that term millennium come from?" It comes from two Latin words. First, the word *milla*, which is the Latin word for one thousand; and then the word *annum*, from which we get our word annual. The Latin word *annum* means year. So *milla annum*, "*one thousand years*," and when you say those two Latin words rather quickly together, you come out with "millennium."

But there's a third thing that God must do to accomplish His purpose for history: when He does restore His theocracy to planet earth, He must lift the curse of man's sin off of nature and restore nature back to the way it was back before the Fall of man took place. In conjunction with that, there's a fascinating statement that Jesus made to His apostles while He was here in His first coming. Matthew records that statement for us in Matthew 19:28: "*And Jesus said unto them, 'Verily, I say unto you, that you which have followed Me in the regeneration, when the Son of man shall sit in the throne of His glory, you also shall sit upon twelve thrones judging the twelve tribes of Israel.'*" What did Jesus mean by "*the regeneration*"? The English word *regenerate* literally means "*to generate again*," and it's referring to the restoration of a lost condition. The idea is that there was an original condition but something happen that caused that original condition to be lost. But then, later, through regeneration, that original condition is restored. What Jesus was referring to through this statement, "*regeneration*," is the fact that when God created planet earth, He created nature perfectly, exactly the way God wanted it to be. But then that perfect condition of nature was lost through the Fall of man because there was a curse of man's sin put upon nature. And nature has been "out of joint" and in turmoil and pain ever since. But Jesus is saying that in the future, that original condition of nature as created by God is going to be regenerated or generated again. Now, that's the English meaning and that's exactly what Christ was communicating.

The Greek word that was translated "*regeneration*" in Matthew 19:28 literally says, "*genesis again.*" Jesus was saying that in the future, this planet will experience "genesis again." The Greek word *genesis*, after which the first book of our Bible is named, literally means "beginning." So even more literally, Jesus was talking about how nature in the future will experience the beginning again. What He is saying is the curse of man is soon to be lifted off of nature, and nature will be put back into joint or restored to the way God originally created it. And Jesus told His apostles when that would happen. He said, "*In the regeneration, when the Son of man shall sit in the throne of His glory.*" In other words, when Jesus, as the last Adam, the Son of man, is back here on the earth in His Second Coming, sitting upon a throne, ruling the whole world as the King of the earth, that's when nature will be regenerated.

Do you know that even animal nature is going to be restored back to the way it was before the Fall of man? Read Isaiah 11. In the first five verses of that chapter, Isaiah is clearly talking about the future rule of the Messiah here on planet earth in the Millennium. But then, beginning in verse 6, Isaiah describes how animal nature is going to be transformed. And he indicates that during the reign of the Messiah, children will be able to lead around as pets, not only what today are tame animals, such as sheep and goats and fatted calves, but even what today would be wild animals, such as lions, bears, leopards, etc. And he says that they shall not hurt; they will be completely tame. And then he says, "*The lion will eat straw like the ox.*" Once again, even the lion will be vegetarian in diet and no longer flesh-eating.

So, through the seven-year Tribulation, plus the Second Coming of Christ, God will crush Satan and get rid of him and his kingdom rule from planet earth altogether. Then, Jesus, after He comes to earth in His Second Coming, will restore God's theocracy and, as the last Adam, will administer God's rule over this entire earth for one thousand years. And when Jesus restores that theocracy, He will lift the curse of man's sin off of nature and restore nature back to the way it was before the Fall of man took place. And by accomplishing those three things before the history of this world ends, God will glorify Himself by demonstrating that He alone is the Sovereign Lord of this universe.

Question #5

Who are the citizens of the Millennium?

THE BIBLE REVEALS SEVERAL significant things concerning the citizens of the future theocratic kingdom. First, no unsaved people (the human members of Satan's kingdom) will be allowed to enter the kingdom at its beginning. All the unsaved who are alive at Christ's Second Coming will be taken from the earth in judgment. Christ clearly taught this in His parables of the tares (Matt. 13:24-30, 36-43) and the dragnet (Matt. 13:47-50) and in His Olivet Discourse (Matt. 24:37-41; 25:31-46). Thus, only saved people will be allowed to enter the theocratic kingdom at its beginning.

Second, *all the saved people of all previous ages of history will enter the theocratic kingdom with Christ.* They will consist of **four groups**:

The Church saints (those saved from the Day of Pentecost of Acts 2 [when the Church was born] until the Rapture of the Church) will comprise one group. Because they will have been raptured to Heaven before the Tribulation, they will return with Christ to the earth at His Second Coming after the Tribulation. Thus, they will be on the earth with Him for the theocratic kingdom. Two things indicate that this is where they will be. First, after the apostle Paul referred to the Church saints being raptured from the earth to meet Christ in the air, he said, "and so shall we ever be with the Lord" (1 Thess. 4:17). This indicates that, once the Church saints have been raptured, they will go wherever Christ goes. Second, Paul also taught that Church saints will reign with Christ in the future (2 Tim. 2:12). As a result of the transformation of their bodies at the Rapture (1 Cor. 15:51-53; 1 Thess. 4:16), the Church saints will have glorified, immortal bodies in the theocratic kingdom.

Old Testament saints (those who became saved and died before the Church began on Pentecost and who, therefore, are not part of the Church) will be a second group of saints in the theocratic kingdom. They will be resurrected in conjunction with Christ's Second Coming after the Tribulation and, therefore, will have glorified, immortal bodies in the kingdom. Daniel 12:1-2 refers to people being resurrected to everlasting life after the unparalleled time of trouble (the Great Tribulation—see Christ's reference to that unparalleled time of trouble in Matt. 24:21). In addition, a statement made to Daniel in Daniel 12:13 seems to indicate that he, as an Old Testament saint, will be resurrected at that time. Daniel was told *"you shall rest, and stand in your lot at the end of the days."* The expression *"you shall rest"* was a reference to the fact that he would die.[9] The expression *"you shall... stand in your lot"* was a promise of resurrection after death.[10] Daniel was told that his resurrection will take place *"at the end of the days."* In the context of Daniel 12, it appears that this indicated that Daniel's resurrection will take place once the days of the unparalleled time of trouble (the Great Tribulation) have ended.[11]

A **third group** in the theocratic kingdom will consist of **resurrected Tribulation saints**. Revelation 7 reveals that large numbers of people will become saved during the Tribulation Period. Revelation 6:9-11 and 20:4 indicate that many of the Tribulation saints will be martyred for their faith during the Tribulation. The apostle John recorded the fact that martyred Tribulation saints will be resurrected from the dead in conjunction with the Second Coming of Christ after the Tribulation and then will reign with Him for one thousand years (Rev. 20:4-6). Because of their resurrection, these Tribulation saints will have glorified, immortal bodies in the theocratic kingdom.

A **fourth group** of saints in the theocratic kingdom will be comprised of **people who will become saved during the Tribulation Period and survive the Tribulation alive**. Because they will have escaped death, they will enter the kingdom with mortal bodies and, therefore, will be able to marry and give birth to children and will still have their sin natures. These are *"the sheep"* of Matthew 25:31-34 and those that are *"left"* in the field and at the mill at Christ's Second Coming (Matt. 24:39-41). Because this fourth group of saints will enter the theocratic kingdom with mortal bodies and sin natures, they will be different from the other three groups of saints. The other groups will enter the kingdom with glorified, immortal bodies and, therefore, will not marry (Mark 12:25) or give birth to children and will be sinlessly perfect (without sin natures—1 John 3:2).

The third significant thing concerning the citizens of the future theocratic kingdom is this: Unsaved children will be born into the kingdom after its beginning. As noted earlier, Tribulation saints who have not died will enter the kingdom with mortal bodies and, therefore, will be able to marry and give birth to children during the kingdom. The prophet Jeremiah foretold the birth of Jewish children during the kingdom (Jer. 30:19-20), and the prophet Ezekiel foretold the birth of Gentile children during the kingdom (Ezek. 47:22). Because the Tribulation saints who will enter the kingdom with mortal bodies will still have sin natures, they will give birth to unsaved children, just as Christians today give birth to unsaved children. Thus, although only saved people will be on the earth at the beginning of the kingdom, after a while, through birth, unsaved people will be present. The fact that a huge multitude of people will flock to Satan to take part in his attempt to overthrow Christ's theocratic kingdom rule, when he is released from the bottomless pit after the Millennium (Rev. 20:7-9), indicates that many of those born during the kingdom will not become saved during that time.

Question #6

Who are the "great multitude" that John saw in Revelation 7 between the sixth and seventh seal?

N THE SECOND HALF of Revelation 7, John said that he saw a great multitude up in Heaven. We read in, Revelation 7:9-14,

> After this I beheld, and, lo, a great multitude which no man could number of all nations and kindreds and people and tongues stood before the throne and before the Lamb clothed with white robes and palms in their hands and cried with a loud voice, saying, "Salvation to our God which sits upon the throne and unto the Lamb." And all the angels stood round about the throne and about the elders and the four beasts and fell before the throne on their faces and worshipped God saying, "Amen. Blessing and glory and wisdom and thanksgiving and honor and power and might be unto our God forever and ever. Amen." And one of the elders answered saying unto me, "What are these which are arrayed in white robes and whence came they?" And I said unto him, "Sir, you know." And he said to me, "These are they which came out of Great Tribulation [the Greek says literally "out of **the** Great Tribulation"] and have washed their robes and made them white in the blood of the Lamb."

Some claim that this great multitude from every tongue, tribe and nation who obviously are up in Heaven are the Church which has just been raptured out of the world to Heaven as one body in between the breaking of the sixth seal and the breaking of the seventh seal. And some would say, "See, the sixth seal is the forewarning that the day of the Lord is about to begin but then after the breaking of the sixth seal the Church is removed from the earth by Rapture and then with the breaking of the seventh seal you have the day of the Lord beginning with God's wrath starting to be poured out upon planet Earth."

But, is *"the great multitude"* in Revelation 7 the Church? It really can't be. Let me explain to you why we would say that. Please note that the apostle John clearly stated that all these people who make up this great multitude came out of the Great Tribulation. In other words, every one of these persons was living here on the earth during at least part of the future Great Tribulation and then came out of that to Heaven. If this is the Church, then you're forced to conclude this would be a partial Rapture of the Church or a part of the Church being raptured out of the world. Only that part of the Church that would be alive on the earth during the Great Tribulation of the second half of the 70th week of Daniel.

Where would be all the rest of the Church that has lived and died in the centuries preceding the Great Tribulation and who, as a result of dying in preceding time, will never be here on the earth during the Great Tribulation and therefore do not come out of the Great Tribulation?

When you look at the Rapture passages, it clearly indicates that all the Church is raptured together at the same time as one group. In light of that, if this is the Church, this is a partial Rapture of the Church, but that goes completely contrary to the clear teaching of the Rapture passages in the Bible.

In addition, when one of the 24 elders said to John, *"These are they which came out of the Great Tribulation,"* the verb translated *"came"* is in the Greek present tense. The normal significance of the present tense, unless the context indicates otherwise—which it doesn't do here—the normal significance of the Greek present tense is continuous action. So in essence, the elder is saying to John, "These are they who are coming out continuously, one after another, from the Great Tribulation to Heaven." How? Through death, through martyrdom, or through natural death.

Interestingly, Dr. A. T. Robertson, who has been regarded as the foremost Greek scholar of America in the twentieth century, talking about the significance of the present tense of this exact verb here in Revelation 7:14, says it's indicating continuous action. And again, what it's stating is these saints are coming out of the Great Tribulation one by one by one by one as they're experiencing death, either through martyrdom or natural death throughout the course of the second half of the Great Tribulation. By contrast, the Rapture passages indicate that the Church is not raptured one person and then another person and then another person, but the Church is raptured in one lump sum, one group, at the same time caught up from the earth to meet the Lord Jesus in the air and taken to the Father's house in Heaven to live in the mansions there that Jesus is preparing for His Church right now.

Question #7

What is God's promise to Satan?

WE'VE BEEN TRACING THE conflict of the ages between the Kingdom of God and kingdom of Satan and seen how this helps us understand the ultimate purpose of history. We noted how God must do certain things before the history of this world ends in order to accomplish His purpose for history: He must restore His theocracy to planet earth; He must crush Satan and get rid of him and his kingdom rule; He must lift the curse of man's sin off of nature.

Now, in light of the fact that God must crush Satan and get rid of him and his kingdom rule from this planet before the history of this world comes to an end, it's very important to note that right after the Fall of man took place in Genesis 3, when God came to man and to Satan to confront them with their roles in the Fall, God made a significant promise, and it's recorded for us in Genesis 3:15. This is what He said; and please note, He's saying this directly to His enemy, Satan: "*And I will put enmity between thee and the woman and between thy seed and her seed. It* [referring to the woman's seed] *shall bruise thy head, and thou shalt bruise his heel.*"

This is what God was doing. God here was giving the very first promise of a man-child Redeemer who would be born of woman during the course of world history. This is what He means by "*the seed of the woman*," an offspring of woman—that some time during the course of world history there would be a unique man-child Redeemer born of woman into the world, and God said to Satan, "*That man-child Redeemer will crush your head.*"

Now, God was using language here that fit the serpent or snake form that Satan had taken upon himself when he came into the Garden of Eden. So what God was saying to Satan was this: "The whole key to My defeating you and thereby accomplishing My purpose for history will be the coming and work of this man-child Redeemer born of woman during the course of world history. That man-child Redeemer will be my instrument to crush you and get rid of you and your forces and your kingdom rule from planet earth altogether."

God went on to say to Satan that Satan would bruise the heel of the Redeemer. Again, using language that fit the serpent form that Satan had taken upon himself there, this is what God was saying: Just as a poisonous snake, if it sinks its fangs into the bare heel of a human being, if that human being doesn't get help in a hurry, that human being will die; so Satan, as a result of his work in the world would cause the man-child Redeemer's death.

Why would this man-child Redeemer die? Well, God made clear through a revelation He gave after Genesis 3 why the Redeemer would die. Here's the reason: If God is going to accomplish His purpose for world history, some time during the course of world history He must get rid of the cause of the terrible predicament that man got himself into by rebelling against God in the Garden of Eden. The cause of the mess that the human race has gotten itself into is human sin. And so some time during the course of world history God must get rid of human sin. But how could He do that? Well, again, through later revelation God made it very clear the only way He could get rid of human sin is through death. *"Without the shedding of blood there is no remission of sin,"* the Scriptures say. *"The soul that sins shall die,"* we're told in the prophets. Paul, in Romans 6 says, *"The wages of sin is death."* A death penalty had to be paid for the sin of mankind.

But the problem is, sinful man cannot offer up an acceptable sacrifice by himself unto God to cancel out his sin. God, through further revelation, made it very clear that this man-child Redeemer who would be born of woman into the world would be a completely sinless, spotless human being. And, when that man-child Redeemer would die, He would die as a substitute for the human race. He would die to pay the penalty for man's sin. This is why, then, when the Lord Jesus was first pointed out by John the Baptist to John's disciples, that John said of Jesus in John 1:29, *"Behold, the Lamb of God who takes away the sin of the world"* (NKJV).

So God here, in this first promise of the Redeemer in Genesis 3:15, was saying to His enemy Satan, "The whole key to My crushing you and accomplishing My purpose for history will be the coming and work of this man-child Redeemer, born of woman into the world." Now, if you were Satan and God had just told you this would be His key to defeating you, and you wanted to prevent God from crushing you, what would you do? You would try to prevent that promised man-child Redeemer from coming into the world and doing the work that God sent Him to do. And that ultimately is what all the rest of Old Testament history is about: As Satan throughout the course of Old Testament history used angels; used nations;

used human beings; used institutions and events as his means of trying to prevent the Redeemer from coming into the world.

Interestingly, centuries after the Garden of Eden and the Fall of man, God made a covenant with one man. That man's name was Abraham. God made that covenant, called the **Abrahamic Covenant**, approximately 2000 BC. . And God made several specific promises to Abraham in that covenant. One is that He would raise up a great nation from Abraham's seed, Abraham's physical descendants. And the Scriptures make it very clear that great nation was the nation of Israel. Israel consists of literal physical descendants of Abraham. But God also gave this promise in the covenant to Abraham, "*And through your seed all families of the earth will be blessed.*"

Now, one of the major things God made through that promise—and later revelation from God made it clear this was true—is that the promised man-child Redeemer eventually would be born through Abraham's physical line of descendants, specifically the nation of Israel. Now, again, if the Redeemer is going to be born through that specific nation, and you're Satan and what you're trying to accomplish through Old Testament history is prevent that Redeemer from coming, what would you do? You would go after the nation of Israel and you would try to destroy the nation of Israel before that Redeemer could be born into the world. And that's what he was doing then throughout most of the rest of Old Testament history.

And just to give an example of that: Several generations after Abraham, because of a famine in the land of Canaan where the people of Israel were living, the people of Israel migrated down to the land of Egypt. And after they had been there and prospered for a number of years, according to Exodus 1, there was a new pharaoh who came to the throne who did not know Joseph. And Satan used that pharaoh as his tool to try to annihilate Israel.

That pharaoh passed a horrible decree to the effect that every boy baby born of a Jew was to be put to death. If you destroy all the males of a nation, that nation very quickly will disappear from the world scene altogether because it will have no means of reproducing itself and continuing its existence on planet earth. Satan, through that horrible decree passed by that Egyptian king, the pharaoh, was going to try to annihilate the nation of Israel from the face of the earth so the Redeemer could not come. Here's a first in world history. Anti-Semitism, hatred of Israelite or Jewish people, started there in the land of Egypt as Satan's way of trying to destroy that nation so the Redeemer could not come into the world.

Now, when you look at God's dealings with the nation of Israel, both in Old Testament times and New Testament times to what God projects for them in the future, God made it very clear that He chose the nation of Israel to have a unique relationship with Him. Not because Israel was greater than any other nation; Moses very clearly stated that more than once in Deuteronomy. He told the people of Israel, "We were not greater in number. That's not why God chose us." But God chose the nation of Israel because He wanted to use that nation as a key to His accomplishment of world history. One part of the key was that through that nation the promised Redeemer would be born into the world that would do the work of crushing Satan and getting rid of him and his kingdom rule from planet earth.

In Deuteronomy 28, God mapped out ahead of time, early in Israel's history, His whole future course in dealing with that particular nation, right up to the Second Coming of the Messiah. In verses 1-14, God told the people of Israel that as long as they would listen to and obey His commandments, He would bless them more than any other nation on the face of the earth. They would always be the head nation, never the tail nation, and He told them why He would bless them that way: in return for their obedience. In verse 10 He says, "*And all people of the earth shall see that you are called by the name of the Lord and they shall be afraid of you*" (NKJV). God would bless them more than any other nation when they obeyed Him to arouse the curiosity of the world, "*Why is this nation being blessed more than we are?*" and bring them to the fact that it is because they have a unique relationship with the true and the living God of the universe.

But then, beginning in verse 15 and going to the end of the chapter, God warned the people of Israel that if they would not listen to and obey His commandments or His Word, He would curse them more than any other nation on the face of the earth. And one of the curses He pointed out was the fact, verses 49-50, "*The Lord shall bring a nation against you from afar, from the end of the earth, as swift as the eagle flies, a nation whose tongue you shall not understand, a nation of fierce countenance which shall not regard the person of the old nor show favor to the young.*" And God went on to point out that these four nations that He would raise up against Israel would scatter them throughout the nations of the world.

And so He said in verse 64, "*The Lord shall scatter thee among all people from the one end of the earth even unto the other.*" And verse 65, "*And among these nations shall you find no ease, neither shall the sole of your foot have rest; but the*

Lord shall give you there a trembling heart and failing of eyes and sorrow of mind and your life shall hang in doubt before you. You shall fear day and night and shall have no assurance of your life. In the morning you shall say, 'Would God it were even,' and in even you shall say, 'Would God it were morning,' for the fear of your heart wherewith you shall fear and for the sight of your eyes which you shall see."

And if you know the history of the nation of Israel, you know that, tragically, the greater part of their history has been characterized by the curses rather than by the blessings because of rebellion and disobedience against God. And so they have been scattered throughout the world for centuries. And just as He said here, they would despair for life itself. You study the history of the Jewish people. As they have been scattered among the Gentile nations of the world, they've been hounded; they've been persecuted more than any other particular group in all of world history. Anti-Semitism has been poured out upon them venomously in Gentile nations all over the world. The Holocaust of World War II is a very classic example. And Satan, because God allows the people of Israel to be chastened because of their rebellion against Him, Satan continues to go after them with a vengeance trying to annihilate them from the face of the earth because they still remain a key to God defeating Satan.

God has made it very clear in the Scriptures that He will not finish the job of crushing Satan until the people of Israel repent of their rebellion against Him and place their trust in Jesus Christ as their true Messiah and Savior. And so, to Satan's way of thinking, *"if Israel must repent and believe in Jesus before God will crush me, if I can totally annihilate Israel from the face of the earth before they repent and believe...God will never crush me."*

And so today, you notice what's happening with the nation of Israel in the Middle East. Over and over again it's in the news because of terrorists attacking it. Islamic forces align themselves together against Israel and declare that they want to annihilate Israel from the face of the earth. And the prophetic Scriptures make it very clear that Israel's worst days are still ahead.

Question #8

What do the dry bones in Ezekiel 37 represent?

A FTER SAYING THAT HE would scatter Israel throughout the nations for their disobedience, in Ezekiel 37, God brought the prophet Ezekiel to a valley that was full of dry bones. And we read in verses 2-3 that Ezekiel says that: "*God caused me to pass by them all around and, behold, there were very many in the open valley, and, lo, they were very dry. And He said unto me, 'Son of man, can these bones live?' And I answered, 'O Lord God, you know'*" (NKJV).

Now, what do these bones represent? We're told in verse 11 that God said to Ezekiel, "*Son of man, these bones are the whole house of Israel.*" He's picturing Israel here as dry bones, scattered, oppressed, with almost no life in them whatsoever as they are hounded and persecuted by the peoples of the world. And that's still even going on in some respects today. But then he goes on to say in verses 4-8:

> *Again He said to me, "Prophesy to these bones, and say to them, 'O dry bones, hear the word of the Lord! Thus says the Lord God to these bones: "Surely I will cause breath to enter into you, and you shall live. I will put sinews on you and bring flesh upon you, cover you with skin and*

put breath in you; and you shall live. Then you shall know that I am the Lord.""" So I prophesied as I was commanded; and as I prophesied, there was a noise, and suddenly a rattling; and the bones came together, bone to bone. Indeed, as I looked, the sinews and the flesh came upon them, and the skin covered them over; but there was no breath in them (NKJV).

God, through the prophets, foretold that toward the end of world history He would restore the people of Israel back to their homeland, the land of Israel, or as the world has known it for many years, the land of Palestine. But interestingly, we've seen a return of hundreds of thousands of Jewish people from all over the world back to their homeland beginning in 1948 when Israel became a new nation state, independent nation state, for the first time in over 1900 years.

But we must recognize that Israel has returned to their homeland starting in 1948 in unbelief, without spiritual life, and that's what's being signified here. The bones being put back together; the flesh being put upon it; but no breath inside of it; no spiritual life inside of it. Empty spiritually. That's the present state of the nation of Israel in the Middle East. It's back there as a nation state, but it's still out of joint with God; no spiritual life there.

But then God goes on to say that the time would come, verses 8-10: "*And when I beheld, lo, the sinews and the flesh came upon them, the skin covered them above, but there was no breath in them; then said He unto me, 'Prophesy unto the wind. Prophesy, son of man, and say to the wind, Thus says the Lord God, Come from the four winds, O breath, and breathe upon these slain that they may live.' So I prophesied as He commanded, and the breath came into them and they lived and stood up upon their feet an exceeding great army.*"

The prophets make it very clear that at the very end of the seven-year Tribulation period when Jesus Christ the Messiah will come out of heaven in His glorious Second Coming, according to Zechariah 12:10 Messiah will say of the Jews who are still alive, *"They shall look upon Me whom they have pierced, and they will go about in great mourning, household by household, beating themselves upon the breast."* What He is saying is, the Jews who are alive at the Second Coming of Christ, when they see Him come out of heaven in His glorified form, they will finally recognize Him as their true Messiah and Savior and they will repent. They will radically change their mind toward Him and take Him, receive Him as their Messiah and Savior. And that's when life will be breathed into the nation, spiritual life, and they will be made right with God.

Now, please note something. Some people say, "What evidence do we have that there's a God who actually exists?" Well, a great line of evidence is what God has said in the Scriptures: How He would deal with the nation of Israel historically and eventually bring them back to the land, first in rebellion, but then finally, bringing them to a saving knowledge of the Messiah. In 1948 God brought them back to the land in unbelief and rebellion, just as He foretold here over 2500 years ago through the prophet Ezekiel. That's evidence that there is a true and living God. He has foretold He would do this with Israel, and He has been accomplishing that with Israel during the lifetime of most of you who are receiving this teaching right now.

Question #9

What is God's
eternal plan for the Jews?

ONE TIME WHEN VOLTAIRE was visiting at the royal court of Frederick the Great, Frederick the Great thought he would have some sport. He would pit Voltaire against his court chaplain. And so he brought in the chaplain and Voltaire gave all of his arguments against belief in the Bible and belief in God. And when Voltaire was done, Frederick the Great turned to his chaplain and said, "*Well, chaplain, how can you rebut what Voltaire has just said?*" And the chaplain said, "*Your majesty, I can rebut it with one word: the Jew.*" And went on to indicate God foretold in the Scriptures what He would do with the Jew and that He would never allow them to be totally annihilated from the face of the earth; He would preserve them throughout history as a people for His unique purposes. And he said, "*When you look at history, that's exactly what God has done.*"

Now, we're living a couple of centuries after the time of Voltaire and Frederick the Great, and we're seeing something even more significant that God foretold about the people of Israel, what He would do in the future. And we've seen it fulfilled beginning in 1948. Just as God foretold here, He would bring Jews from all over the world back to the homeland and restore them as a nation state but in unbelief for right now. But this is one of the strongest evidences that we have in all the Word of God for the existence of God, and that is that He has caused to happen through history exactly what He said would happen with regard to the Jew, the people of Israel.

In Ezekiel 38, God foretold that in the latter times, the latter days, there would be a major military attack against the tiny State of Israel, in the homeland, once Israel would be restored. And God indicated that military attack would be comprised of the armies of six nations as they were known back in Ezekiel's day. God named **five of those nations** in Ezekiel 38:5-6. In verse 5 the **first nation** was **Persia**. Now, that's what it was known as in Ezekiel's day, but modern-day Persia is the nation of **Iran**. God, some 2500 years ago, through this prophecy, was saying that in the end times Iran would be sending military forces against Israel in the Middle East. The radical Muslim government of Iran has publicly declared more than once that its ultimate goal is the annihilation of Israel from the Middle East.

The **second nation** named in verse 5 is **Ethiopia**. Now that again is what that nation was known as in Ezekiel's day, but I must point out that the nation known as Ethiopia back in Ezekiel's day is not the same nation that we know as Ethiopia today. The nation known as Ethiopia in Ezekiel's day is the nation that we know today as the **Sudan**. And Sudan right now, again, is dominated and ruled by a radical Muslim government that hates Israel with a passion and wants to see it destroyed. And, by the way, that Sudanese Muslim government today is attacking Christians in the Sudan; they're literally crucifying Christian pastors on crosses; they are kidnapping many Christian women and children and selling them into slavery to Arab peoples in the Middle East. And God some 2500 years ago was saying Sudan is going to send military forces against Israel in the coming Tribulation period.

The **third nation** named in verse 5 is **Libya**. Libya is located due west of Egypt in North Africa. Libya's leadership in recent years has been very anti-West; anti-American; but even more strongly anti-Israel. And after Netanyahu was elected as the prime minister of Israel in May of 1996, many of the Arab nations of the Middle East got together to hold a conference to try to plan their strategy in light of Netanyahu's election. Libya's leader at that time, Mu'ammar Qaddafi, was one of the most vocal spokesmen at that Arab summit and in essence said, "*We must deal with the nation of Israel.*" He wanted to see Israel destroyed. The leadership in Libya today continues to want to see Israel destroyed from the Middle East.

The **fourth nation** named in verse 6 was **Gomer**. In Ezekiel's day, Gomer was a tribal group of people who were located in the central part of what you and I know today as the nation of **Turkey**.

And then, the **fifth nation** named, verse 6, was "the house of **Togarmah** of the north quarters." In Ezekiel's day Togarmah was another tribal group of people who were located in the eastern part of what you and I know today as the nation of **Turkey**. Now, you're probably aware of the fact that since the end of World War II Turkey, although it's a Muslim nation, has had basically a secular government that has allied itself with the Western nations of the world. Turkey since the end of World War II has been a member of NATO. But that is now radically changing. A radical Muslim party in Turkey won control of the government of the capital city of the nation of Turkey. And when they won that election they publicly stated,

WHAT IS GOD'S ETERNAL PLAN FOR THE JEWS?

"Our next goal is to gain control of the national government of Turkey." And one of the spokesmen for that radical Muslim party said, *"When we do that, we're going to change our relationship with NATO. We're going to establish an Islamic NATO and an Islamic common market."* This radical Muslim party has control of the legislature of the nation of Turkey, and a radical Muslim member of their party was installed as the new prime minister of the nation of Turkey. It looks very much as if Turkey, in the not too distant future, is going to come under complete domination by a radical Muslim element and then it, too, will turn against the nation of Israel and want to see it annihilated from the face of planet earth.

It's interesting to note that every one of these nations named here in Ezekiel 38:5-6 today are Islamic nations. Therefore, God, some 2500 years ago through this prophecy, was indicating that in the end times Israel will have very serious problems with the Islamic nations of the world.

There is an independent secular intelligence agency located in Great Britain that, in light of trends going on in the world, has drawn the conclusion that planet earth is now leaving a major epic of world history and entering a brand new epic of world history. What they meant by that was this. In the present epic of history, the major thing that has determined the decisions of nations and the future direction of the world has been politics. But, they claim, "No longer." In the new epic of history into which we are now entering, the major thing that will determine the decisions of nations and the future direction of the world is religion, specifically the Islamic-Zionist conflict. In other words: Islam against Israel. And they indicate that this is going to alter the whole world situation and involve the world into a new adventure the likes of which the world has never seen before. They are agreeing with what God was foretelling here in Ezekiel 38, that Israel is going to have very serious problems with Islamic nations in the future.

Now, there is a **sixth nation** named here in Ezekiel 38, and interestingly this one is singled out as the leader of this future military attack against Israel. And God gives several identification marks of that leader. Let me deal with two of them. First, the name of the leader, Ezekiel 38:2, where God said to Ezekiel, "*Son of man, set your face against Gog, the land of Magog.*" The land of Magog in Ezekiel's day was located in between the Black and Caspian Seas in the southern part of what we have known historically as **Russia**, or the Soviet Union.

The second identification mark is the geographical location of this leader in 38:14-16: "*Therefore, son of man, prophesy and say unto Gog, 'Thus says the Lord God, in that day when my people of Israel dwell safely shall you not know it? And you shall come from your place out of the north parts*[literally out of the remotest parts of the north] *you and many people with you, all of them riding upon horses, a great company and a mighty army, and you shall come up against my people of Israel as a cloud to cover the land. It shall be in the latter days...'*" Notice, God says this attack against Israel will be in the latter days, but He is saying the leader of this attack will come from the remotest parts of the north.

Keep in mind, Ezekiel was a Hebrew prophet and therefore, when he would refer to geographical locations, he would refer to them from the vantage point of his homeland of Israel. And so he's saying here that the leader of this attack against Israel will come from the remotest parts directly north of Israel. If you were to lay hold of a good world atlas, place one finger on the tiny state of Israel in the Middle East and then move that finger straight north and go as far north as you can and still be in land mass, you would end up in the heartland of what we have known historically as Russia or the Soviet Union.

Both of these identification marks seem to be pointing the same direction, namely, that Russia is going to lead this invasion against Israel in the future Tribulation and that Russia will be allied with several Islamic nations who hate Israel with a passion; will be allied with them and leading them in this attack.

Question #10

Why will Russia lead the attack against Israel?

ONE REASON IS ANTI-SEMITISM. For centuries Russia has been notorious for hatred and persecution and massacring of Jews living in that land. And now that Communism, at least for a while, has lost its grip on the government of Russia, anti-Semitism has been permitted to raise its ugly head again. And there's an organization there in Russia right now called Pamyat that sees ultimate purpose of its existence as that of eliminating every Jew from the land of Russia. And so persecution has begun to break out against the Jews again. And that's why there's been a mass exodus of Jews out of Russia or the Soviet Union, many coming to North America but over half a million of them going back to their ancient homeland of Israel during our present lifetime.

But there is another reason why Russia will lead this attack against Israel. According to the British intelligence service, here is the current thinking of the disgruntled officers of the Russian military. They are saying that in spite of what has happened to Russia since 1991 when it began to fall apart at the seams, Russia can still have superpower status in the world if it will ally itself with the Islamic nations of the world against Israel. And God, some 2500 years ago through Ezekiel 38, was foretelling that is precisely what is going to happen in world history.

Years ago a former Canadian seaman was being honored with other Canadian seamen by the Soviet government for the role they played in the constant supply line of ships from the Western allied nations to Russia's northern seaport during the Second World War. He said that in that ceremony in which these Canadian seamen were honored, they were allowed to ask the Soviet representative some questions. And one question that was asked was this: "Is your government still requiring the young people in your public schools to learn the English language as their second language?" And the government official said, "That had been our policy since the end of World War II but we've changed that." Then he was asked, "To what have you changed it?" He said, "We're now requiring all of our young people in our public schools to learn the Arabic language as their second language." Then he was asked, "Why the change?" He said, "Because my government has concluded that the future of the Soviet Union lies with the Islamic nations of the world." Israel is going to have serious problems with Islamic nations and the nation of Russia in the future Tribulation period.

Question #11

When will the Battle of Gog and Magog prophesied in Ezekiel 38 occur?

WE'RE TOLD HERE IN Ezekiel 38:8, *"after many days, you shall be visited, in the latter years you shall come into the land that is brought back from the sword and is gathered out of many people against the mountains of Israel which have been always waste but is brought forth out of the nations and they shall dwell safely, all of them."* God is saying this attack by Russian Islamic nations will take place after Jewish people had been re-gathered from nations around the world and reestablished in their homeland as a nation. As we've already mentioned, we've seen Israel brought back from many nations and reestablished as a nation state in their homeland beginning in 1948. But God says that this attack will take place when the people of Israel are feeling very safe and secure.

Verse 11, He says to Gog of Magog, *"You shall say, I will go up to the land of unwalled villages; I will go to them that are at rest, that dwell safely; all of them dwelling without walls and having neither bars nor gates."* God is saying that Russia will lead this attack when Israel is feeling so safe and secure in their homeland that they have let down their own defenses; they do not have their own defenses with which to stave off any attack against themselves.

Now, that certainly is not true of Israel at the present time. Israel, because of constant threats, is loaded to the hilt with very sophisticated weaponry. But, according to Daniel 9:27, at the very beginning of the future seven-year Tribulation period, the head of the future revived Roman Empire, the Antichrist, is going to confirm a covenant with the nation of Israel for a seven-year period, and through that covenant, Antichrist will guarantee the national security of Israel. And so Israel initially in the Tribulation period will feel very safe and so secure because of the commitment by the revived Roman Empire ruler to defend Israel against all attackers. But now, according to Daniel 9:27, in the middle of the seven-year Tribulation period, Antichrist himself will turn against Israel and begin desolating it worse than it's ever been desolated in all of world history from the past.

So therefore it's only during the first half of the seven-year Tribulation period that Israel is going to feel safe and secure while Antichrist is still its protector and its great ally. In light of that, we are forced to conclude Russia and these Islamic nations will invade Israel during the first half of the seven-year Tribulation period. And we shall be looking at another prophecy later which will relate to this, and we'll see some of the things that will cause Russia and these Islamic nations to come in during the first half of the Tribulation period against Israel.

Question #12

Is the Battle of Gog and Magog prophesied in Ezekiel 38-39 the same battle as Gog and Magog in Revelation 20:7-10?

WHILE GOG AND MAGOG are mentioned in Ezekiel 38-39 and Revelation 20:7-10, as you read these passages you will see distinct differences. As we have just discussed, the battle in Ezekiel 38 occurs during the first half of the seven-year Tribulation period while Israel is feeling safe and secure under the protection of the Antichrist.

"When the thousand years are completed, Satan will be released from his prison, and will come out to deceive the nations which are in the four corners of the earth, Gog and Magog, to gather them together for the war; the number of them is like the sand of the seashore. And they came up on the broad plain of the earth and surrounded the camp of the saints and the beloved city, and fire came down from heaven and devoured them. And the devil who deceived them was thrown into the lake of fire and brimstone, where the beast and the false prophet are also; and they will be tormented day and night forever and ever" (Rev. 20:7-10, NASB). We see the timing in this battle is at the end of the Millennium when Satan has been released from the abyss.

In the battle of Ezekiel 38-39 the armies come from the north and involve only Russia and specific Islamic nations. The battle in Revelation 20:7-9 will involve all the nations of the earth from every direction, *"the four corners of the earth."*

In the battle of Ezekiel 38-39 it will take seven months to bury the dead. *"On that day I will give Gog a burial ground there in Israel, the valley of those who pass by east of the sea, and it will block off those who would pass by. So they will bury Gog there with all his horde, and they will call it the valley of Hamon-gog. 'For seven months the house of Israel will be burying them in order to cleanse the land'"* (Ezek. 39:11-12, NASB).

There would be no need to bury the dead from the battle in Revelation 20:7-10 because *"fire came down out of heaven, and devoured them."* And the Great White Throne judgment and the New Heaven and New Earth (Rev. 21:1) immediately following this battle.

God uses the battle in Ezekiel 38-39 to bring Israel back to Him (Ezek. 39:21-29). In Revelation 20:7-10, Israel has been faithful to God during the Millennium. Those destroyed in Revelation 20:7-10 were born during the Millennium—so they have never been tempted by Satan. When Satan is released from his prison, he offers them the chance to rebel against God by attacking Jerusalem. Those who rebel are destroyed without any more opportunity for repentance and Satan is sent to the Lake of Fire.

In conclusion, as we look at all of the differences in the Battle of Gog and Magog in Ezekiel 38-39 and the one in Revelation 20:7-10, it is obvious that these are referring to different battles.

Question #13

What was Daniel's vision of the future?

I N DANIEL 7 GOD delivered a very significant prophecy in the form of a vision to the prophet Daniel. The first thing Daniel saw in his prophetic vision, verse 2, was a sea which was being whipped into a stormy condition by the winds of the heavens. Now, keep in mind, this is a vision; and in visions you have symbols, but symbols are very real things. When the *sea* is used symbolically in the Bible, it is used to represent the world of nations, particularly the *Gentile nations*. And that's what it is representing here—the world of Gentile nations in a state of chaos. Because what God was going to portray in this vision is one Gentile nation or kingdom rising up against another and conquering it and assimilating it into itself. As Daniel was watching this vision, one by one **four different animals** came rising out of that storm-tossed sea. God was representing through each of these animals the nations that would effect the whole future course of Gentile world power or dominion from Daniel's day, when Babylon was the great world power, right up to the Second Coming of the Messiah back to planet earth in the future.

The **first wild animal** that came out of the sea was a **winged lion**, and that represented the ancient kingdom of **Babylon** which was the great world power in Daniel's day when he received this revelation from God. Winged lions were the national symbol of the ancient kingdom of Babylon. Standing at the entrances of the royal palaces of the Babylonian kings in the capital city of Babylon were huge stone images of winged lions. It was the national symbol of Babylon, so the winged lion represents Babylon.

But then Daniel saw a **second animal** rising out of the sea, and that was a **bear;** a bear that was lopsided; one side raised higher than the other. This was God's way of indicating that Babylon would not remain the great world power forever but eventually would be conquered by a second great Gentile kingdom represented by this bear as is described for us in verse 5. And from our historic vantage point, we know that second Gentile kingdom, represented by the bear, was the kingdom of **Medo-Persia**. And this part of Daniel's prophetic vision was fulfilled in the year 539 BC, because in 539 BC Medo-Persia conquered Babylon and assimilated it into itself. Why would God ahead of time represent Medo-Persia in the form of a bear? In that part of the world in ancient times a full-grown bear was larger than a full-grown lion. And it's a fact of history that the Medo-Persian kingdom ended up being much larger than the Babylonian kingdom. It not only conquered Babylon, it conquered another great kingdom known as Lydia which was located in the area of the world we know as Turkey today, and then it also conquered the ancient kingdom of Egypt.

By the way, this bear had three ribs between its teeth, representing the remains of three victims it had devoured. Those three victims were Babylon, Lydia, and Egypt—the three great Gentile kingdoms that Medo-Persia conquered. Why was this bear lopsided with one side raised up higher than the other? The Medo-Persian kingdom was a partnership kingdom. In 550 BC, one ruler was able to bring together two national groups, the Medes and the Persians, to form one kingdom. After a while, one of those partners, the Persians, became the dominating partner. It gained more control and authority than the other partner, the Medes, and so God represented one side of the bear—representing Persia—raised up higher than the lower side of the bear, representing the Medes.

But then in Daniel 7:6, Daniel saw a **third beast** rising out of the storm-tossed sea. This was in the form of a **leopard with four wings and four heads**. This was God's way of indicating that the Medo-Persian kingdom would not last forever as the great Gentile world power but eventually would be conquered and assimilated by a third great Gentile kingdom represented by this leopard. From our historic vantage point today, we know that third kingdom was the kingdom of **Greece**—initially under the leadership of Alexander the Great. And this part of Daniel's prophetic dream or vision was fulfilled by the year 331 BC, because by 331 BC Alexander the Great and his Greek Macedonian armies had been able to completely conquer the Medo-Persian kingdom.

Why would God represent this leopard with four heads? Well, it's a fact of history that Alexander the Great died at a very young age, age 32, while out on the field with his men conquering more territory. There was not another man in the Grecian kingdom of the same charisma and administrative ability and influence that Alexander the Great had who was able to replace him and hold that Grecian kingdom together as one unit. And so what happened was, the four leading generals of the Greek army subdivided Alexander the Great's Grecian kingdom into four divisions, and each of those generals took over one of those divisions to rule.

But then in Daniel 7:8, Daniel saw a **fourth beast** come rising out of the storm-tossed sea. And we have to call this a **nondescript beast** because there was no animal alive on the face of the earth that could accurately represent this particular beast. This was God's way of indicating that Greece would not remain the great Gentile power forever but eventually would be conquered and assimilated by this fourth Gentile kingdom, represented by this nondescript beast. And from our historic vantage point today we know what that fourth kingdom was. It was **Rome**. And this part of Daniel's prophetic vision was fulfilled in 146 BC, because by that time Rome had conquered the Grecian kingdom and Greece no longer was an independent kingdom.

Now, the major thing emphasized about this fourth beast was its tremendous strength and overwhelming destructive power. And that was certainly true of the ancient Roman empire. It was able to conquer and bring under its dominion almost all of the ancient Mediterranean Sea world and even some regions beyond the Mediterranean Sea world. It was so powerful that the western half of that Roman Empire was able to last for almost a thousand years and did not fall until 476 AD when barbarian tribes overran it. But the eastern half of the Roman Empire continued to exist for almost another thousand years until finally Muslim forces destroyed it in 1453 AD.

Now, Daniel noticed that this fourth beast had ten horns on its head, and he was really curious as to what this fourth beast and its ten horns was about. He said in Daniel 7:19-20: "*Then I would know the truth of the fourth beast which was diverse from all the others, exceeding dreadful, whose teeth were of iron, his nails of brass which devoured, broke in pieces, stamped the residue of its feet, and of the ten horns that were in his head,...*" He was really curious about this fourth animal and its ten horns.

Thankfully, there was an interpreting angel who attended this vision, and the interpreting angel interpreted the fourth beast and the ten horns. Verse 23, "*The [angel] said, 'The fourth beast shall be the fourth kingdom upon earth which shall be diverse from all kingdoms and shall devour the whole earth and shall tread it down and break it in pieces; and the ten horns out of this kingdom are ten kings that shall arise*'" (NASB).

The angel was indicating that this fourth kingdom, the Roman kingdom, would pass through two phases: the first phase was the beast-conquering phase, and that was certainly true of the ancient Roman Empire. But in the second phase that Roman kingdom would be characterized by ten divisions with ten equal rulers; basically, the idea of a confederation of divisions confederated together for the purpose of strength and influence in the world but not totally integrated. But it would have ten equal rulers ruling over them at the same time.

If you were to study the history of the ancient Roman Empire you would find that never did that empire consist of ten divisions with ten equal rulers ruling over the Roman Empire at the same time. And because that was never true of the ancient Roman Empire, scholars have been forced to conclude that this part of Daniel's prophetic vision has not yet been fulfilled and that therefore, God was indicating that sometime in the long range future there would be a revived form of the Roman Empire that would be established in the world and that revived Roman Empire at first would consist of ten divisions with ten equal rulers.

Now, is there something looming on the horizon today that has the prospect of fulfilling this prophetic vision that God gave to Daniel? Many scholars are convinced, and I believe they are right, that this is the direction that the European Union is heading at the present time.

It looks as if the European Union in the near future will fulfill this phase of Daniel's prophetic vision and it will constitute that revived Roman Empire that initially will have ten divisions with ten equal rulers.

Now, what do we do with the number ten? The number of countries in the European Union fluctuates. Interestingly, it has been indicated that Europe is going to be reorganized into regions rather than nations; that national boundaries will be erased and Europe will be reorganized into regions. And so it could very well be that the number ten that's here in the book of Daniel is referring to ten regions rather than ten nations. Ten regions, confederated together, for the purpose of power and influence in the world but not totally integrated with each other; but ten regions with ten equal rulers ruling over that confederation. These are things that are beginning to form on the horizon during our time right now and it looks as if it's not too far into the future that they will fulfill this prophetic vision that God gave to the prophet Daniel some 2500 years ago.

But as Daniel was considering the ten horns that appeared in this vision - the ten horns representing the ten equal rulers with the ten divisions of the revived Roman Empire - he made this statement in Daniel 7:8: "*I considered the horns, and, behold, there came up among them another little horn* [so this is an eleventh horn] *before whom there were three of the first horns plucked up by the roots. And, behold, in this horn were eyes like the eyes of a man and a mouth speaking great things."*

Daniel said that as he was watching the ten horns that were already on the head of this fourth beast, that after a while, there was an eleventh horn that began pushing its way up through the head of this fourth animal. And as it pushed its way up through the head of that animal, it uprooted three of the original ten horns that were there. Now, in light of the fact that the original ten horns were interpreted by an interpreting angel as representing ten kings or rulers, it's obvious this eleventh horn is also representing a ruler who will rise to power from within this Western European revived Roman Empire, or of the European Union, after that revived Roman Empire has already been established and functioning for some undisclosed period of time with ten equal rulers. And it's indicating that as he rises to power, he will overthrow three of the original ten rulers and thereby gain controlling authority over this Western European revived Roman Empire.

Now, we're told that this little horn had eyes like the eyes of man. Again, this is a vision and we have symbols but symbols of real things. In the Bible, *eyes* are used symbolically for *intelligence*. The implication is, this eleventh ruler will be a very intelligent man. Apparently, he will be noted in the world for his brilliance and perhaps his ability to tackle difficult world problems and come up with very plausible solutions for those world problems and thereby gain tremendous influence in the world. But we're also told that he has a mouth speaking great things.

Now, in order to see what the interpreting angel had to say about this eleventh horn, we look again at Daniel 7:24, where the angel said to Daniel, "*And the ten horns of this kingdom* [of this Roman kingdom] *are ten kings that shall arise. and another* [in other words, an eleventh one] *shall rise after them, and he shall be diverse* [or different] *from the first.*" How will he be different from the first ten rulers? Well, the first ten rulers of the revived Roman Empire will be content to be equal in authority with each other. But not this eleventh ruler; he will not be content to share equal rule with other men. This man will want to be the dominant ruler of the revived Roman Empire.

So the angel says at the end of verse 24, "*He shall subdue three kings.*" He'll overthrow three of the ten and thereby gain controlling power of the revived Roman Empire. What about the mouth "*speaking great things*" that we're told about in verse 8? Here's what the angel says about that in verse 25: "*And he shall speak great words against the Most High.*" Now, in the book of Daniel "*the Most High*" is a reference to the God of Israel, the true and the living God who created the universe and is Sovereign Lord over the entire universe. The Hebrew language literally says of this eleventh ruler that "he *shall speak words at the side of the Most High.*" In other words, on a equal level with the Most High, the implication being that once this ruler of the future revived Roman Empire of Western Europe comes to full power, he's going to, by what he claims about himself, he will try to raise himself to the level of absolute deity, to the level of the true and the living God.

In Daniel 11 this same man is described. In Daniel 11:36 we're told, "*He shall exalt himself and magnify himself above every god and shall speak marvelous things* [literally monstrous things] *against the God of gods.*" Notice, he's going to try to exalt and magnify himself above every God, even including the true and the living God.

In 2 Thessalonians 2 the apostle Paul talks about this same man and he calls him "*the man of sin,*" or literally, "*the man of lawlessness.*" And in 2 Thessalonians 2, Paul says at the end of verse 4, "*The man of sin will be revealed, the son of perdition, who opposes and exalts himself above all that is called God or that is worshipped, so that he as God, sits in the temple of God, showing himself that he is God.*" Paul is indicating here that when this man comes to full power, he is going to walk into a new temple that the people of Israel will have built in Jerusalem by that time and he's going to take control of that temple. And when he does that, he's going to make the bold claim that he is the God of this universe. And the Scriptures make it very clear that people who reject his claim to be God and who refuse to worship him as God, he's going to wage all-out war against them.

And so in light of that, when we come back to Daniel 7:25, the next thing the angel said this man will do is this: "*He shall wear out the saints of the Most High.*" In other words, he's going to wage all-out war against people who are true believers in Jesus Christ during the seven-year Tribulation period. There will be many people saved during this seven-year Tribulation period. Revelation 7 makes that very clear where John saw 144,000 Jewish men who will get saved during the Tribulation period, plus John saw "*a great multitude from every tongue, tribe and nation*" on the face of the earth who will be washed in the blood of the Lamb of God, the Lord Jesus, during the Tribulation period. Many people will get saved during that seven-year period of time, and those Tribulation saints will refuse to acknowledge that Antichrist is God, will refuse to worship him, and as a result, he will wage all-out war against those Tribulation saints.

Interestingly, this same man is described for us again in Revelation 13 where he is presented as a *"beast who comes out of the sea."* And this is what we're told about him: that the beast was worshipped. Verse 4: *"They worshipped the dragon (who is Satan) which gave power unto the beast* [the Antichrist], *and they worshipped the beast, saying, 'Who is like unto the beast? Who is able to make war with him?' And there was given unto him a mouth speaking great things and blasphemies and power was given unto him to continue for forty and two months. He opened his mouth in blasphemy against God to blaspheme His name and His tabernacle and them that dwell in them. And it was given unto him to make war with the saints and overcome them; and power was given him over all kindreds and tongues and nations and all that dwell upon the earth shall worship him whose names are not written in the book of life of the Lamb slain from the foundation of the world."*

Tribulation saints will not go along with the masses of people in the world who will worship the Antichrist. Tribulation saints will refuse to worship him as God and so he's going to wage all-out war against those saints. And passages in Revelation make it very clear that Tribulation saints will be martyred by the Antichrist. Revelation 20:4-5 make that very clear, for example, that many of these Tribulation saints will be put to death by Antichrist and his forces.

But then, coming back to Daniel 7:25 again, the angel told Daniel that this man would also think to change times and laws. Now, we're not told how he will do that, but let me point out *"times and laws,"* time periods and laws, such as natural laws, spiritual laws, etc., are things that were established and ordained by God to bring order into the life of man here on planet earth. And apparently as this man, Antichrist—by the way, John calls him the Antichrist in 1 John 2—as this man, the Antichrist, the future ruler of the revived Roman Empire of Western Europe, claims that he is God, he's going to try to usurp priorities that belong exclusively to the true and the living God and try to change time periods and laws different from the way God had established them in order to demonstrate the fact that he is deity. This man is going to be a tyrant, an absolute dictator.

God, some 2500 years ago, through this prophecy that He gave to Daniel and other prophets, made it very clear that's exactly what Western Europe is going to get. When the European Union has been functioning for a period of time with ten equal rulers and ten divisions, there will be an eleventh ruler that will rise to power within that European Union, that revived Roman Empire, gain control of it, but he's going to be energized and dominated by Satan. He's going to be an absolute dictator. He's going to be a tyrant. He will demand that he have his own way and anyone who rejects his claim to be God, he will try to put to death.

You see, this again demonstrates there is a true and a living God, that He knows the end from the beginning. And some 2500 years ago He could foretell these things that are going to take place as we move into the end times. And it looks as if the world is very quickly moving in this direction, even in Western Europe at this time in which we are now living.

We've seen on the basis of Daniel 7 that the Antichrist will rise to power from within the future revived Roman Empire, or as we expressed a conviction, the direction that the Western Europe nations are heading right now with the European Union.

There's a very significant prophetic passage in Daniel 11 that sheds a lot more light on this man and, particularly, significant world events that are going to impact him. In Daniel 11:36-39, we have the character of the Antichrist being portrayed. And the first thing we're told in verse 36 is that *"he will do according to his will,"* indicating that once this man comes to power, he's going to be a strong-willed individual. He will demand that he have his own way; he will not tolerate anyone else being in authority over him telling him what he may do and what he may not do.

The next thing we're told about his character is that he will oppose all established forms of worship. For example, near the middle of verse 36, we're told that he shall speak marvelous, literally monstrous, things against the God of gods. As we've noted earlier, he'll be a blasphemer against the true and the living God, and that's what is being declared here. Verse 37 says, *"Neither shall he regard the god of his fathers."* Now, some have concluded that this indicates the Antichrist will be a Jew because, you know, the Jews talked about the God of their fathers Abraham, Isaac and Jacob. Maybe he will be a Jew, but I'm not convinced we can conclude that on the basis of this one statement. The reason I say that is, the word translated *"god"* in the expression *"god of his fathers"* has a pluralized ending so it could also be translated *"the gods of his fathers."* The point here is this: not whether he is a Jew or Gentile, but the fact that **this man will oppose the worship of any god or gods that his ancestors revered and worshipped**.

What does Daniel 11:37 mean when it says the Antichrist will have no regard for the desire of women?

Then we're told in Daniel 11:37 that *"he will have no regard for the desire of women."* Now, many have taken that to mean this man will be a bachelor;

that he will not experience a man's normal physical desire toward a woman. But the context suggests *"desire of women"* is not referring to a man's normal physical desire toward a woman. Right before the expression *"the desire of women"* the text is talking about objects of worship: He'll have no regard for the god or gods of his fathers. Right after the expression *"the desire of women"* it says, *"nor regard any god."* The whole context surrounding *"the desire of women"* is talking about object of worship. In light of that, it appears *"desire of women"* is referring to an **object of worship**. What could it be? Well, historically, *it was the supreme desire of many Jewish women to be the mother of the Messiah*, and because of that, the Messiah historically was also known as *"the desire of women."* And what this is saying is, this **Antichrist will have no respect, regard, whatsoever for the true Messiah, the Lord Jesus**. He will oppose everything that Jesus is or that Jesus has done or that Jesus stands for. That's why John in 1 John 2 calls him "Antichrist."

Then we're told at the end of verse 37 why he will oppose all established forms of worship: *"He shall magnify himself above all."* He's going to try to magnify himself above every god or goddess that's ever been worshipped by mankind. And in 2 Thessalonians 2 Paul indicates that **Antichrist, when he's at the peak of his power, will take control of a new Jewish temple in Jerusalem and will set himself up there as God.**

Who is the god that the Antichrist will worship?

Daniel 11:38 tells us that he himself will have a god whom he will worship. We're told in verse 38, *"But in his estate shall he honor the god of fortresss,"* literally the *"god of munitions or armaments."* The point is that this man is going to make war his god. Whatever a man is totally sold out to and devoted to, whatever is the center of his life and drives and motivates him, is that man's god. And war is going to be the Antichrist's god. He's going to try to conquer the whole world and bring it under his dominion on behalf of his master, Satan.

And we're told here that's a god whom "*his fathers knew not.*" His ancestors didn't make war their god. And we're also told in verse 38 that he shall honor this god "*with gold, silver, with precious stones and precious things.*" Apparently, he will expend huge amounts of wealth in equipping, training, preparing and then marching his armies out across the landscape of planet earth and that's how he will honor his god of war. And it would appear that he will enjoy a great deal of military success because verse 39 says, "*Thus shall he do in the most strongholds with a strange god.*" The idea seems to be that by making war his god, he will be successful in conquering some of the strongest military outposts on the face of the earth.

And then verse 39 says, "*Whom he shall acknowledge and increase with glory.*" Now, the Hebrew text gives the idea that he shall honor those who acknowledge him. In other words, he will reward his most devoted followers. And the end of verse 39 tells us **two ways he shall reward them**. **First**, "*he shall cause them to rule over many.*" As the Antichrist conquers new groups of people, he will turn over the rule of those newly conquered peoples to some of his most devoted followers. In other words, he will put some of his most devoted followers into positions of rule within his government. And the **second** way that he will reward them is, "*he shall divide the land.*" As he conquers new geographical territory, he shall turn over choice pieces of land as gifts to his most devoted followers as rewards for being so devoted to him. This is a very interesting insight into the character of the coming Antichrist.

But when we come to **Daniel 11:40-45**, we have the military career of the Antichrist being revealed. Verse 40 says, "*And at the time of the end*"—this is going to be in the future Tribulation—"*shall the king of the south push at him, and the king of the north shall come against him like a whirlwind with chariots, with horsemen and with many ships.*" Who is the "*him*" of verse 40? Well, in light of the fact that it's the Antichrist that's just been described in the immediately preceding verses, it's obvious that the "*him*" of verse 40 is the *Antichrist*. So Daniel is being told in verse 40 that at the time of the end, Antichrist will be attacked militarily by the king of the south and the king of the north. But who are the king of the south and the king of the north in verse 40?

Thankfully, the events in **Daniel 11:2-35** have already been fulfilled historically. In fact, they were fulfilled even before the first coming of Christ. In light of that historic fulfillment it's interesting to note that the king of the south and the king of the north are referred to several times in Daniel 11:2-35. So we know who they were in that passage. The **king of the south** in those verses was always the nation of **Egypt**, directly south of Israel. And the **king of the north** in verses 2-35 was always the nation of **Syria**, directly north of Israel, the same Syria and Egypt that are in the Middle East today and that sometimes cause problems for Israel.

And so **Daniel 11:2-35 is past history**; but here, the king of the south and the king of the north are referred to again in verse 40 which has not yet been fulfilled, and since Daniel is not told these are different from the king of the south and the king of the north of verses 2-35, we can draw the conclusion they are still the same two nations. Therefore, what Daniel is being told here by God in verse 40 was this: that in the future Tribulation period, Antichrist will be attacked jointly by Egypt and Syria at the same time. But that revelation poses a problem. How will they attack Antichrist? At this time, our understanding is, Antichrist will be headquartered over in Western Europe as the head of the Western European revived Roman Empire, and as you know, Syria and Egypt are two Middle Eastern nations. If they're in the Middle East and he's in Europe, how will they attack him? I want to make a proposal to you as to how this could happen.

According to Daniel 9:27, at the very beginning of the seven-year Tribulation, Antichrist is going to confirm a covenant with the nation of Israel in the Middle East. The Hebrew language of Daniel 9:27 makes it very clear that this will be a strong, binding covenant. The implication seems to be that through the confirming of that covenant, Antichrist will so strongly bind the nation of Israel in the Middle East to its Western European revived Roman Empire, that he will actually regard Israel as an extension of himself and his revived Roman Empire in the Middle East. And therefore, any attack against Israel will be an attack against him. In light of that, I would propose that the way in which Syria and Egypt will jointly attack the Antichrist is by those two Middle Eastern nations jointly attacking his Middle East ally, Israel, at the same time. Syria will come down from the north against Israel, while Egypt comes up from the south against Israel in a pincher type military movement.

How will Antichrist (while over in Western Europe) react when he receives news to the fact that his Middle Eastern ally, Israel, has been jointly attacked by Syria and Egypt? At the end of Daniel 11:40 we're told, "*and he shall enter into the countries and shall overflow and pass over.*" Keeping his covenant commitment to

Israel, Antichrist will move his Western European armies into the Middle East and will begin overflowing the nations of the Middle East.

Now, when you begin reading at the end of verse 40 and you read down through verse 43, it becomes obvious that once he invades the Middle East, his movements will be from north of Israel to south of Israel. Apparently, he will invade Syria north of Israel first, and other peoples probably around there—probably Lebanon as well—and take control of them. But then, verse 41 says, "*He shall enter also into the glorious land.*" Obviously to Daniel, the "*glorious land*" is the land of Israel. After Antichrist has finished his conquest of Syria in the north, he will march his Western European army south through the land of Israel. And we're told, "*many shall be overthrown, but these shall escape out of his hand, even Edom and Moab and the chief of the children of Ammon.*"

In Daniel's day, Edom, Moab and Ammon were nations located due east of Israel right across the Jordan River. Today that is the nation of Jordan. The implication is, that when Antichrist marches his army south through Israel, he is so anxious to get down to Egypt, the other enemy that attacked his ally, Israel, that he won't take the time to cross east of the Jordan River to take control of the nation of Jordan. And he will get down to Israel.

We are told in verse 42, "*He shall stretch forth his hand also upon the countries and the land of Egypt shall not escape, but he shall have power over the treasures of gold and of silver and over all the precious things of Egypt, and the Libyans and the Ethiopians shall be at his steps.*" What this is saying is, he will get to Egypt and he will be able to conquer the entire nation of Egypt. When it says here "*the Libyans will be at his steps,*" literally at his heels, the point is, he will conquer Egypt clear over to its western border with Libya and stop there and turn around so that when he turns around, the Libyans will be at his back, at his heels. And then he will conquer Egypt, as far south as you can go to its border with its southern neighbor, so that when he turns around, that southern neighbor of Egypt will be at his heels as well. This is God's way of saying the Antichrist will be able to conquer the entire nation of Egypt. And it will look as if the whole Middle East is going to come under this Western European ruler's control.

But look at the contrast word that begins Daniel 11:44: "*But....*" In other words, in contrast to the way it will appear, "*tidings out of the east and out of the north shall trouble him.*" What will be the substance of this disturbing news from the north and from the east that Antichrist will receive while he's down in Egypt taking a spoil of the resources of the nation of Egypt?

We noted earlier a prophecy that God gave to the prophet Ezekiel in Ezekiel 38 to the effect that during the first half of the Tribulation period, Israel will be jointly attacked by Islamic nations and Russia, Russia leading this multi-nation attack against Israel. We saw there that Russia is going to come from the north against Israel. We also saw that one of the Islamic nations that is going to attack will be Iran and Iran is due east of Israel. I would propose to you that the disturbing news that Antichrist will hear while down in Egypt is to the effect that his ally Israel has been attacked again, this time by the joint forces of Islamic nations and Russia—Ezekiel 38.

In **Daniel 11:44**, Antichrist will receive disturbing news down in Egypt, disturbing news from the north and from the east. And we've noted that Russia and Iran are going to come together with other nations against

Israel in the first half of the Tribulation period—Russia from the north, Iran from the east—and it would appear that's the disturbing news that Antichrist will hear when he's in Egypt.

How will he react to this disturbing news? In the middle of verse 44 we are told, *"Therefore, he will go forth with great fury to destroy and utterly to make away many."* In other words, keeping his covenant commitment to Israel, Antichrist will rush his Western European armies north out of Egypt to the land of Israel with the goal of trying to totally destroy the invading armies of Russia, Iran and other Islamic nations.

But if you know the Ezekiel prophecy, Ezekiel 38 and 39, God makes it very clear that in the day that Russia, Iran and other Islamic nations attack Israel, God says, *"Then my fury will come up in my face,"* and God indicates that He will intervene supernaturally, through supernatural means, and God will supernaturally wipe out these massive armies of Russia, Iran and other Islamic nations. Read Ezekiel 38 and 39 where that is made very clear.

The end result is that by the time Antichrist gets up to Israel, the armies of these other invaders have already been wiped out supernaturally, and that will give the Antichrist a free hand to do what he wants in the Middle East. And so notice what he will do in Daniel 11:45: *"And he shall plant the tabernacles of his palace between the seas in the glorious holy mountain."* Once he gains control of the Middle East, he will decide to plant his palace, in other words, his headquarters for what he hopes will become the capital of a worldwide kingdom; he's going to plant it there in the Middle East between two seas. That would be between the Dead Sea on the east and the Mediterranean Sea on the west, and that palace between the seas will be in the glorious holy mountain. The glorious holy mountain to Daniel would be Mount Zion where the Temple stood in Old Testament times. In other words, once Antichrist gains complete control in the Middle East, he's going to make Jerusalem the capital of what he hopes will become his worldwide kingdom.

Then the world will come to the exact middle of the seven-year Tribulation period and it's at this point that what Paul described in 2 Peter 2:4 will take place: "*For if God spared not the angels that sinned, but cast them down to hell, and delivered them into chains of darkness, to be reserved unto judgment.*"

Now that he has complete control of Jerusalem, Antichrist will walk into a new temple that the people of Israel will have built there by that time, and according to Daniel 9:27 he will put a stop to sacrifices and offerings that the Jews will have reinstituted there in their temple by that time.

And then Paul says in 2 Thessalonians 2:4, "*who opposes and exalts himself above every so-called god or object of worship, so that he takes his seat in the temple of God, displaying himself as being God*" (NASB). He will claim that he's absolute deity. It would not be surprising if he tried to claim the credit for the supernatural destruction of the armies of Iran and Russia and their Islamic allies and said to the world, "*Look at what I was able to do without using one man-made weapon. It's obvious these massive armies have been destroyed supernaturally. This demonstrates I'm more than a man. I am supernatural. I am God. And you either worship me as God, or I try to put you to death.*"

And according to Daniel 9:27, when Antichrist does that, that's when Israel will begin to be desolated worse than it's ever been desolated in all of past history. And that's when Antichrist now will turn against Israel and the man that Israel thought would be its great protector in the Tribulation period will end up becoming its great attacker. And he will go after Israel with a vengeance and try to annihilate it from the face of the earth because his master, Satan, wants Israel annihilated before it can repent so that God will not crush Satan and his forces and get rid of them from planet earth altogether.

Now, it's interesting, right after Daniel 11:45 we are told in Daniel 12:1, "*And at that time...*" At what time? The time that Antichrist will take control of Jerusalem in the middle of the Tribulation and claim that he is God, "*At that time shall Michael stand up, the great prince which stands for the children of your people, and there shall be a time of trouble such as never was since there was a nation, even to that same time.*"

What God is revealing is this: When Antichrist makes that claim to be God, Michael, the great Archangel whom God has assigned to the nation of Israel to prevent that nation from being fully annihilated from the face of the earth, Michael is going to have to stand up and go into all-out action. And the reason is because Antichrist and other satanic forces are going to go after Israel now. Throughout the entire second half of the seven-year Tribulation period, they'll go after Israel with a vengeance trying to annihilate them from the face of the earth. And Michael is going to have to go into all-out action to prevent Israel from being totally annihilated from the face of the earth. And this passage is saying that is going to be the unparalleled time of trouble in all of world history.

In light of that, Jesus made some very significant statements in Matthew 24. Speaking to Jews who will be living in the land of Israel, at the middle of the Tribulation period, this is what Jesus said, Matthew 24:15: *"When you therefore shall see the abomination of desolation spoken of by Daniel the prophet"*—Jesus going back to Daniel 9:27—*"When you see the abomination of desolation spoken of by Daniel the prophet stand in the holy place."* Israel's holy place would be the temple. What He's referring to is an image of the Antichrist that Antichrist will set up in that Jewish temple in Jerusalem claiming that he's God. And so Jesus is saying when you see that abominable, detestable thing, an image of a man, the Antichrist, standing in your holy place, your temple, claiming that the man represented by that image is God, Jesus said, this is what you Jews had better do. Matthew 24:16: *"Then let them which be in Judea flee into the mountains."* Get out into the mountain wilderness. *"Let him which is on a housetop not come down to take anything out of his house. Neither let him which is in the field return back to take his clothes. Woe until them that are with child and to them that give suck in those days! But pray that your flight be not in the winter, neither on the sabbath day."*

What He's saying to Jews who will be living in the land of Israel at that time, when that image of the Antichrist goes up in your new temple and the Antichrist claims that he's God, you drop everything, no matter what you're doing, drop everything and run from where you are. Get out into the mountain wilderness to hide out as fast as you can. And then He told them why they should do that. Matthew 24:21—and here He practically quotes Daniel 12:1—*"For then shall be great tribulation such as was not since the beginning of the world to this time, no nor ever shall be. And except those days should be shortened, there should no flesh be saved; but for the elect's sake, those days will be shortened."*

Jesus indicating when Antichrist announces he's God in the middle of the Tribulation period, that will begin the Great Tribulation, the unparalleled period of time in all of world history. It'll be so disastrous here on planet earth that if God hadn't determined ahead of time to cut it off after another three and a half years, all flesh would perish from planet earth. The second three and a half years of the Tribulation period will be that terrible.

Question #14

What if you have not trusted Jesus Christ as your Savior before the Tribulation?

MAY I POINT OUT to you that if you've never trusted Jesus Christ, the Son of God, as your Savior, even though He died personally for your sins on the cross, was buried bodily in the grave, and rose bodily from the dead three days later, if you've never trusted Jesus Christ as your Savior, please heed the warning of the prophecies we've been examining.

God has revealed these future events not to satisfy our curiosity about what's going to happen, but instead to change hearts and lives. And God has revealed these future events to issue a warning to unbelievers that if you're an unbeliever on the earth when Christ comes and raptures the Church out of the world, you're going to be left here on the earth to go into this horrible Tribulation period. And you're going to have to go through the unparalleled time of trouble on planet earth in which great masses of humanity are going to disappear from the face of the earth through horrendous judgments. And you're going to be under the tyrant rule of this Antichrist.

And when he makes his claim to be God, you're going to have to make a horrible decision. If you accept the Antichrist's claim to be God and worship him as God, according to 2 Thessalonians 2, that will seal your doom forever. You will not be able to get saved once you accept Antichrist's claim to be God and worship him as God, and you will spend eternity in the eternal lake of fire under the conscious torment and judgment of God forever.

But if, in order to escape that wrathful judgment of God, you reject Antichrist's claim to be God, then you will be subject to that man's wrath. And he will pursue you and hunt you down together with his forces and try to put you to death because you reject his claim to be God. What a horrible, horrible decision people are going to have to make at that time.

But our understanding is that Christ is going to Rapture the true believers in Himself from the earth before this seven-year Tribulation period begins. And the Bible makes it very clear that the Rapture could take place at any moment. We can't count on any time between now and the Lord coming to Rapture the Church out of the world. And so if you're an unbeliever, in light of these things, heed the warning from God; trust Jesus Christ as your Savior now before it may be too late for you. We cannot impress upon you strongly enough for your sake the urgency of your doing it at this time; for your sake, but also for the honor and for the glory of God.

Question #15

Who are the 144,000 in Revelation?

THE FIRST MENTION OF the 144,000 is in Revelation 7:1-8:

And after these things I saw four angels standing on the four corners of the earth, holding the four winds of the earth, that the wind should not blow on the earth, nor on the sea, nor on any tree. And I saw another angel ascending from the east, having the seal of the living God: and he cried with a loud voice to the four angels, to whom it was given to hurt the earth and the sea, Saying, Hurt not the earth, neither the sea, nor the trees, till we have sealed the servants of our God on their foreheads. And I heard the number of them who were sealed: and there were sealed a hundred and forty and four thousand of all the tribes of the children of Israel. Of the tribe of Judah were sealed twelve thousand. Of the tribe of Reuben were sealed twelve thousand. Of the tribe of Gad were sealed twelve thousand. Of the tribe of Asher were sealed twelve thousand. Of the tribe of Naphtali were sealed twelve thousand. Of the tribe of Manasseh were sealed twelve thousand. Of the tribe of Simeon were sealed twelve thousand. Of the tribe of Levi were sealed twelve thousand. Of the tribe of Issachar were sealed twelve thousand. Of the tribe of Zebulun were sealed twelve thousand. Of the tribe of Joseph were sealed twelve thousand. Of the tribe of Benjamin were sealed twelve thousand.

We see from these verses that God has sealed 144,000 Jewish men; 12,000 from each of the twelve tribes of Israel before He allows the angels to hurt the earth. While that sealing may not grant them physical protection from what Satan and his helpers will want to do to them, it will enable them to spread the good news about redemption through the Lamb.

In Revelation 14:1-5 we see the Lamb (Jesus) and the 144,000 on Mount Zion. This is a heavenly scene:

> And I looked, and, lo, a Lamb stood on Mount Zion, and with him a hundred and forty-four thousand, having his Father's name written in their foreheads. And I heard a voice from heaven, as the voice of many waters, and as the voice of a great thunder: and I heard the voice of harpers harping with their harps: And they sung as it were a new song before the throne, and before the four beasts, and the elders: and no man could learn that song but the hundred and forty-four thousand, who were redeemed from the earth. These are they who were not defiled with women; for they are virgins. These are they who follow the Lamb wherever he goes. These were redeemed from among men, being the first fruits unto God and to the Lamb. And in their mouth was found no guile: for they are without fault before the throne of God.

Apparently God is not finished with the Jews yet. There are many prophecies that are partly fulfilled on the literal nation of Israel, and we await their total fulfillment. Many cults claim that they are the 144,000, but we read in these verses that they are not accurately interpreting the Scriptures.

Question #16

Why do we assume there will be a new Temple built in Jerusalem, and what preparations are being made for it?

WE'VE MADE SOME REFERENCES to a new temple that the people of Israel will have at least by the first half of the seven-year Tribulation period. We note in 2 Thessalonians 2:4 that the apostle Paul referred to the fact that Antichrist in the middle of the Tribulation will walk into that temple and announce that he's God. He noted in Daniel 9:27 that when Antichrist does that in the middle of the Tribulation, he'll put a stop to sacrifices and offerings that the Jews will be offering by that time. The Jews will not offer sacrifices and offerings to God without a temple. That implies there will be a temple. We noted in Matthew 24:15 Jesus said to the Jews of the future Tribulation, "*When you see the abomination of desolation stand in your holy place.*" Jesus, again, was referring to the temple. All these things indicate that the people of Israel, the nation of Israel, will have a new temple for at least the first half of the Tribulation period. How does that relate to some of the current trends going on?

Today, there's an interesting organization in Jerusalem called The Temple Institute. And scholars and skilled craftsmen, as a result of research, have already reproduced many of the instruments of worship that were used in the Old Testament temples of Israel. They've reproduced the high priests' garments. They've reproduced the long silver trumpets that were played in the worship services of the Old Testament temples.

In addition, they have set up a training school where they are taking Jewish men whom they are convinced are physical descendants of the priestly tribe of Israel and they are training them how to perform the ritual and worship of the Old Testament priesthood; even how to perform the animal sacrifices. They want everything ready to go so that when they can build the new temple, everything will be set for the worship that's there.

In addition, there's a Jewish couple that migrated to Jerusalem from the United States a number of years ago. Through their research they have rediscovered the kinds of harps that were played in the worship services of the Old Testament temples, and they're in the process of reproducing those harps so that those will be available for the new temple. In addition, there is an elderly Jewish woman living in France who has been a professional musician for most of her life and she, through intensive research, has rediscovered the kind of music that was played in the worship services and that was sung in the worship services of Solomon's temple and the second temple which Herod eventually had called his temple. And she's already set some of the Old Testament poetic books such as the Song of Solomon to that temple music. She's in the process of setting all 150 of the psalms from the Old Testament to that temple music so that the music will be ready when the temple is built.

It is very interesting to note that it's just been within the last number of years that all this activity toward a new temple has been taking place. And God, through the prophetic Scriptures in Daniel 9:27, Matthew 24:15, and in 2 Thessalonians 2:4, is making it very clear that Israel will have a new temple during the first half of the Tribulation period. And when Antichrist takes control of Jerusalem in the middle of that Tribulation period, he's going to confiscate that temple for his purposes and announce that he is God.

Interestingly, again, this demonstrates there is a God who knows the end from the beginning; that He could foretell even thousands of years ago there would be a temple in this future period of time. And we notice how movement in that direction is taking place right now during our present lifetime. So Israel will have a new temple.

But we also noted that once Antichrist takes charge of that and announces he's God, he's going to turn against Israel and begin persecuting it worse than it's ever been persecuted in all of past history. And one of the reasons is, Satan wants to annihilate the nation of Israel and the Jewish people from the face of the earth. Why does Satan want to do that? Well, the reason is, there's a program to which God has committed Himself and it's revealed in the Scriptures in various ways. The program is this: That God will not finally crush Satan and get rid of him and his kingdom rule from planet earth until the people of Israel as a nation repent of their rebellion against God and believe in Jesus Christ as their true Messiah and Savior. To Satan's way of thinking, "If God will not crush me until Israel repents and believes in Jesus Christ as its Messiah and Savior, if I can totally annihilate Israel, the Jewish people, from the face of the earth before they repent and believe in Jesus, then God will never crush me." So in light of that, here's a significant thing that Satan is going to do in the second half of the seven-year Tribulation period.

In Revelation 16: 12-16, the apostle John records something that's going to happen when the sixth bowl judgment is poured out upon planet earth, the sixth bowl or vial judgment. Now, this will be the next to the last judgment of the seven-year Tribulation period, so this is what's going to transpire almost at the very end of the seven-year Tribulation period. John says, Revelation 16:12, *"And the sixth angel poured out his vial upon the great river Euphrates, and the water thereof was dried up that the way of the kings of the east might be prepared."*

The Euphrates River, historically, at least in ancient times, was the major dividing line between most of Asia and the Middle East. It was a natural barrier. Interestingly, it was a natural barrier between the Roman Empire, which extended that far east to the Euphrates River, and the Parthian Empire which was east of the Euphrates River. And the Romans were never able to conquer the Parthians. It was a dividing line there. It was always a natural barrier that invading forces against Israel had to cross to come against Israel. The Medo-Persians had to come across it; the Babylonians had to come across it; the Assyrians had to come across the Euphrates River from Asia to attack Israel.

This prophecy is indicating that right near the end of the seven-year Tribulation period, the Euphrates River is going to be dried up to make it possible for the rulers of Asia, the rulers of the Far East, to march their massive forces west across the Euphrates River to come to the land of Israel. This could include all the Asiatic nations, China, India, Indonesia, Thailand, Japan and on and on you could go; all the Asiatic forces are going to move their armed forces westward across the Euphrates River at the very end of the seven-year Tribulation period to come to the land of Israel.

But that's only the beginning of this particular prophecy. Revelation 16:13 goes on to say, "*And I saw three unclean spirits like frogs come out of the mouth of the dragon.*" The dragon in the book of Revelation is clearly identified as Satan. We're told that, for example, in Revelation 12. "*And out of the mouth of the beast...*" the beast in Revelation is the Antichrist. We referred to him earlier in Revelation 13, the one who will be worshipped as God. He will blaspheme the true and the living God and will wage war against the saints.

"*And out of the mouth of the false prophet.*" The false prophet will be another man who will be energized and controlled by Satan who will lead the unsaved people of the world in the worship of the Antichrist as God. So here are Satan, his Antichrist and his false prophet near the end of the Tribulation period sending demons out into the world. We're told in verse 14 of these unclean spirits, "*for they are the spirits of devils,*" literally "of demons".

Here's what these demons will do: They'll be working miracles. "*They go forth unto the kings of the earth and of the whole world to gather them to the battle of that great day of God Almighty.*" Verse 16, "*And he,*" now, the Greek literally has a force of "***they,***" referring to these demons, "*And they gathered them* [they gathered the rulers of the nations of the world] *together into a place called in Hebrew, Armageddon.*"

This is what John has revealed to him here. Almost at the end of the Tribulation period Satan, his Antichrist and his false prophet are going to use demons, demonic influence, to persuade the rulers of all the Gentile nations of the world, all the Gentile nations without exception—including the kings of the East, the Asiatic kings, but all the Gentile nations from all the rest of the world as well—to bring their combined military forces into the Middle East to the land of Israel. One of the major reasons that Satan will want the combined military might of the Gentile world gathered there in Israel by the end of the Tribulation period will be to be his tool to try to annihilate the nation of Israel from the Middle East before it can repent and believe in the Lord Jesus so that God will not crush him.

When you study the prophet Zechariah, chapters 12-14, this same gathering of the Gentile armies of the world to the land of Israel is very graphically described for us. Zechariah 12:1-3, *"The burden of the word of the Lord for Israel, says the Lord, which stretches forth the heavens and layeth the foundation of the earth and forms the spirit of man within him, Behold, I will make Jerusalem a cup of trembling unto all the people round about when they shall be in the siege both against Judah and against Jerusalem, and in that day will I make Jerusalem a burdensome stone for all people, all that burden themselves with it shall be cut in pieces, though all the people of the earth be gathered together against it."*

And then he goes on to describe how these Gentile armies of the world will wage war against Judah. And when we come to Zechariah 14:1-2: *"Behold, the Day of the Lord comes, and thy spoil shall be divided in the midst of thee, for I will gather all nations against Jerusalem to battle and the city shall be taken and the houses rifled and the women ravished and half of the city shall go forth into captivity and the residue of the people shall not be cut off from the city."*

Now, you might be saying, but this passage has **God** saying He's going to gather the nations of the world into the land of Israel against Judah and against the city of Jerusalem. But we saw earlier in Revelation 16 that **Satan**, the Antichrist and the false prophet are going to use demons to gather the nations there. Isn't that a contradiction? No. Both are true. Both

God and Satan will play a role in bringing those forces there, but for different purposes. Satan will bring them there for one reason: to try to annihilate Israel before it can repent so that God will not crush him. But God will bring them there as well to be His instrument to break Israel's stubborn rebellion against Him and bring them to faith in Jesus Christ as their Messiah and Savior.

So while these armies are there decimating the land of Israel and the city of Jerusalem—and, by the way, Zechariah 13:8,9 make it very clear that things will be so terrible for the people of Israel that two-thirds of the Jews will perish very shortly from the face of the earth; only one-third of them will survive what in scope will be the worst holocaust that Israel has ever experienced in all of history—but when Israel is backed to the wall with every other nation on the face of the earth fighting against it and it looks as if they're about ready to be annihilated, God, through this tremendous pressure, will bring them to repentance; will break their stubborn rebellion against Him.

And so according to Zechariah 12:10, when the Lord Jesus will come out of Heaven in His glorious Second Coming, at this point, at this worst hour in Israel's history, this is what the Messiah will say of the one-third remnant of Jews that are left. In the middle of verse 10 of Zechariah 12: *"They shall look upon Me whom they have pierced, and they shall mourn for Him as one mourns for his only Son and shall be in bitterness for Him as one that is in bitterness for his first born."* He's describing here that when the one-third remnant of Jews see the glorified Christ come out of Heaven and it dawns upon them that the very One whom their nation had crucified centuries earlier was indeed after all their true Messiah and Savior, they will repent. The word *repent*

THE MOST ASKED PROPHECY QUESTIONS

means "*a change of mind;*" they'll go through a radical change of mind with regard to God and Jesus Christ. They'll stop the rebellion against God. They will receive Jesus Christ as their Messiah and Savior.

And according to Zechariah13:1, God says, "*In that day, there shall be a fountain opened to the house of David and to the inhabitants of Jerusalem for sin and for uncleanness.*" In response to their repentance, God will wash away the sins, will cleanse the people of Israel from their sins and will save them.

And then, according to Zechariah 14:3-4, now that Israel has repented, we read: "*Then shall the Lord go forth and fight against those nations as when He fought in the day of battle, and His feet shall stand in that day upon the Mount of Olives*" and the rest of chapter 14 describes how the Lord Jesus, now that Israel has repented, will destroy the rulers and armies of the world that are gathered there. And this parallels with what John recorded in Revelation 19:11 and following.

When Christ comes out of Heaven, here will be the Antichrist, the false prophet, the rulers and armies of all the Gentile nations gathered there in Israel, and Christ at that time will wage war against them. John tells us in Revelation 19 He will destroy these godless forces and then, according to Revelation 20, Satan will be bound; will be cast into the bottomless pit where he'll be held as a prisoner of God throughout the thousand-year Millennium. And according to Zechariah 14:9, "*The Lord shall be King over all the earth; in that day shall there be one Lord and His name one.*" Jesus, having totally crushed Satan and his forces in light of Israel repenting, Jesus will then take over the rule of the earth on behalf of God and as the last Adam, will be King over all the earth for the next one thousand years for the honor and the glory of God.

Question #17

When does the Rapture take place?

THREE DIFFERENT PASSAGES IN the New Testament are the basic foundational passages for the whole doctrine of the Rapture of the Church.

The **first one** is in **John 14:1-3,** Jesus, the night before He went to the cross, gathered with His apostles in the upper room. At the end of John 13, where we have the record of this gathering, Jesus forewarned His disciples that He would leave them soon. That really caused them to be disturbed. In order to calm their fears He made a great promise to them in John 14:1-3. This is what He said: "*Let not your heart be troubled. You believe in God believe also in Me. In My Father's house are many mansions. If it were not so I would have told you. I go to prepare a place for you. And if I go and prepare a place for you I will come again and receive you unto Myself so that where I am there you may be also.*"

Now Jesus was referring here to a future coming of His, and we are convinced that He is talking here about His coming to rapture the church from the earth. How do we know that He is referring here to His coming to Rapture the church instead of His Second Coming after the end of the great tribulation? Well, for one thing He indicates here that when He comes He will receive the believers unto Himself. Notice in this coming He's not going to come down to where they are and live where they are. In other words, He's not the only one that's going to be moving here. He's going to removing them from where they are to be where He is. And so He says here, "*I will come again and receive you unto Myself.*"

Then notice the purpose of this coming. It's a purpose clause—*that where I am there you may be also.* He's saying here, "The whole purpose of My coming in this particular coming I'm referring to is so that you can be *where I am,* not so that I can be where you are." So He's not saying in this coming *"come so I can live where you are on the face of the earth,"* but, *"I'm going to come in this coming so that you can be where I am,"* namely in the Father's house. And the very fact that He ties this promise in with the concept that He's going to be preparing dwelling places for them in the Father's house in heaven strongly infers that when He receives them to Himself He's going to take them back to live with Him in those dwelling places in the Father's house in heaven. This is definitely a Rapture passage.

The **second key passage** is **2 Corinthians 15: 51-52**, where Paul says to his readers, "*Behold, I show you a mystery; we shall not all sleep but we shall all be changed in a moment, in the twinkling of an eye, at the last trump. For the trumpet shall sound and the dead shall be raised incorruptible and we shall be changed.*" Paul is emphasizing the fact that there would be an entire generation of Christians who would never experience physical death; and the reason they wouldn't is because the Lord was going to come and remove them from the earth while they're still alive before they would experience physical death. So he's saying not every Christian will die, but everyone will be changed.

He emphasizes that the change will involve a *change in their body*. They now have a *mortal* body, which is subject to disease, deformity and death; but when this change takes place, they will receive an *immortal* body, which will never die again, which will never be subject to disease and deformity. Paul's also emphasizing the extreme rapidity of the change in the body of Christians when this event takes place. The change in that body will take place faster than the twinkling of an eye. The twinkling of an eye meant the amount of time it takes for a ray of light to hit and bounce off of the eye—its' quicker than just having your eye blink. Before your eye can blink, it hits your eye and bounces off. So this emphasizes the rapidity of the change in their bodies that will happen at the Rapture of the Church.

But the **third** and really the most extensive **passage** on the Rapture is found in **1 Thessalonians 4:13-18**. Jesus is indicating there that the day is coming when He will come out of Heaven, He will bring with Him the souls of those Christians who have already died. When they died, their souls were separated from their bodies; their bodies were buried in the ground; and their souls were ushered immediately into the presence of God in Heaven. Paul in 2 Corinthians 5 says for the Christian *"to be absent from the body is to be present with the Lord."* And that's where they stay, in Heaven, until Christ comes to rapture the Church. He will bring their souls with Him out of Heaven down toward the earth.

We are told that He will come with the blast of a trumpet, the trump of God, with the voice of the archangel. Apparently there will be a great archangel who will accompany Him as an escort from the Father's house in Heaven.

And then Paul says when that happens, some intriguing things will begin to transpire here on the face of the earth. The bodies of the Christians who have died will be resurrected from the dead. And the implication is that their descending souls that are coming down from Heaven with Christ will be reunited with their resurrected bodies.

But then Paul says those Christians who are still alive on the earth when the event of the Rapture takes place, that they, together with the resurrected Christians, will be caught up from the earth to meet the Lord Jesus in the air.

Now, there are a couple of significant things about that. The whole concept of being snatched up or caught up from the earth, that's where the concept of the Rapture comes from. The English word *Rapture* is derived from a Latin verb form which means to be snatched or caught up and so the Bride of Christ, the Church, involving the resurrected believers but those as well who have never died will be caught up from the earth, Paul says, "*together, to meet the Lord Jesus in the air.*"

Another significant thing about that is, that tells us that in this coming of the Lord He stops in the air above the earth. He doesn't come the whole way down to the surface of the earth. As He descends from Heaven from the Father's house, He stops in the air above the earth and He waits there as His believers are caught up to meet Him in the air. And then Paul concludes with these words at the end of verse 17, "*and so shall we ever be with the Lord.*" That's significant because that means once we are raptured to meet Christ in the air, from that time on we shall never be separated from Him again. Wherever Jesus goes, we go with Him. And that has significance for other future events that the Bible spells out.

So to put it all together: Christ ascended to the Father's house in Heaven on the day of His ascension—Acts 2. He's been away from us here on the earth, ever since His ascension, in the Father's house. But according to John 14, while He's away, He's busily engaged in His Father's house preparing living accommodations or mansions to which He can bring His Bride, the Church, later on. At the appropriate time, He will come out of the Father's house in Heaven, bringing with Him the souls of those Church saints who have already died. He will descend toward the earth but not the whole way down. He will stop in the air, will resurrect the bodies of the Christians who have died, reunite the returning souls with those resurrected bodies, will transform the bodies of the living Christians also into a resurrection-type or immortal-type body and together those resurrected Christians and living transformed Christians will be caught up from the earth to meet the Lord in the air.

And the implication of Jesus' promise in John 14 is that He's coming to take them back to the Father's house in Heaven so that they can live in the dwelling places that He's preparing for the believers now while He's in the Father's house in Heaven.

Question #18

What is a mystery?

T HE WORD MYSTERY REFERS to new revelation that has been given for the first time. It's never been told before to mankind. It's a whole new revelation from God. First to the apostle Paul, and then he passes it on to the believers to whom he is addressing this. And what he's saying is, it's something new.

Now, it wasn't about resurrection from the dead because even in the Old Testament indicated that people would be resurrected from the dead. Daniel 12 indicates that. Abraham believed when God told him to sacrifice his son Isaac that God would resurrect him from the dead as well. And so that was not what this was dealing with here at all. But what it's saying is that the new thing that's being revealed here is the fact that not all Christians will die. There's going to be a time when Christians who are alive on the earth, they will escape death all together, because it's going to be an event that the Bible calls the Rapture of the church. And it mentions that not all Christians are going to experience death, but all Christians will be changed. They'll be transformed from a mortal human body, which can suffer, die, etc., to one that will never die again.

The implication is that those who have already died their bodies will be resurrected from the dead with an immortal body—which will never experience death again. And the Christians who are alive when this event takes place, their bodies will be changed instantaneously from a mortal body subject to death to a body which will never die in the future whatsoever. And so that's the new truth that he was delivering to them as well.

Question #19

Why is Jesus' teaching in John 14:1-3 an analogy of a Jewish wedding which also infers a Pre-Tribulation Rapture of the Church?

NOW, YOU AND I who live in this twenty-first century world do not catch the full impact of the promise that Jesus made in John 14:1-3, and the reason we do not is because in delivering this promise Jesus inferred in analogy with the way which Jewish people conducted their weddings in Bible times. The first major step in a Jewish wedding between a young man and young woman in Bible times was the establishment of the marriage covenant. The Jews called the establishment of such a covenant betrothal or espousal.

Usually the way that covenant would be established was as follows: The groom would leave his father's house and travel to the home of his prospective bride. By analogy, Jesus, over 1900 years ago, left His Father's house in heaven and traveled to the home of His prospective bride, the Church, here on planet earth. When the Jewish bridegroom would arrive at the bride's home, he would come for the purpose of establishing a marriage covenant. And in order to establish that covenant he had to

pay a purchase price. Jewish young men had to buy their wives in Bible times. By analogy, when Jesus came in His first coming to the earth He also came for the purpose of establishing a **covenant**, a covenant through which He would obtain His bride the Church. And the covenant He came to establish is the one that the Bible calls the *New Covenant*. And He did that when He died on the cross. And He too had to pay a purchase price in order to establish that covenant and through that purchase price to obtain His bride the Church.

The purchase *price* that Jesus had to pay was the *shedding* of *His* own life *blood*. That's why Paul says at the end of 1 Corinthians 6, "*What, know ye not you are not your own; you have been bought with a price. Therefore, glorify God in your body and spirit.*"

After the Jewish bridegroom had established the marriage covenant at the bride's home and thereby had obtained his bride to be his wife, he would leave her at her home and would return to his father's house and they would remain separated for a period of time—normally for approximately one year. And during that year of separation the Jewish bridegroom would be busily engaged in his father's house preparing living accommodations to which he could bring his bride later on.

By analogy, Jesus, less than two months after He established the New Covenant through the shedding of His blood on the cross of Calvary, left the home of His prospective bride, the Church here on planet earth, and on the day of His ascension He returned to His Father's house in heaven. And He's been away ever since. And you and I, right now, are living in the period of separation between the time of His departure and the time of

His return. And as He promises here in John 14, while He is away from us in the Father's house in heaven right now, He's busily engaged preparing living accommodations or mansions to which He can bring His bride, the Church, later on.

The Jewish bridegroom at the end of the year of separation would come on an unannounced night to take his bride to be with him. The bride never knew exactly what night he would come. She knew it would be some night near the end of the year of separation, but she never knew exactly when. And so on that unannounced night the Jewish bridegroom would call to himself at his father's house, his best man and other male escorts, and together those young men would begin a torchlight procession through the streets of the city from the groom's father's house over to the home of the bride. Here was the bridegroom coming to take his bride to be with him.

As those young men would be weaving their way through the streets of the city, bystanders, recognizing what was happening, would pick up a shout, "*Behold the bridegroom comes.*" That shout would be carried from block to block to block until finally it would arrive at the bride's home. The major purpose of that shout was to forewarn the bride to the effect that she'd better get ready in a hurry because tonight was the night and her groom was already on his way to take her to be with him. As soon as she would hear that shout, she sent out word to her bridesmaids to come to her home get her dressed in her bridal garment and all prepared, because this was the night.

Now, by analogy, the Bible teaches that at the end of the present period of separation from Christ in which we are now living, Jesus too will come from the Father's house in heaven toward the earth, toward the home of His bride here on the earth, at an unannounced time. The Bible makes it clear that nobody living on planet earth knows exactly when the Lord Jesus will come for His bride the church. It's an imminent event; it could happen at any moment. In fact, it could even happen today.

The Scriptures also teach by analogy that when Jesus will come at that unannounced time for His bride, He too will come with an escort. Paul, in 1 Thessalonians 4, refers to one great archangel, Michael, who apparently will be the escort for the Lord Jesus from the Father's house in heaven. And Paul also indicates in 1 Thessalonians 4 that just as the Jewish bridegroom's coming was accompanied by a loud shout, so Jesus' coming will be accompanied by a loud shout. And I surmise that the content of that shout will be the same, *"Behold, the bridegroom comes."*

Now interestingly, when the Jewish bridegroom came on that unannounced night, he and his male escorts would wait outside the bride's home until she was ready and then she and her bridesmaids would come out of her home and meet her groom and his male escorts in the streets of the city. By analogy, Paul tells us in 1 Thessalonians 4 when Jesus comes for His bride, the Church, He will not come the whole way down to planet earth where His bride is living, He will stop outside the earth in the air and wait there, and then His bride the church will come out and meet Him in the streets of the city.

After the Jewish bride would come out of her home with her bridesmaids and meet her bridegroom and his male escorts, now the enlarged wedding party would have a return torchlight procession back to the groom's father's house. By analogy, after Jesus has caught up His bride the Church from the earth to meet Him in the air, we are convinced in light of this passage in John 14 that He will return with His bride from the air above the earth back to His Father's house in heaven to begin living in the living accommodations He's prepared there.

After the Jewish bride and groom arrived at the groom's father's house, they went into hiding privately into a room that the Jewish people called the *chuppah*, in English that means the *bridal chamber*. And there in the privacy of that room, they would enter into physical union with each other for the first time and thereby consummate their marriage.

Now intriguingly, they would stay hidden in that bridal chamber for seven days. This is known therefore in the Jewish encyclopedia as the seven days of the bridal chamber. And then at the end of the seventh day, the groom would come out of hiding from the bridal chamber and he would bring his bride out of hiding with him out in the open with her veil removed so that everyone could see who his bride truly was.

Now, by analogy with this aspect of the Jewish marriage customs, after Jesus and His bride the Church will arrive by Rapture at His Father's house in heaven, He and His bride will also go into hiding for a period of seven, but in this instance for seven years. For while the seven-year Tribulation period will be transpiring down here on planet earth, Jesus and His bride the Church will be hidden away from the view of everyone who is still living down here. They will be hidden away in the Father's house in heaven.

But finally at the end of the seventh year of the tribulation period, Christ will come out of hiding from the Father's house in heaven in His glorious Second Coming, this time the whole way down to planet earth to take over the rule of the earth on behalf of God. And when He will come out of hiding at that time, He will bring His bride out of hiding with Him from the Father's house in heaven, now out in the open on full public display so that everyone who's still living here on planet earth can see who His bride the church truly is.

This analogy which Jesus inferred indicates a pre-Tribulation Rapture of the church before the seven-year Tribulation period begins.

Question #20

Could Jesus return at any moment?
What does imminency mean?
Is Christ's return imminent?

WE'VE DISCUSSED THE SEVEN-YEAR Tribulation period, the Second Coming of Christ, and also to a certain extent the thousand-year reign of Jesus during the Millennium here on the earth. But we've mentioned in passing that it is our understanding that before the seven-year Tribulation period begins, that Jesus Christ will come from Heaven to the air above the earth and will Rapture His bride, the Church, out of the world to meet Him in the air and then to return with Him to the Father's house in Heaven. In other words, we believe that Christ will rapture the Church in a pre-Tribulation Rapture before the seven-year Tribulation period will begin. Why do we believe that? What are some of the reasons?

One reason is that the New Testament, in a number of passages, teaches the imminency of Christ's return. The word "imminent" carries with it the idea of something that is always hanging overhead, and because it's always hanging overhead, it could fall at any moment, an *any moment* happening of this particular event. Other things may happen before it transpires, but we can't count on anything else happening. Nothing else *must* happen before it transpires.

The Scriptures teach that there's a coming of the Lord that has that characteristic of imminency. **First**, in **1 Corinthians 16:22**, the apostle Paul said to the Corinthian Christians, "*If any man love not the Lord Jesus Christ, let him be anathema*," and then Paul interjected at the end of this verse, an interesting expression, "*Maranatha!*" Now, what does that term mean? It's very interesting to note that that word was derived from the Aramaic language. Let me explain. The Aramaic language was the language that was spoken in the land of Israel during Jesus' day. From all we can discern, that was even the language the Jesus spoke while He was here in the world. It was kind of a mixture of Hebrew and importing things from other languages where the Jews had lived over the centuries. This was an Aramaic expression.

"*Maranatha*" is made up of three Aramaic words. The first one is the word "*Mar,*" which meant "Lord, and then the next one is "*Ana,*" which means "Our" and the third was "*Tha,*" which means "*Come.*" So putting it together, *Maranatha* means "*Our Lord, Come.*" The interesting thing is, this was in the form of a petition. So when Christians would make that statement, as Paul did here, he was actually petitioning the Lord to come.

Now, the question is, why petition the Lord to come if He can't come at any moment? If you know that He can't come until a year from now or ten years from now or a hundred or a thousand years from now, it would really be useless to be petitioning the Lord as if He could come right now. Another intriguing thing about this is that although this is an Aramaic expression which apparently began with Jewish believers in the Lord Jesus in the land of Israel during the first century, here Paul uses this word to Greek speaking people at a Greek Church in the city of Corinth, and he's writing it in a letter that he wrote in the Greek language.

And so scholars have asked the question: "*Why would Paul throw out an Aramaic term at people who knew the Greek language and in a Greek book that he's writing?*" Scholars have concluded that the reason is that this expression had become a widespread expression by Christians all over the ancient world. Even though they may not have known any other expression in the Aramaic language, they learned what this one meant, so they used it as a byword; some feel they even used it as a greeting when they would see each other to identify themselves as believers. They would say, "*Maranatha*" (Our Lord, Come.) But again, it's conveying a concept that the Lord could come at any moment, otherwise, why petition Him to come? It's imminency that's being conveyed here.

A **second** significant passage out of many others in the New Testament on the imminency of the Lord's return is **1 Thessalonians 1:10**. Here the apostle Paul is talking about an outlook or attitude that the Thessalonian Christians had in the first century. He indicates they were "*waiting for His Son,*" God's Son, "*from heaven whom He raised from the dead, even Jesus.*"

It's interesting that the tense of the verb "*wait*" here is that of a continuous action. They were *continually waiting* for Jesus to come from Heaven. And the words translated "*to wait*" literally mean "*to wait up for.*" What Paul was implying was that people will wait up for the arrival of an individual if they are convinced that individual could arrive at any moment. They will not go to bed at their normal time. They will wait up for him to arrive because they are convinced that he could come at any moment. If they knew he could not come, say, for another five hours, they wouldn't wait up for him beyond their normal time to go to bed. They'd go to bed; they'd sleep for the five hours; and then have their alarm wake them up five hours later so they'd be awake whenever he would come.

And so the concept is that the Thessalonian Christians had the understanding that they should be in essence constantly waiting up for the Lord Jesus to come from Heaven to take them to be with Him. And the reason they should have that constant attitude is because He could come at any moment and take them out of the world to be with Him. That is the idea of imminency.

Another interesting thing about this term, and scholars point this out, is that this indicates patience and confidence. And in addition it's in the present tense; and normally in the original language of the New Testament the present tense, unless the context tells us otherwise, has the idea of a continuous action.

So Paul was teaching here that the Thessalonian Christians were continuously and patiently awaiting the Lord's coming, waiting up for Him to come, because they were confident that He could come at any moment. Again, the idea is, they believed in the imminent return of the Lord Jesus.

Now, a question we could ask at this point is this: Where did they get this idea from—that the Lord could return at any moment? When you read the book of Acts which records what Paul did when he went to the city of Thessalonica on one of his missionary journeys we find that Paul is the one who taught them what they knew about the Scriptures and the truth of God.

And when you read 1 Thessalonians there are several indications. Paul reminds them of things that he had taught them when he was with them. So, if the apostle Paul had been their major teacher of God's truth, to my way of thinking that implies that Paul was the one who had taught them of the imminent coming of Christ, that He could come from Heaven at any moment for His believers to take them home to glory to be with Him. It's very intriguing to notice as well that Paul did not rebuke them or correct them for having this expectation and this attitude, and there's no indication that he rebuked them or corrected them at all. In fact, when you read the context, he seems to be commending them for having this attitude. So I get the distinct impression that Paul was fully convinced himself that the Lord could return at any moment and therefore they were right in having this expectancy.

Now, as soon as you say that He cannot come, say, for another three and a half years—say He cannot come until the middle of the Tribulation, since the seven-year Tribulation hasn't started yet—then you're saying, "Well, He can't come for at least another three and a half years," that destroys the concept of imminency because you're saying, therefore, He couldn't come today. He couldn't come at any moment. He can't come for another three and a half years. If you're going to say that He can't come for about three fourths of the Tribulation period, again, that destroys the concept that He could come at any moment. Or if you're going to say, as some sincere Christians do, that He can't come until the Second Coming after the Tribulation period, in other words, you're saying that He can't come for another seven years, that destroys the concept of imminency.

Really, the only view of the timing of the Rapture of the Church that fits the New Testament concept of imminency is the pre-Tribulation Rapture view which says, although many things may happen before the Lord comes, biblically there's nothing that must happen. He could come at any moment. We can't count on any time period between now and the Lord's coming and therefore, we should be ready every moment, moment by moment, for the Lord to come and we meet Him face to face. So imminency of the Lord's coming is one of the reasons why we believe that the Lord will Rapture the Church out of the world before the seven-year Tribulation period begins.

But there's something else in 1 Thessalonians 1:10 that is significant with regard to this. Paul says that they were waiting for God's Son from heaven, the end of the verse, *"which delivers us from the wrath to come."* The implication being that this coming of the Lord at any moment to Rapture His bride, the Church, out of the world will deliver the Church from a future unique period of wrath, the wrath to come. And the Greek construction indicates this was a future period of wrath that the Thessalonians already knew about. And it's a specific, unique period of wrath that we will be delivered from as Church saints as a result of the Lord coming first and taking us at any moment out of the world.

Question #21

Where is the imminent return of Christ taught in the book of James?

THEN, A THIRD PASSAGE that I'd like to focus our attention upon for the imminency of the Lord's return is in the book of James, and this is found in **James 5:7-9**: "*Be patient, therefore, brethren, unto the coming of the Lord; behold the husbandman waits for the precious fruit of the earth and has long patience for it until he receive the early and latter rain. Be you also patient; establish you hearts, for the coming of the Lord draws nigh. Grudge not one against another, brethren, lest you be condemned. Behold, the Judge stands before the door.*"

I'd like to draw your attention to two verb forms that James uses here. At the end of verse 8 he says, "*the coming of the Lord draws nigh,*" and then in verse 9, "*the judge stands before the door.*" A very important thing to note here is that in the original language in which James wrote, both of those verbs are in what the Greeks called the *perfect tense*. And the significance of the Greek perfect tense was that it is referring to *an action that was completed in the past but then there is a resultant state that continues on from that action*. It just continues on indefinitely.

What James is indicating there is this: That the Lord's coming had already drawn near before James wrote this letter, and the Lord's coming continues to be near at hand, even while James wrote the letter, and it would continue thereafter. And as well, the judge stands before the door, he was saying that there's a sense in which Jesus Christ as the Judge of believers took His position of the door of Heaven and was standing there; He even took that position and began to stand there before James wrote this epistle and He continues to stand at the door of Heaven.

A number of scholars have said James is trying to emphasize to his readers the imminency of the Lord's return. The idea is, the Lord could come as the Judge of Heaven through that door of Heaven at any moment and then immediately, Christians would stand before Him at the Judgment Seat of Christ; they have their works as believers evaluated by the Lord. It's imminency that he's talking about here. And we are convinced that just as it was imminent back then, the Lord could have stepped through the door of Heaven at any time; the same is true today—that Christ could step through the door of Heaven at any moment and we who are believers in Jesus Christ would be ushered into His presence and then would stand before Him at the Judgment Seat of Christ to have our works evaluated by the Lord.

Now, one of the very interesting things by way of practical application is that James says to the believers to whom he is writing in verse 9, "*Grudge not one against another, brethren, lest you be condemned; behold, the Judge stands before the door.*" What James is emphasizing is the fact that Jesus Christ could return at any moment and take us as believers before Him in the Judgment Seat of Christ.

It ought to be a tremendous motivating factor for believers for godly, holy living, proper conduct, and how we treat one another. The distinct impression you get from God's Word when you look at all the imminency passages in the New Testament is that God intends the whole fact that Christ could come at any moment to perhaps be the greatest motivating factor that we as Christians have for godly living, moment by moment, day by day. Because we don't know when it is that the Lord is going to come out of Heaven and we see Him face to face and our works will be evaluated by Him at the Judgment Seat of Christ. This is a very critical truth of the Word of God and one that ought to be emphasized tremendously in Bible believing circles today because of the implications it has for us in how we live out our lives day by day by day for His honor and for His glory.

Question #22

If you do not trust Jesus Christ to be your Savior, what will God declare to be your future?

THE BIBLE TEACHES US very clearly different things about the personal Sovereign Creator God of the Universe. One thing is that He is a God of love and that He has exhibited that love, demonstrated it, by sending His only beloved Son, Jesus Christ, into the world to become incarnated in human flesh. In other words, to become a human being so that Jesus, toward the end of His life here on the earth, could die as our substitute—take our place as fellow human beings on the cross of Calvary. And when Jesus was on the cross, God poured out all His wrath that we deserved to receive for our sins and rebellion against God, He poured out all that wrath upon His Son, the Lord Jesus, so that Jesus paid the penalty for your sins and for my sins.

Paul tells us in one of his Corinthian letters that *"God made Him,"* referring to Christ, *"who knew no sin to be sin for us, in order that we might be made the righteousness of God in Him."* In other words, Jesus Christ traded places with us, in essence, when He went to the cross.

The Bible very clearly teaches, **Romans 3:23**, that *"all have sinned and fallen short of the glory of God."* That's true of every human being who has ever been born through normal means into the world. That's true of you; that's true of me. We've all sinned against God. Whether we recognize it or not, that's what God, who is the ultimate Judge of the universe with whom we have to deal, says about us from His perspective; we've all sinned against Him. We therefore stand condemned; we deserve His wrathful judgment upon us.

But He demonstrated His love toward you and me by sending someone else, namely His only begotten Son Jesus Christ, to take our place that we deserved on the cross of Calvary. And Jesus received that wrath of God for our sins so that we would not have to go through that, as long as we appropriate personally what Jesus Christ has done for us. And the Bible makes it very clear how we do that: we place our faith in the Lord Jesus; we acknowledge that we are sinners who stand condemned before God; we acknowledge there are no good works we can do to cancel out our sins and make us right with a holy God, and that's why we need a Savior. And we acknowledge that Jesus Christ is God's Son who died for our sins and, acknowledging that, we put our trust in Jesus Christ and Jesus Christ alone. Not our church, not our works, not baptism or anything else—totally in Jesus Christ and what He did for us in His death, burial and resurrection to save us from our sins.

But what about people who don't accept what Christ has done for them? They refuse to acknowledge they are sinners, or even if they do acknowledge that they've sinned and maybe stand condemned before God, they refuse to acknowledge Jesus Christ as the Son of God and as their Savior. What about them? Well, the apostle Paul writes about those people in **Romans 2:5ff**. He says, "*But after your hardness and impenitent heart,*" in other words a heart that refuses to repent of your sinfulness, "*treasure up unto yourself wrath against the day of wrath and revelation of the righteous judgment of God who will render to every man according to his deeds, to them who by patient continuous and well doing seek for glory and honor and immortality, eternal life; but unto them that are contentious and do not obey the truth,*" the truth here being the Gospel message of Jesus Christ, "*but obey unrighteousness,*" here's what they build up for themselves: "*indignation and wrath, tribulation and anguish, upon every soul of man that does evil, of the Jew first, and also of the Gentile.*"

Paul is making it very clear here, it doesn't matter who you are, what your status in life is; it doesn't matter what other people think of you or what your own evaluation is of yourself, you've got to be concerned about the personal sovereign Creator God of the universe, the ultimate Judge, how He evaluates you. And He says, "*You've sinned, and unless you trust His Son as Savior, you're headed for His wrath.*"

Question #23

What is meant by the biblical expression, "the Day of the Lord"?

THE BIBLE INDICATES THAT there's going to be a future period of time here on planet earth that will be an unparalleled time of God pouring out His wrath upon planet earth. The Bible uses a particular title for that future period of time. It's called *"the Day of the Lord."*

The Scriptures indicate that the Day of the Lord will begin first with a seven-year period of this unprecedented pouring out of God's wrath upon the face of the earth. That seven-year period will culminate with the Second Coming of Jesus Christ the whole way down to earth and then it will continue on, the Day of the Lord , with a great period of unparalleled blessing for the world which has been called the Millennium, when the Lord Jesus as God's representative will administer God's rule worldwide. But the point is that people who are alive on the earth when that seven-year period of the Day of the Lord where God pours out His wrath comes, they are going to be incredibly subject to that outpouring of God's wrath.

The book of Revelation spells out three series of judgments, all of which are expressions of God's wrath upon the unbelievers at that period of time.

First, seven seal judgments; second, seven trumpet judgments; and then third, seven bowl judgments. If you've never done this, take a Bible and look at the last book of the Bible, the book of the Revelation, and begin reading with chapter 6 where Jesus begins breaking these seals, unleashing the first series of judgments. Read from there right up through chapter 19 and you will see the awesome things that are going to transpire here on the face of the earth as God pours out one expression of His wrath after another after another upon the unbelievers that are here upon the face of the earth.

The Scriptures indicate in **Revelation 3:10** that seven-year period will be a time of testing the earth dwellers. And if you were to go through the book of Revelation and see every place the expression "earth dwellers" appears, it's referring to people who are hardened in their heart against God, who rebel against Him, they refuse to acknowledge Him or His ways; they refuse to acknowledge that they are sinners; they refuse to repent and accept God's way of salvation, they're going to be the major targets of God's wrath during that period of time. But interestingly, that's not going to be the end of God's wrath for those unbelievers; because when they die unsaved, through time they're going to go into eternal wrath, not just a seven-year period which will be here on the earth at the beginning of the Day of the Lord, but according to Revelation 20 and later, they're going to be subject to the wrath of God in the eternal lake of fire in conscious torment forever and ever and ever throughout eternity.

It's interesting to note that terminology, "*the Day of the Lord*," because when you go back to **Genesis 1**, when God used the term "*day*" there, the days there always started out with a period of darkness followed by a period of light. The evening and the morning were the first day; the evening and the morning were the second day. Interestingly, historically the Jewish people begin their day at sundown, so the first part of their day chronologically is darkness followed by a period of light when the sun rises in the morning. And so you have this same pattern for this designation *"the Day of the Lord."* First a period of spiritual darkness and chaos upon the face of the earth, the seven-year Tribulation period; then followed by a period of spiritual light and blessing in the world, the thousand-year Millennial Reign of Christ.

Question #24

Will Christians escape God's wrath in the time period called "the Day of the Lord"?

WHAT HAPPENS TO THOSE who have trusted the Lord Jesus as their Savior when this future period of the wrath of God called the Day of the Lord will break forth upon planet earth, again, the last seven years before Christ returns in His glorious Second Coming? Will true believers in the Lord Jesus experience any of that wrath? Will they go through all seven years of that wrath or maybe three fourths of the way through or just half of the way through? Or, will they escape that period of time altogether by being removed from the earth by Rapture before that seven-year period of God's wrath begins?

Sincere Christians disagree with regard to this. There are those who believe that the Church will be removed from the earth by Rapture before the seven-year Tribulation period begins, and those who hold to that view call their view the **pre-tribulation** Rapture view. *Pre* means *before*, and so pre-tribulation means "*before the Tribulation.*" And so they say, "We're raptured out before that seven-year Tribulation period when God's wrath will be poured out upon the earth."

There are those who believe that the Church will be raptured out in the middle of the seven-year Tribulation period. In other words, they will go through the first three and a half years of the outpouring of God's wrath, then be removed; although some of those who hold to that say that you won't have the wrath of God until the middle and so that if they're raptured out in the middle, they'll escape the wrath of God because it'll come in the second half. That's called the **mid-tribulation** Rapture view because they *believe the Church will be removed right in the middle of that seven-year period of time.*

But then there are those who believe that the Church will go through all seven years of the Tribulation and then will be raptured out immediately after the Tribulation when Jesus comes out of Heaven in His Second Coming the whole way down to planet earth to take over the rule of the earth on behalf of God. Those who hold to that view call their view the **post-tribulation** Rapture view. *"Post"* means *"after,"* and so post-tribulation means *"after the Tribulation"* is when the Rapture would take place. The issue that's involved here is this: What will be the relationship of Christians to this future period of God's wrath?

There are significant passages in the Bible which shed some light on that. One of those significant passages is in **1 Thessalonians 1:10**. It clearly teaches the imminency of the Lord's return to take the Church saints out of the world, but Paul goes on to teach some other interesting concepts in that verse. This is what he said to the Thessalonians Christians: That they were waiting for His Son, for God's Son from Heaven, whom He raised from the dead, even Jesus, *"which delivered us from the wrath to come."*

Now, interestingly, the verb translated "*delivered*" there is a fascinating verb. For one thing, it's in the *present tense*. Some of our English translations translate it as past but it's in the present tense, and normally the *Greek present tense*, unless the context indicates otherwise, is referring to *continuous action*, and that appears to be what it is here. And it's indicated that Christ has already given to us, as a continuous thing, deliverance from this future time of wrath. It's already a present reality for us because of what Jesus Christ did for us on the cross of Calvary and through His resurrection. So that's a guarantee, in essence, to us that Church saints will be delivered from the wrath to come.

Now, the verb translated "*delivered*" here also carries with it the idea of deliverance from something that's threatening you, or *deliverance from an enemy*. And the idea is God's wrath is certainly a threat to a human being. No human being who has any degree of sanity would ever want to come under the full weight of God's wrath. That would be a horrible, horrible thing to experience, and so human beings would regard the wrath of God as an enemy or a threat to them. And so Paul is saying that Jesus has already provided for those who have trusted Him as Savior deliverance from that wrath, deliverance from that thing that would threaten the wellbeing of a human being.

But there's another fascinating idea that's associated with the verb that Paul used here translated "*delivered*," and that is it refers to *deliverance by a mighty act of power*. That's very significant in light of what he said earlier in this verse: That the Thessalonians were waiting for God's Son to come from Heaven, as we saw earlier, to come to Rapture them out of the world.

The Rapture will certainly be a mighty act of divine power when Jesus Christ will catch up from the earth the whole body of born again Christians for all the centuries that the Church has ever existed. He'll bring with Him the souls of those Church saints that have already died; He'll bring those souls with Him from Heaven, He'll resurrect their bodies from the grave, reunite the returning souls with their bodies, so they'll be here on the earth by resurrection. And then the Christians who are alive when He comes to Rapture the Church, He'll instantaneously transform their bodies into an immortal body. But then He's going to catch up all the millions of Christians who have trusted Christ as Savior and lived throughout all the centuries, the Church that existed here on planet Earth. In one mighty act of power, He will snatch them up from the earth to meet Him in the air and then return with them back to His Father's house to Heaven to live in the mansions or dwelling places He's prepared for them there. *A mighty act of power*. Since Paul is inferring the Rapture earlier in this verse, that's the mighty act of power through which He will actually carry out this deliverance that He's already provided for us from the wrath to come.

But what does he mean by *"the wrath to come"*? . Let me give you a very literal translation to show you what the Greek language says here: *"The wrath, the coming."* Paul uses the *definite article "the" twice* in there, and many Greek scholars pointed out the reason he does that is because he's referring to a very specific, unique, period of intense wrath that is so unique because of the **intensity of God's wrath** being poured out that it's in a class all of its own, totally distinct from any past outpourings of God's wrath in previous history.

Scholars recognize it's going to be an incredibly unparalleled intensity of God's wrath being poured out upon the earth for a particular period of time. And most scholars are of the conviction that he's referring to that beginning seven-year phase of the future Day of the Lord that will be the unparalleled time of an outpouring of God's wrath through seal judgments, trumpet judgments, and bowl judgments. Paul is saying here that Jesus, through a mighty act of power—through the Rapture—will carry out the deliverance that He's already granted to us and provided for us as Christians from that future Day of the Lord wrath here on planet Earth. The implication is that the way He will deliver us from that is by removing us from the earth by Rapture before that seven-year phase of God's wrath of the future Day of the Lord will begin. That implies a pre-tribulation Rapture; that the Church will be removed before this period of time of unparalleled wrath of God is poured out upon the face of the earth.

Question #25

When will the Lord come
"as a thief in the night"?

ANOTHER SIGNIFICANT PASSAGE WHICH bears on the relationship of Church saints to this future time of wrath is **1 Thessalonians 5:9.** If you were to look at the opening verses in this chapter, you would find that Paul is talking about the future Day of the Lord. First Thessalonians 5, beginning with verse 1: "*But of the times and the seasons, brethren, ye have no need that I write unto you, for yourselves know perfectly,...*" the Greek says really "*accurately,*" "*...yourselves know **accurately** that the Day of the Lord so comes as a thief in the night, for when **they,...**"* Paul is putting "*they*" in a different category from himself and the believers; he's referring here to unbelievers. "*When they* [the unbelievers] *shall say, 'Peace and safety,'*" when the unsaved people of the world think they have finally established peace and safety in the world, "*then sudden destruction comes upon them.*"

In other words, they're going to get the opposite of what they believe they have. "*Sudden destruction comes upon them, as travail*" —literally as the birth pang upon a woman with child, "***and they shall not escape.***" Notice the contrast. Verse 4, "*But you, brethren,*" notice, he's been talking about *they;* they, them, the unbelievers, "*sudden destruction is going to come upon **them**,*" the Day of the Lord. But by contrast, "*you, brethren, are not in darkness that that day should overtake you as a thief.*" In other words, you're not going to be overtaken by the thief in the night phase of the Day of the Lord, which is characterized by darkness. You're not going to be caught in that. He's saying that to the Christians, to church saints.

Why won't they be caught in it? He tells us why in verse 9: "*For God has not appointed us to wrath but to obtain salvation by our Lord Jesus Christ.*" What wrath of God? Since in the context in this passage he's talking about the future Day of the Lord that's going to bring sudden destruction upon the unbelievers upon the face of the earth, it seems very obvious by context he's talking about the future Day of the Lord wrath. Therefore he's saying to Church saints, those people who have trusted Christ as Savior since the Church began on the day of Pentecost in **Acts 2** right up to the present day, he's saying to Church saints, "*God hasn't appointed you to that Day of the Lord wrath, instead, He's appointed you to obtain salvation*"—and in this context the salvation is deliverance from the future Day of the Lord's wrath. And then he says, that salvation comes to us by our Lord Jesus Christ. He's provided for us, how? Verse 10, "*who died for us, that whether we wake or sleep, we should live together with Him.*" We should live together with Him.

He's saying what's going to be involved in our salvation—it doesn't matter whether you've already died as a believer or whether you're going to be alive as a believer in the future—we all, the dead believers and the living believers, are going to live together with Christ. And then he says, in verse 11, "*wherefore, comfort yourselves together and edify one another, even as also you do.*" He's saying, comfort and build each other up with this truth that you've not been appointed to the Day of the Lord wrath; instead, God has appointed you to be saved from that future Day of the Lord wrath and He's able to do that because of what Christ did for us when He died on the cross.

And instead of our destiny being that Day of the Lord wrath, our destiny as Christians is to live together with the Lord Jesus. Paul says that should be a comforting truth that will edify or build us up. An intriguing thing about this: The wording Paul uses in **1 Thessalonians 5:10-11**, "*we should live together with Him, wherefore comfort yourselves, edify one another,*" are almost parallel to what Paul says at the end of **1 Thessalonians 4**. At the end of **1 Thessalonians 4:17**, after talking about how the dead Christians will be resurrected and then they and the living Christians together will be caught up to meet the Lord in the air, he says, "*so shall we ever be with the Lord.*" Paul said in **1 Thessalonians 5:10**, our destiny is to live together with the Lord.

In **1 Thessalonians 4:18**, after talking about our being caught up in the Rapture to meet the Lord so we'll ever be with Him, he says, "*Wherefore, comfort one another with these words.*" By parallel, in **1 Thessalonians 5:11**, after saying we're not appointed to the Day of the Lord wrath, instead we're appointed to be saved from that through Christ so we can live together with Him he says, "*Wherefore, comfort yourselves together.*" This is very parallel. And many scholars say this language is parallel to **1 Thessalonians 4** which is dealing with the Rapture of the Church. So the whole implication seems to be that the way in which we will be saved or delivered from the future Day of the Lord wrath is by the Lord Jesus coming out of Heaven before this seven-year period of God's wrath or the future Day of the Lord will begin. The Lord will come from Heaven; He will by Rapture remove the Church saints from the face of the earth for the purpose that we can be together with Him, which, by the way, is parallel with **John 14** where Jesus said, *"In my Father's house are many mansions, if it were not so, I would have told you. I go to prepare a place for you, and if I go and prepare a place for you, I will come again and receive you unto myself"*—and here's the purpose of this coming to receive us—*"so that where I am there you may be also."*

Again, the idea is, "so you can live together with Me." All these passages seem to be referring to the same thing: The Rapture of the Church. And so Paul is teaching here in **1 Thessalonians 5** that Church saints will not even enter into that future period of the Day of the Lord wrath which will last for seven years here on planet earth. And the way in which we will not enter into it is by being raptured out of the world by the Lord Jesus before the seven-year Tribulation period begins.

Question #26

When will that future Day of the Lord begin?

NOW, THE QUESTION IS, when will that future Day of the Lord wrath begin? Well, it's interesting that when you look at **Revelation 5**, we are told, in the future Jesus will take from the hand of God a scroll, sealed with seven seals. And as Jesus begins to break those seven seals, very traumatic events will begin transpiring upon planet earth.

For example, when He breaks the fourth seal, one fourth of the world's population will be destroyed through four means: the sword, which means war; famine; pestilence; and wild beasts. Now interestingly, in **Ezekiel 14:21** God makes this statement: *"These are my four sore judgments: the sword, famine, pestilence and wild beasts,"* the same four things that in the fourth seal of Revelation will destroy one fourth of the people of the world. What we're saying is that **fourth seal is certainly an expression of God's wrath upon planet earth.**

It's very interesting to note who is breaking the seals, all seven seals. It's Jesus Christ who is breaking the seals. Not Antichrist, not Satan, not some human ruler here on the face of the earth. Jesus Christ, the Son of God, is breaking the seals. And so He is the One who is unleashing all these devastating things upon the face of the earth through the breaking of the seals. And so these are expressions of God's wrath and judgment upon the earth. If you were to compare the first four seals of **Revelation 6** with what Jesus called in **Matthew 24** "*the beginning of sorrows,*" more literally, "*the beginning of birth pangs,*" you would see that by comparison, the beginning of sorrows of Matthew 24 are the same thing as the first four seals of Revelation 6.

It's interesting, Jesus put the beginning of birth pangs or sorrows before the abomination of desolation spoken of by Daniel the prophet. And the abomination of desolation, according to **Daniel 9:27**, will take place in the exact middle of the seven-year Tribulation, or we could call it the seventieth week of Daniel 9. Well, if the abomination of desolation takes place in the middle of the seven-year Tribulation, and Jesus placed the beginning of sorrows or the first four seals before the abomination of desolation, this indicates that Jesus was putting these first four seals, or the beginning of sorrows, in the first half of the seven-year Tribulation period. And since those will involve an outpouring of God's wrath upon the world, this means therefore that even the first half of the seven-year Tribulation period will be characterized by an outpouring of God's wrath upon the earth. And since as we saw in **1 Thessalonians 1:10** that Jesus, through His imminent coming, "*delivers us from the wrath to come,*" and in **1 Thessalonians 5:9** the Church saints "*have not been appointed to the Day of the Lord wrath,*" we conclude, therefore, that the Church will be raptured by the imminent coming of Christ before even the first half of the seven-year Tribulation period; which, again, would indicate a pre-Tribulation Rapture out of the world before the wrath of God is poured out upon planet earth.

When we go to Revelation 16, John is recording what will happen in the world when the sixth bowl is poured out. Now, when you read Revelation 6-19 you will find that throughout the 70th week of Daniel 9, throughout that seven-year Tribulation period, there will be three series of judgments poured out: first, seven seals; then, seven trumpets; then seven bowls. So the bowls are the last series of judgments and John is seeing here the sixth of those seven bowls. In other words, this is the next to the last judgment of the 70th week of Daniel 9. What happens?

Revelation 16:12-16: "*And the sixth angel poured out his vial upon the great river Euphrates and the water thereof was dried up that the way of the kings of the east might be prepared. And I saw three unclean spirits like frogs come out of the mouth of the dragon* [in Revelation the dragon is Satan], *Out of the mouth of the Beast* [in Revelation the beast is the Antichrist], *out of the mouth of the false prophet, for they* [these unclean spirits] *are the spirits of devils* [literally of demons] *working miracles which go forth unto the kings of the earth and of the whole world to gather them to the battle of that great day of God Almighty. And he gathered them together into a place called in the Hebrew tongue Armageddon.*"

What John is witnessing here is this: The armies of all the nations of the world do not even begin to gather to the land of Israel for Armageddon until the sixth bowl. In other words, they don't even begin to gather until the next to the last judgment, almost at the very end of the seven-year Tribulation Period. According to Joel 3, once they are gathered there, there's a Day of the Lord that is near that will have great cosmic disturbances tied in with it.

When you go over to Joel 2, and in the context, this is referring to the same type of thing as is described in Joel 3. In Joel 2 he talks about cosmic disturbances. Joel 2:30, *"I'll show wonders in the heavens and in the earth, blood, fire, pillars of smoke. The sun will be turned into darkness, the moon into blood, before the great and terrible Day of the Lord come."* It's referring to the same Day of the Lord with the same cosmic disturbances as in chapter 3, but here he calls that future Day of the Lord, *"the great and terrible Day of the Lord."*

What is this Day of the Lord? It's the day when Christ will come out of Heaven in His glorious Second Coming immediately after the seven-year Tribulation period, accompanied by great cosmic disturbances that Jesus describes in Matthew 24:29-30: *"Immediately after the Tribulation of those days shall the sun be darkened, the moon shall not give her light; the stars shall fall from heaven, the powers of the heavens shall be shaken. Then shall appear the sign of the Son of Man in heaven and then shall all the tribes of the earth mourn and they shall see the Son of Man coming in the clouds of heaven with power and great glory."*

This great and terrible Day of the Lord with its cosmic disturbances is the precise day that Jesus Christ will come out of Heaven in His glorious Second Coming immediately after the seven-year Tribulation Period. And according to Revelation 19, when He does that, here will be all the rulers and armies of the nations of the world gathered together against Him under Antichrist and the false prophet. And Jesus unleashes the wrath of God upon them and destroys them.

Now, let us say some more about the Day of the Lord. When you look at everything the Bible teaches about the future Day of the Lord, it's used in a broad sense, and we've already referred to that, covering a period of time, including the seven-year Tribulation period, the Second Coming of Christ, and then the thousand-year Millennial reign of the Lord Jesus here on the face of the earth.

But there are passages which at least imply that there's also a more narrow sense of the future Day of the Lord. And that is referring to one specific 24-hour day, namely the day that Jesus Christ will come out of Heaven after the seven-year Tribulation period in His glorious Second Coming in order to set up the theocratic Millennial kingdom. That day is referred to in the Bible as *"the great and terrible Day of the Lord"* (see Joel 2:11,31 and Malachi 4:5). In other words, the most intense time of God's wrath upon planet earth because in that day, that's when the saved who are still alive on the earth (those who have accepted the Lord during the Tribulation) are going to be exposed to the full glory of the Son of God. And that's when all the armies of all the nations of the world and all the rulers of the Gentile nations of the world are going to be judged and destroyed by the Lord Jesus at His glorious Second Coming. And Satan is going to be bound and removed from the earth and cast into the abyss together with his demonic fallen angels. That is the great and terrible Day of the Lord.

Now, how do we know that there is this more narrow future Day of the Lord, the one specific day of Jesus' Second Coming? We saw earlier that according to Revelation 16, the armies and rulers of all the nations of the world do not even begin to gather into the land of Israel until the sixth bowl or vial judgment, which is the next to the last judgment of the Tribulation, which means that the armies and rulers of the Gentile nations don't even start coming to the land of Israel until almost the very end of the seven-year Tribulation period.

When you go to the prophet Joel 3, there's another prophetic reference to the armies of all the nations of the world gathering together there in the land of Israel at one location; the same gathering that's described for the end of the Tribulation period of Revelation 16. But when you read Joel 3, we're told there that once the armies are gathered there, there is a Day of the Lord that is at hand or that is near, indicating there's a more specific Day of the Lord that's about to transpire when all the armies of the world are gathered there against Israel at the very end of the Tribulation period.

But notice, there's already been a Day of the Lord going on throughout the seven-year Tribulation period as God's been pouring out His wrath during the first half of the Tribulation period and during the second half of the Tribulation period. But now that the Gentile armies are gathered in Israel at the very end of the Tribulation period, there's another Day of the Lord that's at hand. When you tie that in with Revelation 16, it says that the armies are gathered there in Israel for the battle of the great Day of the Lord, or the great day of God, and it will be Armageddon.

Armageddon is going to transpire on the day that Jesus Christ comes out of Heaven in His full glory in His glorious Second Coming, and He pours out the wrath of God upon the rulers and armies of the world that are gathered there together against Him and who are trying to destroy the nation of Israel. And Armageddon is not so much one nation fighting against another, Armageddon is going to be the confrontation between the greatest accumulation of Satan's forces here on the earth on the one hand, and Jesus Christ and His heavenly forces, His holy angels and saints of God, on the other hand. The final showdown between Christ and the forces of Satan, and Christ will crush Satan. And so, according to Revelation 19 and Zechariah 14, when the Lord comes out of Heaven, He'll go to war against the rulers and the armies of the world that are gathered there in Israel and He will destroy them.

In Daniel 11:45 we saw how the Antichrist, in the middle of the Tribulation, will take control of Jerusalem and make it the capital of what he hopes will become a worldwide kingdom. We did not finish verse 45. The end of that verse says of Antichrist, "*Yet he shall come to his end and none shall help him.*" Revelation 19, where John records the Second Coming of Christ on His great and terrible Day of the Lord when He comes out of Heaven to confront these forces of Satan, Revelation 19:19 says this to us: "*And I saw the beast* [that's the Antichrist] *and the kings of the earth and their armies gathered together to make war against Him that sat on the horse* [that's the Lord Jesus] *and against His army, and the beast* [the Antichrist] *was taken and with him the false prophet that wrought miracles before him with which he deceived them that had received the mark of the beast and them that worshipped his image. These both* [the Antichrist and the false prophet] *were cast alive into a lake of fire burning with brimstone.*"

In other words, when the final showdown comes between God's ultimate Man—His last Adam, the Lord Jesus, the true Messiah—and Satan's ultimate man—the Antichrist, the false Christ—the Antichrist will be no match for the Lord Jesus. Christ authoritatively will have him removed from the earth, cast into the eternal lake of fire where he'll be tormented forever throughout eternity. No wonder therefore Daniel says of the Antichrist in Daniel 11:45, "*Yet he shall come to his end and none shall help him.*" Antichrist will be no match for the true Christ.

And then Revelation 19:21 says, "*And the remnant* [the other political rulers and their armies that were there] *were slain with the sword of Him that sat upon the horse; and all the fowls were filled with their flesh.*" Here's the great and terrible Day of the Lord, the specific day that Christ comes out of Heaven, and the conglomeration of Satan's world forces are gathered together there against Him to try to prevent Him from coming back to the earth. And Christ will destroy these godless forces of Satan and Satan himself will be finally crushed and removed from the earth and imprisoned in the abyss or bottomless pit for the next one thousand years.

Question #27

What is the mark of the beast?

THE MARK OF THE beast is going to be instituted about midway through the seven-year Tribulation period. Satan tries to be like God in every way. He has his unholy trinity (Satan, Antichrist and False Prophet) in response to God's trinity of the Father, Son and Holy Spirit. Satan, with his unholy trinity, desires to be worshiped as God is worshiped. And part of the worship is going to be taking an identification mark.

Then I saw another beast coming up out of the earth, and he had two horns like a lamb and spoke like a dragon. And he exercises all the authority of the first beast in his presence, and causes the earth and those who dwell in it to worship the first beast, whose deadly wound was healed. He performs great signs, so that he even makes fire come down from heaven on the earth in the sight of men. And he deceives those who dwell on the earth by those signs which he was granted to do in the sight of the beast, telling those who dwell on the earth to make an image to the beast who was wounded by the sword and lived. He was granted power to give breath to the image of the beast, that the image of the beast should both speak and cause as many as would not worship the image of the beast to be killed. He causes all, both small and great, rich and poor, free and slave, to receive a mark on their right hand or on their foreheads, and that no one may buy or sell except one who has the mark or the name of the beast, or the number of his name. Here is wisdom. Let him who has understanding calculate the number of the beast, for it is the number of a man: His number is 666 (Rev. 13:11-18).

The mark of the beast is simply a way to force people to worship someone out of fear. If you worship the Antichrist then you get the mark.

The Bible doesn't tell us if it is going to be (for example) a computer chip on the forehead or the back of the hand. But we do know that it will be an identification mark that is needed to buy and sell. As we look at the direction that the world is going in, we know that we are not going to have any paper money or coins in the future—it's going to be all electronic. That is part of what's happening in our world technologically today that sets the stage for these prophecies to be fulfilled. The Antichrist will require every single person on earth to have this identification mark. If you don't want to worship the Antichrist you're not going to take the mark, but then you can't buy anything.

The Bible uses the number 666 to describe the mark of the beast. While we are not sure exactly what that means, we do know six is the number of man; it's a number of incompleteness. The mark of the beast represents everything that man can do that falls short of what God can do. God's number is seven (the number of completion), man's number is six. And this number is going to be used to intimidate the people of the world. And those who do not allow this number to be placed on their body will not be allowed to live.

WHAT IS THE MARK OF THE BEAST?

Many Christians today are wondering if they have to worry about the mark. No. Remember, the mark happens in the middle of the Tribulation. We have been caught up to be with the Lord in the air and we won't be here then.

Question #28

Will Christians go through the Tribulation? What does the phrase "the hour of temptation" mean?

A PASSAGE WHICH IS VERY significant in regard to this is **Revelation 3:10** where Jesus is making a promise to Christians and He says, "*Because you have kept the word of my patience, I also will keep you from the hour of temptation.*" Literally, **the hour of testing** "*which shall come upon all the world to try them that dwell upon the earth.*" Literally, "*to try the earthdwellers.*"

Notice, He's saying here that He will keep His saints, His true believers, out of the hour of testing. Many scholars agree that the testing here is referring to a future period of wrath upon the face of the earth. It's obviously referring to a time period because He talks about the "*hour*" of testing. So, many agree that He's promising here to believers to keep them out of **that** hour of testing, but some say, "*Well, it's just the testing that He's preserving them from. They'll be here during the time of the testing but God somehow will shelter them or protect them from the testing.*"

But notice John doesn't say here, quoting the Lord's promise, that He will deliver them or keep them out of the testing, He says He will keep them out of "*the hour of testing.*" In other words, He will keep them out of the very time period when the testing is taking place. And then He says here the purpose of that time period of testing is not to do something with regard to Church saints, but the purpose of that hour of testing is to test or to try the earthdwellers.

When you go through the book of Revelation, the earthdwellers consistently is referring to rebellious unsaved people who refuse to repent and who are so hardened against God that they will never repent. They will never get saved.

It's interesting to note the very next expression after **Revelation 3:10**, Jesus says, "*Behold, I come quickly. Hold that fast which you have that no man take your crown.*" Very interesting the Lord Jesus throws that in. "*Behold, I come quickly,*" after His promise, "*I will keep you from the hour of testing.*" The implication seems to be the way He will keep the believers out of that hour of testing is by His coming quickly to remove them from the face of the earth by Rapture before that hour of testing begins.

So, we are convinced in light of **1 Thessalonians 1:10, 1 Thessalonians 5:9, and Revelation 3:10**, that the Church saints will have no relationship at all to this future period of God's wrath upon the face of the earth. And the reason we shall not is because Jesus will come to the air above the earth before that future period of divine wrath begins and He will remove His Bride the Church, all of His Church saints, from the earth by Rapture and take them back to the Father's house in heaven. And then after we're there, sometime after, then this future period of God's wrath will be poured out upon the unbelievers here on planet earth.

Question #29

Does the Bible teach two separate comings of the Lord?

WE BELIEVE ON THE basis of biblical teaching that the Church will be raptured out of the world before this seven-year period of divine wrath the beginning part of the Day of the Lord, the seven-year period many call the Tribulation period. But then we've also made reference to the effect that Christ will return in His glorious Second Coming back to the earth immediately after that seven-year period. The implication is that this is talking about two separate comings of the Lord here—the one before the seven-year Tribulation period for the purpose of rapturing the Church out of the world; the other one after the seven-year Tribulation period when Christ will come back, not to Rapture the Church out of the world but He's coming back to crush Satan, get rid of him and all of his rebellious forces from the face of the earth, and then take the rule of the earth back on behalf of God.

This poses a question in many people's minds. Does the New Testament actually at least infer if not outright teach two future comings of the Lord, one before the Tribulation period to Rapture the Church; the other one after the Tribulation period to crush Satan and set up God's Kingdom rule?

We believe that the Scriptures do teach that very strongly, by inference at least. Let us point out to you perhaps one or two reasons why we are convinced of that.

First, when you look at the order of things that the Bible teaches that will take place at the Rapture and then you look at the order of the things that the Bible teaches will take place at the Second Coming of Christ and after the Tribulation period, you will find that the order of things between those two comings of the Lord are just the opposite of each other.

What do I mean by that? We have seen from 1 Thessalonians 4 that when the Rapture takes place, it is the believers who will be removed from the earth in blessing to meet the Lord in the air and to go back with Him to the Father's house in Heaven.

So at the Rapture, believers are removed from the earth and by implication the unbelievers are left here. But when you go to passages such as Matthew 24, which are describing the Second Coming of Christ immediately after the Tribulation period, you have just the reverse order of that being taught, namely, that at the Second Coming of Christ it's the unbelievers who are alive on the earth at that time who are going to be removed from the earth but removed from the earth in judgment, and it's the believers who will be alive on the earth at that time who will be left here to go into the next period of world history. So, at the Rapture it will be the reverse order of things at the Second Coming of Christ.

Question #30

At the Rapture, who will be taken to heaven, who will be left on earth? At the Second Coming, who will be left on earth, who will be taken away?

WE HAVE LOOKED AT some of the passages with regard to the Rapture, so we've already seen from the Scriptures that it's the believers who are removed at the Rapture, but what about passages that are talking about who will be removed, who'll be left, at the Second Coming of Christ after the Tribulation period?

In Matthew 13 where Jesus taught some parables concerning the Kingdom, one of those parables has been called *"the parable of the tares."* And Jesus taught about a man who had sowed good grain or wheat in a field. Later on, his enemy came along and sowed tares in that same field. As time passed, the wheat and the tares sprang up together; they were growing together during the growing season.

The farmer's servants noted what had happened and they came and reported to him and they said to him, "What do you want us to do? Should we go out during the growing season and root out the tares from among the good grain or the wheat?" And he said, "No. Don't do that." **Matthew**

13:29-30 says, *"But he said, 'No, lest while you gather up the tares you root up also the wheat with them. Let both grow together until the harvest and in the time of harvest I will say to the reapers, Gather you together **first** the tares.'"* That word *"first"* is very critical here. *"Gather together **first** the tares and bind them in bundles to burn them but gather the wheat into my barn."*

Now drop down to **verse 36**, *"Then Jesus sent the multitude away and went into the house and his disciples came unto him saying, 'Declare unto us the parable of the tares of the field.'"* In other words, they said, "Explain to us; give us the interpretation of that parable." *"He answered and said unto them, 'He that sows the good seed is the Son of man.'"* So He is saying that the farmer that sowed the wheat represented Himself, Jesus, the Son of man. *"The field is the world. The good seed are the children of the Kingdom."* In other words, righteous human beings, those who have gotten saved, they're believers in the Lord Jesus who will eventually go into the future Millennial Kingdom.

Then He says, *"But the tares are the children of the **wicked one**."* Now, in the Bible the wicked one is **Satan** and the Bible identifies the **children of Satan** as **unbelievers**. First John 3 draws a contrast between believers and unbelievers and indicated that the **believers** are **children of God** but the **unbelievers** are **children of Satan**. The Bible makes that very clear. So that the children of the wicked one here are the unbelievers who are in the world. They are represented by the tares.

Verses 39-43: *"The enemy* [God's enemy] *that sowed them is the devil; the harvest is the end of the world,"* literally **the end of the age**, not when this world comes to an end but **when this present age comes to an end**. *"And the reapers are the angels. As therefore the tares are gathered and burned in the* *fire, so shall it be in the end of this age. The Son of man shall send forth his angels and they shall gather out of His Kingdom all things that offend and them which do iniquity and shall cast them into a furnace of fire. There shall be wailing and gnashing of teeth. Then shall the righteous shine forth as the sun in the kingdom of their Father. He who has ears to hear, let him hear."*

What Jesus is saying on the basis of this parable is this: that at His glorious Second Coming, at the end of the age which will be immediately after the future seven-year Tribulation period, He will send forth His angels into the world and they will gather out of the world the tares, the unbelievers, the children of Satan, and will cast them into a horrible place of fire where there will be gnashing of teeth.

So He's teaching that all the unbelievers who are alive on the earth at the glorious Second Coming of Christ, after the seven-year Tribulation period, are going to be removed from the earth in judgment by God's angels. And then He says, the righteous, those are the believers, the saved, "*will shine forth in the Kingdom.*" In other words, the believers who are alive on the earth at the Second Coming of Christ will go into the next period of world history, namely, the Millennial kingdom age of world history.

That's the order of the Second Coming. All the unbelievers are removed from the earth in judgment at the Second Coming of Christ and the believers who are alive at that time left are here to go into the next period, namely, the Kingdom.

Question #31

What does the Parable of the Dragnet tell us about the order of events during the Second Coming?

L ET US CALL YOUR attention to **Matthew 13:47**, "*Again the kingdom of heaven is like unto a net that was cast into the sea and gathered of every kind, which, when it was full they drew to shore and sat down and gathered the good in the vessels but cast the bad away.*" Here Jesus gives the application of that parable to His Second Coming. "*So shall it be at the end of the age. The angels shall come forth and sever the wicked from among the just* [the angels are going to in essence cut off the wicked, remove them, from among the just, the righteous] *and shall cast them into the furnace of fire. There shall be wailing and gnashing of teeth.*"

Notice the same order, for His glorious Second Coming immediately after the seven-year Tribulation period, His holy angels will remove all the unbelievers who are alive on the earth at that time from the earth in judgment and put them into a horrible place of judgment characterized by fire where there will be wailing and gnashing of teeth, but the good fish, representing the believers, are left here to go into the Kingdom. He's teaching that the order of things at His Second Coming will be just the reverse of the order at the Rapture. At the Rapture it's all the believers who are removed from the earth to meet Christ in the air to return with Him to His Father's house in Heaven; and it's the unbelievers who will be left here on the face of the earth.

Question #32

In Matthew 24, is Jesus referring to the Rapture or His Second Coming?

YOU HAVE THE IDENTICALLY same order as Matthew 13:47, again for the Second Coming after the Tribulation period, taught by Jesus in Matthew 24. Many sincere Christians, believe that the Rapture is being presented in Matthew 24 and they believe it's being presented two places in Matthew 24.

Let me give you some background. In **Matthew 24:15** Jesus refers to the abomination of desolation which was spoken of by Daniel the prophet back in Daniel 9:27. In **Daniel 9:27**, we are told that the abomination of desolation will take place precisely in the middle of the seven-year Tribulation period. On the basis of Daniel 9:27 you could call it the 70th week, right in the middle of that 70th week, of Daniel 9. In other words, the **abomination of desolation** will take place **before the second three and a half years of that seven-year period of time**. Then Jesus, after saying the abomination of desolation will take place, He warns Jews who will be living in Israel at that time, He says, *"When you see that abomination of desolation taking place, then those who are in Judea should flee to the mountains."* They should get out of there as fast as they can, and He tells them why in **verse 21-22**, *"for then shall be great tribulation such as was not since the beginning* *of the world till this time, no nor ever shall be, and except those days should be shortened* [literally "**should be cut off**] *there should no flesh be saved but for the elect's sake, those days shall be cut off."*

What He is saying here is this: that when the abomination of desolation takes place in the middle of that seven-year period of time, that will be the starting point of what Jesus calls *"the great Tribulation."* So the Great Tribulation will begin in the middle of the 70th week of Daniel 9 or, if you prefer, in the middle of the seven-year Tribulation period. And Jesus clearly indicates here in verses 21-22 that that Great Tribulation will be the unparalleled time of trouble in all of world history, the likes of which He said have not been since the beginning of the world, nor will ever be again in all of history. This will be the unparalleled time of trouble for planet earth.

Now, with that as background, we come to **verses 29-31**. Having just referred to the Great Tribulation Jesus says, *"Immediately after the tribulation of those days* [so He's talking about what's going to happen immediately after the Great Tribulation] *shall the sun be darkened and the moon shall not give her light and the stars shall fall from heaven and the powers of the heavens shall be shaken."* He's saying, immediately after the end of the Great Tribulation there will be great cosmic disturbances in the heavenly realm. *"And then,"* Jesus said, *"shall appear the sign of the Son of Man in Heaven* [the sign that He's coming out of Heaven] *and then shall all the tribes of the earth mourn and they shall see the Son of man coming in the clouds of heaven with power and great glory and He shall send His angels with the great sound of a trumpet and they shall gather together His elect from the four winds from one end of Heaven to the other."*

He's clearly talking here about His glorious Second Coming immediately after the end of the future seven-year Tribulation period and He's saying that one thing that His holy angels will do when He sends them out into the world at His glorious Second Coming is this: they will gather together His elect from the four winds, from one end of heaven to the other.

Question #33

Who are "the elect"
referred to in Matthew 24:31?

SOME PEOPLE SAY, "WELL, obviously, the elect here would be God's people and so this has to be a reference to the Church saints and so this is referring to the gathering of the Church saints out of the world to take them to Heaven in conjunction with His glorious Second Coming out of heaven after the Tribulation period." And so they would say this has to be a reference to the Rapture of the Church, that the Church will be raptured out of the world in conjunction with the glorious Second Coming of Christ back to planet earth immediately after the Tribulation period. And so they would say, "Look, this would indicate a post-Tribulation Rapture of the Church.

Who are the elect that he gathers with a great sound of a trumpet from the four winds of heaven? Are they the Church saints? We are convinced that they are not. Let us tell you why. For one thing, if you're going to say these are Church saints, you're overlooking some extensive revelation that was given to us in the Old Testament. What kind of revelation?

There are passages in the Old Testament where God calls the whole nation of Israel "*His chosen,*" literally "*His elect.*" Then there are passages in the Old Testament where God specifically refers to the remnant of believers within the nation of Israel who are His elect. There are passages in the Old Testament where God said that because Israel so stubbornly and persistently rebelled against Him for centuries that He would *scatter them to the four winds,* or some places say that He would scatter them to the four corners of the earth. And He did through their captivities, the Assyrian captivity, the Babylonian captivity. He scattered them in every direction.

Then there are passages, these are prophetic promise passages in the Old Testament, to the effect that in the end times that He would gather together His chosen ones, *His elect,* particularly the believing remnant of Israel from all corners of the earth, gather them together even *from the four winds,* gather them together again so that they could go into the Millennial kingdom with the Messiah whenever He reigns.

Now, here's an intriguing thing. We are told in Matthew 24:31, "*He shall send his angels with a great sound of a trumpet and they shall gather together his elect from the four winds.*" The Greek literally says, "*with the sound of a great trumpet.*"

Here is a fascinating promise that God delivered to Israel through the prophet Isaiah in Isaiah 27:12-13: "*O ye children of Israel, and it shall come to pass in that day that the great trumpet shall be blown and they shall come which were ready to perish in the land of Assyria and the outcasts in the land of Egypt and shall worship the Lord in the holy mount of Jerusalem.*" God here was promising toward the end times, if you read the whole context, that He's going to regather His scattered people of Israel from many different places around the world and He will do that in conjunction with the blowing of the great trumpet.

Again, a literal translation of Matthew 24:31 where Jesus says "*immediately after the tribulation...*" the cosmic disturbances and then He comes as the Son of man, "*He shall send his angels with the sound of a great trumpet and they shall gather together his elect from the four winds from one end of heaven to the other.*"

Now, there's a second reason we believe this is referring to the elect of Israel and not to the Church elect or Church saints. The whole context of Matthew 24 is a Jewish context, not a Church context. In Matthew 24:15, Jesus, speaking ahead of time to Jews of that future Tribulation period, said, "*When you see the abomination of desolation spoken of by Daniel the prophet standing in your holy place,...*" well, who had the holy place? The Gentiles? No, the people of Israel did. That's a reference to a temple of God in Israel, "*... your holy place, then let them which be in Judea* [these are Jews living in their own land of Israel] *flee unto the mountains. Let him which is on the housetop not come down to take anything out of his house,*" etc. And then He says to them that they really ought to be concerned that their flight not be on the Sabbath day, verse 20, "*but pray that your flight be not in the winter, neither on the Sabbath day.*"

He's talking here about Jews and how this will affect Jews. The whole context is a Jewish context. So the elect here are Jewish people whom He will gather together through His holy angels from the four winds, really the idea is from all four directions under the heavens here on planet earth, back to their homeland of Israel in conjunction with His Second Coming.

In light of those Old Testament parallels, we are convinced that the *elect* in Matthew 24:31 are not Church saints but the people of Israel who have been scattered throughout the world; perhaps even more specifically the *faithful remnant of Jews* who have become believers in the Lord during the seven-year Tribulation period and are still alive on the face of the earth at His glorious Second Coming back to the earth immediately after the Tribulation period. He will gather together this faithful remnant of Jews from all over the world with the sound of a great trumpet back to the land of Israel.

Question #34

In Matthew 24, is Jesus referring to believers or unbelievers as the ones being removed who are similar to those in the days of Noah?

SOME SAY THAT THERE'S another place in **Matthew 24** where it has to be the Church being removed from the earth and that's beginning with **verse 37** where Jesus says, "*But as the days of Noah were, so shall also the coming of the Son of man be. For as in the days that were before the Flood, they were eating and drinking, marrying and giving in marriage until the day that Noah entered into the ark and knew not until the Flood came and took them all away, so shall also the coming of the Son of man be.*"

What Jesus is saying here is this: the order at His glorious Second Coming immediately after the seven-year Tribulation period will be identical to the order of things in Noah's day in conjunction with the Flood. One of the ways in which the order would be the same is this: the Flood came and took them all away. Which group of people did the Flood take away from planet earth—the believers or the unbelievers? The Flood removed all the unbelievers of Noah's day from the earth in judgment. And the believers in Noah's day, namely, Noah and his family, were left here on the earth in the ark to go into the next period of world history after the Flood.

After pointing that out, Jesus says, again, at the end of **verse 39**, "*So shall also the coming of the Son of Man be.*" It'll be the same order of things then as it was in the days of Noah with the Flood. And then to illustrate that, He goes on in **verses 40-41** to explain in the day that the Son of man comes, after the Tribulation period, "***then*** *shall two be in the field, the one shall be taken and the other left. Two women shall be grinding at the mill, the one shall be taken and the other left.*"

Now the question is, "**Who is the one taken from the field and the one taken from the mill?**" If it's the same order of things as in Noah's day with the Flood and **the Flood took all the unsaved away** and **Jesus says it'll be the same order at His Second Coming**, then it seems that you're forced to conclude that the one who is taken from the field and the one who is taken from the mill are **not believers** taken by Rapture but unbelievers who are alive on the earth at Jesus' Second Coming. They are taken by Christ's holy angels from the earth in judgment just as we saw with the Parable of the Tares and the Parable of the Dragnet in Matthew 13.

Therefore the one that's left in the field and the one that's left at the mill is the believer who is left here on the earth, the believer who is alive at the Second Coming of Christ after the Tribulation period left here on the earth to go into the next period of history, namely, the Kingdom. Just as in Noah's day it was the unbelievers who were removed in judgment, Noah and his family were left here on the earth to go into the next period of world history.

Now, to demonstrate even more clearly that that's the order of things Jesus is describing, we go to the parallel passage, Luke's record of Jesus' same teaching as recorded for us in **Luke 17**. Just to show you Jesus is presenting the same teaching here, we read in **verse 26**: "*As it was in the days of Noah, so shall it be also in the days of the Son of Man. They did eat, they drank, they married wives, they were given in marriage until the day that Noah entered into the ark and the flood came and destroyed them all.*"

Then Jesus says in **verses 30-31**, "*Even thus shall it be in the day when the Son of man is revealed. In that day, he which shall be on the housetop and his stuff in the house let him not come down to take it away; he that's in the field, let him likewise not return back.*"

Then He goes on to say in **verse 34**, "*I tell you, in that night there shall be two men in one bed, the one shall be taken and the other shall be left. Two women shall be grinding together, the one shall be taken and the other left. Two men shall be in the field, the one shall be taken, the other left.*" This is the same teaching that Matthew recorded in Matthew 24.

But now Luke records something that Matthew did not record. We read in **Luke 17:37**, "*And they answered and said unto Him, 'Where, Lord?'*" What they're saying is, "Lord, you keep talking about people being taken somewhere; **to where are they being taken?**" They're not asking, "Where are those that are left?" They don't have to ask that. If a person was in the field and is left in the field, obviously he's still in the field. And if a person was in the bed and he's left in the bed, obviously he's still in the bed. So they're not asking, "Where are those that are left?" Instead, they're asking, "Where are those that are taken? You keep talking about people being taken from the field and from the mill, etc., to where are they being taken?"

Listen to Jesus' answer in verse 37: "*He said unto them, wheresoever the body is, there will the eagles* [literally "there will the vultures"] *be gathered together.*" Vultures are flesh-eating fowl.

What Jesus is saying is this, "*You want to know where those who are taken, where they are taken? They are taken into the realm of death. That's where they're taken at my Second Coming. And their dead bodies, their carcasses, will be left here on the earth for the vultures and flesh-eating fowl on planet earth to come and feast upon their dead bodies.*" Jesus is making it very clear that the ones taken here are taken in judgment into the realm of death. These are not believers being taken into the realm of blessing as will be true at the Rapture.

So the order of things at the glorious Second Coming of Christ immediately after the seven-year Tribulation period will be just the reverse of the order of things at the Rapture of the Church. And that's one of the major reasons why we are forced to conclude that the Rapture of the Church will be a totally separate, distinctive event from the glorious Second Coming of Christ after the seven-year Tribulation period; not only separate and distinct but therefore also at a totally separate, distinct time than the Second Coming of Christ after the Tribulation period.

This forces us to conclude there are two future comings of the Lord: one, down to the air above the earth to Rapture the Church out of the world; the other, after the seven-year Tribulation period, a coming of Christ the whole way down to planet earth, not stopping in the air as at the Rapture but the whole way down to planet earth to crush Satan, his rebellious forces removed, all of his unbelievers removed from planet earth in judgment, and then go with the righteous into the Millennial kingdom for the honor and the glory of God.

Question #35

Are the Rapture and the Second Coming two different events? (Summary)

IN THE PREVIOUS MATERIAL we have given the details of the differences between the events described for the future comings of the Lord, which lead us to believe that there are two separate, distinct events. The first one is the Rapture the Church out of the world before the seven-year Tribulation period; the second one immediately after the seven-year Tribulation period when Christ comes to rule the world.

Here is a summary of the eight reasons why we believe they are different:

1. **There is a difference in the place Christ will meet believers.**

    Rapture — Christians will meet the Lord in the air. *1 Thessalonians 4:16-17*

    Second Coming — Christ descends to earth, and steps onto the Mount of Olives in Jerusalem. *Zechariah 14:2-4*

2. **There is a difference in who removes people from the earth.**

    Rapture—**Christ Himself** comes and takes believers out of the world. *1 Thessalonians 4:16-17*

↻ **Second Coming**—Matthew 24, Christ sends **His angels**
to take (wicked) people to judgment. *Zechariah 14:2-4*

3. **At each event there is a difference in those who are taken from the earth and those who are left. The order of things at the Second Coming is the reverse of that at the Rapture.**

⤵ Rapture—**Believers** are **taken** from the earth to heaven
while unbelievers are left on earth. *1 Thessalonians 4:17*

↻ Second Coming—**Believers** are **left** on the earth to go
into the millennial kingdom while **unbelievers** are **taken**
to judgment . *Matthew 13:41-42; Matthew 13:49-50*

4. **There is a difference of when Jesus comes in relationship to the Tribulation.**

⤵ Rapture—Jesus comes to rescue Christians before
the hour of trial, the Tribulation, and the wrath to come
Revelation 3:10; 1 Thessalonians 1:10

↻ Second Coming—Jesus comes after the Tribulation to
inflict final punishment, conquer His enemies and to
begin to rule the world from Jerusalem. *Matthew 24:29-30:*

5. **The Bible indicates that there is a difference in the number of signs given for each event.**

⤵ Rapture—There are no signs given which must take

place before the Rapture can occur. Rather, the Rapture is an imminent event: It could happen at any moment. *1 Thessalonians 1:9-10; James 5:9 (NASB); Revelation 3:11; Philippians 3:20*

Second Coming—Detailed signs are given that must take place before Christ will come to earth.

1. Many shall come in my name and deceive many.

2. Wars and rumors of wars; nation against nation.

3. Famines

4. Pestilences—plagues

5. Earthquakes

6. They shall kill you.

7. Many shall betray one another.

8. False prophets shall deceive many.

9. Love of many will grow cold.

10. Gospel shall be preached in all the world.

11. Abomination of desolation shall take place.

12. Flee Jerusalem.

13. Great Tribulation.

14. More false Christs.

15. Immediately after the tribulation of those days...the sun darkened...moon will not give its light...stars will fall from the sky.

16. Then they will see the Son of Man coming.

6. **There is a difference between these two events as to when judgment takes place.**

    ↻ **Rapture**—There is no mention made of God's judgment taking place, only promises connected with looking for His return and our going to heaven. *1 Thessalonians 4:16-18; Revelation 3:10*

    ↻ **Second Coming**—Tribulation and judgment do take place *Zechariah 14:2-4 (NASB); Matthew 25:31-32, 46*

7. **There is a difference in the timing of the resurrections which take place.**

    ↻ **Rapture**—A resurrection of the dead in Christ takes place when Christ descends to above the earth and we meet him there in the air, and He takes us to heaven. *1 Thessalonians 4:16-18*

    ↻ **Second Coming**—A resurrection of the righteous dead who died during the Tribulation takes place only after Christ has descended to earth.

    Revelation 19:11-21 and 20:1-5:

    1. The descent of Christ.

    2. Christ slays His enemies.

    3. The Antichrist—the Beast and the false prophet are cast into the lake of fire.

    4. Satan is then bound and thrown into the pit.

    5. And finally, after all of these events there is a resurrection

of the saints.

"...and those who had not worshipped the beast or his image, and had not received the mark upon their forehead and
upon their hand; and they came to life and reigned with
Christ for a thousand years."

8. **The Bible indicates there is a difference in the kind of bodies
believers will possess.**

At the Second Coming of Christ, everybody at that time who is a
believer will receive a glorified body, which will not marry, which will
not give birth to children, will be sinless, and will not experience death.
In light of the fact, this other biblical truth that we've seen—that all
unbelievers alive on the earth at that time will be removed from the
earth in judgment, will not be allowed to go into the Kingdom - this
would mean therefore that everyone who would go into the Kingdom
would go into the Kingdom with glorified bodies, which again, do not
marry, do not give birth to children, are sinless and do not die.

Notice, there are prophecies in the Word of God which teach that
during the Millennial Reign of the Messiah on the face of the earth,
number one, there will be marriage; **number two**, there are prophecies
to the effect that both Jews and Gentiles will give birth to children
during the thousand-year reign of the Messiah. **Number three**, there
are Scriptures that indicate that by the end of the Millennium, when
Satan is set loose from the abyss and comes back to the earth, there
will be a huge horde of human beings who will flock to him and follow

him in one final revolt against Christ's rule. Obviously, those who flock to Satan are unsaved people.

If no unbelievers went into the Kingdom at the beginning, then everyone that goes into the Kingdom goes in with mortal bodies who are sinless and who do not die and who don't give birth to children, where do these unbelievers come from by the end of the Millennium?

In addition, there are prophecies to the effect that at least any who choose to outwardly rebel against Christ during the Millennium will be put to death so that there will be some who will die during the Millennium. But if everyone who went into the Kingdom went in with a mortal body which cannot die, how would that prophecy be fulfilled?

So if the Rapture were to take place at the Second Coming of Christ, the prophecies to the effect of people marrying, people giving birth to children, unsaved rebels being on the face of the earth during that period of time and people dying could not be fulfilled.

So there **must** be two separate events.

↩ **Rapture**—Believers are given glorified bodies.
   1 Corinthians 15:51-53; 1 Thessalonians 4:15-17; Luke 20:34-36 (NAS
↩ **Second Coming**—Believers who are alive (those who were
   saved during the Tribulation who made it through the
   Tribulation alive) will enter the Millennial kingdom and
   marry and bear children. *Isaiah 65:22-23 (NASB)*

That fact of Scripture, together with the fact that the order of things at the Rapture, together with the order of things at the Second Coming force us to conclude that the Rapture of the Church and the Second Coming after the Tribulation period are two totally separate, distinct events separated by a period of time of seven years.

At the Rapture Christ comes to the air; at the Second Coming He comes the whole way down to earth.

At the Rapture Jesus comes by Himself to remove the believers from the earth; at the Second Coming He comes with His holy angels and sends them throughout the world.

At the Rapture we have all the believers being removed from the earth to blessing; at the Second Coming after the Tribulation, all the unbelievers removed from the earth in judgment.

At the Rapture, the believers go to a glorious destiny, to the Father's house in Heaven with Christ; at the Second Coming the unbelievers go into a horrible place of judgment of fire where there's wailing and gnashing of teeth.

And as we have just seen, certain prophecies in the Bible could not be fulfilled if the Rapture takes place at the Second Coming.

In light of these biblical facts, every believer must honestly deal with these facts in dealing with the issue: are the Rapture and the Second Coming of Christ one and the same event? And it seems to that to be consistent with these biblical facts you are forced to conclude that the Rapture and the Second Coming are two totally separate events distinct from each other.

Question #36

How do we know the Tribulation will last for seven years?

W E HAVE REFERRED TO a seven-year period of time between the Rapture of the Church from the world and the glorious Second Coming of Christ immediately after the Great Tribulation. What's the basis for this idea of this seven-year period of time between those two events? The foundational passage for that seven-year period of time is in the Old Testament, specifically in Daniel 9:27.

Just to give a little background so we understand, when you begin with verse 24 of Daniel 9, Daniel is receiving some incredible revelation from God through the angel Gabriel. In that revelation God was mapping out ahead of time His long-range extended program for Israel in the future.

He says in verse 24 that *"seventy weeks* [literally "seventy sevens"] *are determined for your people* [Daniel's people—that would be Israel] *and for your holy city,"* the city of Jerusalem.

What he's saying here is this: God had determined seventy periods of time for Israel in the future, but each one of those seventy periods of time would consist of seven years. That's the idea of seventy sevens.

Why seven-year periods? Well, when you go through the Old Testament you find that God had set up a unique calendar system for Israel that was based upon seven-year cycles. For six years they were to till the ground and grow their crops. But then every seventh year was to be a sabbatical year in which they would allow the land to rest and restore its energy. Then for six more years they would till the ground and then the next seventh year would be a sabbatical year and they would let it rest.

So God had designed Israel's calendar system in seven-year cycles, and that's what He's doing in this prophecy: Seventy cycles of time, each one of those cycles consists of seven years. So seventy times seven means that 490 years were involved altogether.

When you read that prophecy from verses 24-26, we find that the first 69 of those cycles was fulfilled when Jesus presented Himself to Israel officially as its Prince, its coming King. The New Testament would indicate that Jesus did that when He made His triumphal entry into Jerusalem on Palm Sunday.

Then when you examine that prophecy in depth you find that there is a gap of time between the end of the 69th cycle of seven years and the beginning of the 70th, or last cycle of seven-years. We are living in that gap of time right now.

That tells us, therefore, that the last cycle of seven-years has not yet begun. We could call that the 70th week, or the 70th seven. The last seven-year period, the seventieth period of seven years, has not yet transpired and that will take place in the future. And as we've already noted, the historic event that will actually begin that seven-year period of time will be the confirming of a covenant between Antichrist and the nation of Israel in the Middle East.

Then we're told that in the middle of that seven-year period the Antichrist will commit the abomination of desolation. And Jesus, referring to that abomination of desolation in Matthew 24:15, then indicated in verse 21 that will begin the Great Tribulation, indicating that the second half of that seven-year period will be the unparalleled time of trouble for the earth. But Daniel 9:27 is indicating that this Tribulation period lasts seven years. That's where we know that it's seven years in duration.

Now, some have raised the question, "Okay, Jesus applied the term Tribulation to the second half of that seven-year period, but the Bible does not specifically apply it to the first half of this seven-year period. So how can we say that all seven years are the Tribulation period?" Well, for one thing, people who make the claim that there's no reference to tribulation in the first seven years are overlooking the fact that many of the things that will transpire during the first half of the seven-year period of time are foretold in the Old Testament prophets. For example, war, famine, pestilence, wild beasts being instruments of God's wrath, destroying people here on the face of the earth.

The Septuagint is a translation of the Hebrew Old Testament into the Greek language that was prepared by Jewish Hebrew scholars back about 200 years before the birth of Christ into the world. In that Greek translation, by Hebrew and Greek language scholars, when they translated some of the Old Testament prophets describing some of the dramatic things that will take place during the first half of the seven-year period, they used the Greek word *thlipsis* to describe some of the turmoil there. And the Greek word *thlipsis* is the word for tribulation. And that tells us that the Jewish language scholars who prepared this Greek translation of the Hebrew Old Testament, the Septuagint, they understood that the Old Testament prophets were saying by revelation of God that even events of the first half of that seven-year period will be characterized by tribulation.

And so this is indicating that the Scriptures are teaching that even the first half of that seven-year period will be characterized by tribulation. And so it is valid to apply the word tribulation even to the first half of that seven-year period of time, not just to the second half which Jesus called "the Great Tribulation."

Question #37

Why does it matter to us that certain Hebrew words were translated a certain way in the Greek Septuagint?

SOME RAISE THE QUESTION, "It doesn't matter what the translators called that, you know, what do the Scriptures say?" But they're overlooking the fact that Jesus and the apostles in their statements recorded in the New Testament frequently quoted verbatim the Septuagint, that Greek translation, and applied what the Septuagint said to these events. And so Jesus took the Septuagint as being an accurate translation. And the apostles took the Septuagint as an accurate portrayal of what God was saying through the Old Testament prophets would be characteristic of even the first half of that seven-year period of time. And so if we're going to say it doesn't matter what the **translators** said would be true of it, then what do we do with Jesus accepting what the translators say as being valid and the apostles accepting what those translators said as being valid?

In Zephaniah 1:14, the subject of the Day of the Lord is introduced. In fact, the Day of the Lord specifically is referred to. In verse 15, Zephaniah described characteristics of the future Day of the Lord. That day is a day of wrath, a day of trouble and distress, a day of waste and desolation, a day of darkness and gloominess, a day of clouds and thick darkness.

Now, when he talked about a day of trouble and distress, one of the Hebrew words there, either trouble or distress, translated trouble or distress, was the Hebrew word for tribulation. And when the Jewish scholars who produced the Greek translation of the Hebrew Old Testament, the Septuagint, when they translated, they translated that with the Greek word *thlipsis*, which is the Greek word for tribulation. But Zephaniah was making it very clear that the Day of the Lord would be characterized by tribulation.

Interestingly, in Romans 2, Paul says, *"But after thy hardness and impenitent heart treasurest up unto thyself wrath against the day of wrath and revelation of the righteous judgment of God who will render to every man according to his deeds,"* etc., then he goes on to point out what God will render to man in the day of God's wrath. Verse 9: *"tribulation and anguish upon every soul of man that does evil, of the Jew first and also of the Gentile."* Now, notice, Paul here is saying that the day of God's wrath, which is the Day of the Lord, will also be characterized by tribulation. And it's the Greek word *thlipsis*, which is what the Septuagint translators used for the Day of the Lord in Zephaniah 1.

Now, the point is, when does the Day of the Lord begin? When does God begin pouring out His wrath? Well, again, as we saw, certainly it is the wrath of God in the first four seals. Those first four seals are the same as what Jesus referred to as "the beginning of sorrows" or beginning of birth pangs in Matthew 24, and Jesus put that before the abomination of desolation which according to Daniel 9:27 takes place in the middle of the seven-year period. So Jesus is putting the beginning of sorrows, beginning of birth pangs, in the first half of that seven-year period, which means that the "Day of the Lord's" wrath is in the first half of that seven-year period. And Paul here is indicating that the day of God's wrath is characterized by tribulation and anguish. That term is not applied just to man's wrath against man; it's specifically used in the Bible here in Zephaniah 1 for God's wrath being poured out upon the earth as well, tribulation.

Question #38

Will the Rapture begin the seven-year Tribulation period?

THE RAPTURE IS NOT the event that will begin the seven-year Tribulation period. What do we base that upon? Well, it appears as if there will be a period of transition between the time of the Rapture and the beginning of the Tribulation period. Now, we base that upon two things in 1 Thessalonians 5. In 1 Thessalonians 5:1 Paul says to the Thessalonian Christians, *"But of the times and the seasons, brethren, you have no need that I write unto you, for you yourselves know perfectly that the Day of the Lord so comes as a thief in the night."* At the beginning of 1 Thessalonians 5:1, Paul introduces that verse with a combination of two words in the Greek language: *peri de*. And every other time the apostle Paul used that combination of those two Greek words, he used it to introduce a new subject that's different from the subject he just dealt with previously.

At the end of chapter 4 Paul was referring to the Rapture of the Church. Now, when he comes to 5:1, he uses *peri de* to say, "Now, as I'm going to talk about the Day of the Lord;" this is a different subject from the subject of the Rapture of the Church I just dealt with at the end of chapter 4." Now, the second thing is that in 5:2 he tells the Thessalonians that they already had an accurate or perfect knowledge about the Day of the Lord. By contrast, when you go back to 4:13 where he introduces the subject of the Rapture he says, "*But I would not have you to be ignorant, brethren, concerning them which are asleep that you sorrow not, even as others which have no hope.*"

Notice, Paul is saying that before Paul wrote this 1 Thessalonians epistle to these believers, they were ignorant about certain things with regard to the Rapture of the Church. But by contrast, in 5:2, he indicates that before he wrote 1 Thessalonians to these believers, they already had an accurate knowledge about the Day of the Lord. Well, if the Rapture of the Church is part of the Day of the Lord, even the beginning part of it, the start of it, and they had an accurate knowledge about the Day of the Lord, then they would not have been ignorant about some aspects of the Rapture. So that indicates, again, that the Rapture is not part of the Day of the Lord, not even the starting point of the Day of the Lord. It's an event that's totally separate from the Day of the Lord.

Both of these items we've seen here, the *peri de* and the contrast between ignorance about the Rapture and yet accurate knowledge about the Day of the Lord, both of these indicate that the Rapture is a totally separate, distinct event from the Day of the Lord. It is not part of the Day of the Lord. It's not even the beginning or starting point of the Day of the Lord. And that says there must be a transition period between the Rapture and the beginning of the Day of the Lord. And since we saw earlier that the Day of the Lord is even in the first half of the seven-year Tribulation period, even from the beginning, that says that there's a gap of time, a transition period between the Rapture and even the beginning of the seven-year Tribulation period.

Question #39

What do Daniel 9:27 and 2 Thessalonians 2 tell us about the Antichrist?

CCORDING TO **DANIEL 9:27**, we are told, "*and he* [referring to the Antichrist] *shall confirm the covenant with many for one week,*" literally for one seven. Now, there is an interesting implication of this. Many have thought that the event which will actually start the seven-year Tribulation period (Daniel's 70th week) will be the Rapture of the Church. That's not what the biblical text is saying. Instead, Daniel 9:27 is saying that the actual event which will officially begin that seven-year period of time will be the establishment of the seven-year covenant between Antichrist and the people of Israel in the Middle East.

Then we're told as we read on in verse 27, "*and in the midst of the week,*" literally in the middle of the week, in the middle of the seven, so it's talking here about what will happen in dead center of this seven-year period of time. After the first three and a half years of this period of time have transpired, in the middle of the week, "*he* [Antichrist] *shall cause the sacrifice and the oblation to cease.*" That implies that by this future period of seven-years Israel will have a new temple and they will have reinstituted the Old Testament sacrifices and offerings in that temple. What's being revealed to Daniel here is that in the middle of that 70th week of Daniel 9 Antichrist will put a stop to the sacrifices and the offerings offered there in Israel's new temple.

In 2 Thessalonians 2, the apostle Paul describes this same man whom we have called the Antichrist as "*the man of sin.*" We read in **2 Thessalonians 2:3,** "*Let no man deceive you by any means, for that day* [the Day of the Lord] *shall not come except there come a falling away first and that man of sin be revealed, the son of perdition, who opposes and exalts himself above all that is called God or that is worshipped so that he as God sits in the temple of God, showing himself that he is God.*"

That is the abomination of desolation spoken of in **Daniel 9:27.** And so Daniel is told that right in the middle of this seven-year period of time the Antichrist will enter into this new temple of Israel in Jerusalem and will put a stop to their Old Testament sacrificial system that they've re-instituted. The reason he does that is because he wants to clear the way for the worship of himself as God. And he will set himself up in that temple as the true and the living God, make the bold claim that he is that, and then he will begin desolating the nation of Israel. The implication is, he will break his covenant with Israel and begin persecuting that nation worse than it's ever been persecuted in all of past history.

Zechariah 12-14 makes that very clear. In fact, the last couple of verses of Zechariah 13 indicate that things will be so terrible for the people of Israel during that period of time that two-thirds of the Jews will perish very quickly. **Zechariah 13:8,** "'*It shall come to pass that in all the land,*' says the Lord, '*two parts therein shall be cut off and die, but the third shall be left therein.*'"

In scope, this will be far worse than the Holocaust of World War II, as inconceivable as that might be. So, during the first half of the 70th week, which is during the first three and a half years of the seven-year period of time, Antichrist appears to be Israel's great benefactor and protector. But in the middle of the week he will turn against the people of Israel, break his covenant with them, and now become their great desolator as he commits this abomination which brings desolation, his declaring that he is God.

Now the Antichrist goes to war against the people of Israel, plus against any believers who are in the world at that particular time. In Daniel 7 we are told that he will wage war against the saints. Revelation 13 declares the same thing. And that's why Jesus in **Matthew 24:15**, said, *"When you see the abomination of desolation spoken of by Daniel the prophet standing in your holy place, then let them who are in Judea flee to the mountains, and pray that your flight is not on the Sabbath day."* And He told them why, **verse 21**, *"because then will be such great tribulation such as has not been since the world began or ever will be, and except those days be cut off, all flesh would perish; but for the sake of the elect, those days will be cut off."*

So what we have here is this seven-year period basically divided into two halves. In the first half, Antichrist appears to be the great benefactor and protector and friend of Israel, but in the middle of that seven-year period he will turn against the people of Israel and begin desolating it severely. And that's why Jesus called then the second half *"the great tribulation, the likes of which has never been since the beginning of the world or ever will be again."* So, the second half of this 70th week of Daniel 9 will be the unparalleled time of trouble for the world.

Question #40

When will the Tribulation time period begin?

SOME HAVE RAISED THE question, "What does Paul mean, though, in 2 Thessalonians 2:3 by the man of sin being revealed? How will he be revealed and when will that take place? Some hold the view that he won't be revealed until the middle of the Tribulation period whenever he announces that he is God. According to the Scriptures, there are several other things that will transpire long before he announces he is God in the middle of the Tribulation period. Several other things will transpire that will indicate who the Antichrist is.

According to Daniel 7, the Antichrist will be an eleventh ruler who will rise to power from within the revived Roman Empire that will have ten divisions with ten equal rulers. And as this eleventh ruler rises to power, he will overthrow three of the original ten rulers that were already there. Daniel 7 makes it very clear that's who the Antichrist is—that eleventh ruler who overthrows three and thereby gains controlling authority over the revived Roman Empire. Now again, he's going to have to be in that position of authority in order to confirm a covenant with Israel, and according to Daniel 9:27, the confirming of the covenant between

Antichrist and Israel is the historic event that will officially begin the seven-year Tribulation period. It's not the Rapture of the Church that begins the seven-year Tribulation period, it's the confirming of this covenant between Antichrist and Israel that officially begins the seven-year Tribulation period. And, even that event, the confirming of the covenant, will identify who the Antichrist is three and a half years before he announces that he is God.

But some would say, "But wait a minute. The unsaved world isn't going to recognize that he is an evil man until he announces that he is God in the middle of the Tribulation period." Paul's not talking here about this man being recognized by the unsaved world. He's talking about this man of sin being revealed, whether the world recognizes it or not. God has given a lot of revelation to the world and it's here and it's genuine; but the world, the unsaved world won't recognize the revelation God has given. We're talking here about revealing the man of sin. And Daniel 7 and Daniel 9 points out some things that will transpire by the beginning of the Tribulation period that will reveal the Antichrist: his rising to power as an eleventh ruler within that ten division revived Roman Empire and overthrowing three of the original ten rulers; and then once he's in that position of authority, then at the very beginning of the Tribulation period, confirming a covenant with the nation of Israel.

Question #41

In Matthew 24, what did Jesus teach about the seventieth week of Daniel and the abomination of desolation?

WHEN YOU GO TO Matthew 24, before Jesus introduced the abomination of desolation in verse 15, He said this in verses 5-14: *"For many shall come in my name saying, 'I am Christ,' and shall deceive many. And you shall hear of wars and rumors of wars. See that ye be not troubled, for all these things must come to pass; but the end is not yet. For nation shall rise against nation and kingdom against kingdom, and there shall be famines and pestilences and earthquakes in divers places. All these are the beginning of sorrows. Then* [and the *"then"* here seems to imply *"at the same time"* these things are going on] *shall they deliver you up to be afflicted and shall kill you and you shall be hated of all nations for my name's sake. And then shall many be offended and shall betray one another and shall hate one another; and many false prophets shall rise and shall deceive many, and because iniquity shall abound, the love of many shall wax cold. But he that shall endure until the end, the same shall be saved. And this gospel of the kingdom shall be preached in all the world for a witness unto all nations, and then shall the end come."*

He seems to be describing here, before verse 15, major things that will be taking place before the abomination of desolation; because in verse 15 He then introduces the abomination of desolation. The impression is that Jesus is spelling out things in chronological order for this future period of time.

The abomination of desolation takes place in the middle of the 70th week. That's followed by the three and a half year Great Tribulation. But He's saying here—at least the implication is—before the abomination of desolation in the 70th week you will have transpired in the world what Jesus called *"the beginning of sorrows,"* literally, *"the beginning of birth pangs."*

He's telling the things that will be involved in the beginning of birth pangs. You will have false messiahs, those who will appear upon the world scene saying, *"I'm the Messiah."* In addition, the earth will experience wars and rumors of wars. You'll have nation rising against nation, kingdom against kingdom. The earth will experience famines, pestilences, earthquakes in many different places. Jesus says all those are the beginning of birth pangs.

Question #42

In Matthew 24, what period of time do the words "birth pangs" refer to?

YOU HAVE THE TERM "birth pangs" used by the Lord Jesus for the first half of that seven-year Tribulation period. He puts the beginning of birth pangs before the mid event of the seven-year period, namely, the abomination of desolation. So he's using the term "birth pangs" for the first half.

You have the term "birth pangs" for the whole Day of the Lord; you have birth pangs in Jeremiah 30 associated with "the Time of Jacob's Trouble" which is in the second half. So the Bible consistently uses the same terminology for both halves of that seventieth week, that seven-year period.

He has been describing what will be transpiring on the face of the earth before the abomination of desolation in the middle of the 70th week, so the implication is these beginning of birth pangs will be taking place during the first half of the 70th week, which is during the first three and a half years. So that it's not going to be an easy time in many places in the world, even during the first three and a half years.

The interesting thing is, when you go to the Old Testament, you have references there to these kinds of things which will happen in the future and you have Hebrew words which are the parallel of our English word *tribulation*, even the parallel of the Greek word for tribulation. So, the implication is that these beginning of birth pangs are also descriptive of what you could call tribulation.

Notice an interesting implication here. He talks here about the **beginning** *of birth pangs*. That very expression indicates that there will be **more birth pangs coming after**: the beginning of birth pangs and then there will be later birth pangs. He's drawing a metaphor with the birth cycle of birth pangs of a woman as she's about to deliver a new life into the world. She has birth pangs at the beginning; they're severe, they cause pain. But, there will be more severe birth pangs, what we often call hard labor birth pangs, after her beginning birth pangs. So Jesus is saying that during the first half of the 70th week you have severe things going on in the world, but not as severe as the things that are going to come later on. In the beginning, in the first half of the 70th week, you have the beginning birth pangs or tribulation; but in the second half you're going to have great tribulation, much more intense agony than with just tribulation of the first half. Therefore in the second half, the Great Tribulation, also means that's when you have the severe, hard labor birth pangs transpiring here on planet earth.

This seven-year period of time, whether you call it the Tribulation period—since you have tribulation the first half and great tribulation the second half—or whether you choose to call it the 70th week of Daniel 9:27, either way, we're talking about this seven-year period of time immediately before the glorious Second Coming of Christ back to planet earth to set up God's Millennial kingdom here on planet earth.

Question #43

Does the Book of Revelation teach that the Rapture will take place before the Tribulation?

E'VE DISCUSSED A SEVEN-YEAR period of time between the Rapture and the Second Coming of Christ immediately after this seven-year period of time. Are there any indications as to why it's before this seven-year period of time, in light of what we've been seeing—that the Church will be raptured out of the world? Yes, there are implications. We noted earlier that the Scriptures teach that the Church saints will be raptured out of the world before the wrath of God begins to be poured out upon planet earth.

Will the wrath of God be poured out on planet earth throughout the seven-year Tribulation period? If the wrath of God will be poured out throughout the entire seven years, 70th week of Daniel 9, and the Church is to be removed before the wrath of God begins, then that would clearly indicate a pre-Tribulation Rapture, a Rapture of the Church out of the world before the wrath of God begins throughout this whole seven-year period of time, the 70th week of Daniel 9.

Are there any implications in Scripture to the effect that you will have the wrath of God here on the earth even during the first half of this seven-year period of the 70th week of Daniel 9? We are convinced that there are implications to that effect. We notice here that Jesus talks about the beginning of birth pangs and we noted that this will be during the first half of the 70th week, before the abomination of desolation in the middle of the 70th week.

When we go to Revelation 6 we have a description of seals that Jesus is breaking on a scroll, and as He breaks each seal some incredible things transpire upon the face of the earth. What we want to point out before we begin next examining the seals and what happens is that when you compare the first four seals with what Jesus called the beginning of birth pangs in Matthew 24, you will find that by comparison they are referring to identically the same thing. For example, in Matthew 24 Jesus talked about (as part of the beginning of birth pangs) false messiahs coming upon the world scene. Parallel to that, in **Revelation 6:1-2**, we read: "*And I saw when the Lamb opened one of the seals, and I heard as it were the noise of thunder one of the four beasts saying, 'Come and see.' And I saw, and, behold, a white horse and he that sat on him had a bow and a crown was given unto him and he went forth conquering and to conquer.*"

Some have said that the rider on the white horse is the Lord Jesus and that this is giving a preview again of His glorious Second Coming after the Tribulation period. When you go to Revelation 19 where we clearly are given a preview of His Second Coming, Christ comes riding out of Heaven on the back of a white horse. But it must be noted that there are several things different about the rider on this white horse than the Lord Jesus in

Revelation 19, although both are riding on a white horse. This rider *has a bow*; **Jesus**, by contrast, **had a sword**. This rider has *one crown* on his head; **Jesus**, by contrast, had **many crowns** on His head in **Revelation 19**. The rider on the white horse here in **Revelation 6**, the **name that's used for the crown is an altogether different name than that for the crowns that Jesus has on His head**, indicating this is not the Lord Jesus.

But the very fact that he's **riding a white horse** (as Jesus will at His Second Coming) may be the idea that this is **a false messiah**, one who is coming in place of the true Messiah who will come out of Heaven to rule the world in His glorious Second Coming. You notice as well that this **rider goes forth conquering and to conquer**. Jesus is going to conquer Satan and all his forces at His glorious Second Coming so this seems to be an imposter, a false messiah. That parallels what Jesus said for part of the beginning of birth pangs, the false messiahs. We'll come back to this later and give a more specific identification of this rider.

We go to the second seal in Revelation 6:3-4: "*And when He had opened the second seal, I heard the second beast say, 'Come and see.' And there went out another horse that was red and power was given to him that sat thereon to take peace from the earth and that they should kill one another, and there was given unto him a great sword.*" Here we have the sword, which is the idea of warfare taking place when Christ breaks the second seal; people killing one another. When you read about the beginning of birth pangs that Christ describes in **Matthew 24**, He talks about "*war, rumors of wars; nation rising against nation.*" The idea is of warfare and people being killed.

We go on to the third seal in Revelation 6:5-6. John said, *"When He had opened the third seal, I heard the third beast say, 'Come and see.' And I beheld, and lo, a black horse, and he that sat on him had a pair of balances in his hand. And I heard a voice in the midst of the four beasts saying, 'A measure of wheat for a penny and three measures of barley for a penny and see you hurt not the oil and the wine.'"* The third seal brings famine to the face of the earth and food is scarce, not totally gone. People are able to buy food, but it's so expensive because of scarcity, and so this implies famine. When you look at the beginning of birth pangs Jesus described in **Matthew 24**, He indicated that part of the birth pangs will be **famine**. That's parallel.

Then we come to the fourth seal, Revelation 6:7-8: *"And when He had opened the fourth seal, I heard the voice of the fourth beast saying, 'Come and see.' And I looked and, behold, a pale horse, and his name that sat on him was Death and Hell followed with him. And power was given unto them over the fourth part of the earth to kill with sword and with hunger and with death and with the beasts of the earth."* When you go over to **Matthew 24**, Jesus talks about *famine and pestilence* taking place; again, a parallel to the fourth seal.

So when you compare the beginning of birth pangs in Matthew 24 with the first four seals of Revelation 6, it's apparent we are dealing with the same thing. Now here's the significance of that. We noted earlier that Jesus refers in Matthew 24 to the beginning of birth pangs before He refers to the abomination of desolation in the middle of the seven-year period of the Tribulation. The implication is that the beginning of birth pangs will take place during the first half of the seven-year Tribulation period before that mid-week abomination of desolation. Since the beginning of birth pangs of Matthew 24 are in the first half of the 70th week, and since they are the same thing as the first four seals of Revelation 6, then we can conclude rightly that the first four seals are also in the first half of that seven-year 70th week period of time.

Question #44

Do the first four seals in the book of Revelation teach that this is God's wrath upon the world or man's wrath?

WITH THE FIRST FOUR seals being in the first half of the 70th week, an issue we have to grapple with is, do those first four seals involve an outpouring of God's wrath upon the world, or are they just man's wrath?

Why is that so critical to answer with regard to the timing of the Rapture? The reason it is critical is this. We have previously noticed—in 1 Thessalonians 1:10, 1 Thessalonians 5:9, and Revelation 3:10—implications to the effect that the Church will be removed from the earth by Rapture before the "Day of the Lord" wrath of God begins to be poured out upon planet earth. If the wrath of God is being poured out in these first four seals during the first half of the 70th week of Daniel 9, this would indicate that the Church must be removed from the earth before those first four seals; or to put it another way, before the first half of the 70th week of Daniel 9.

So the issue we must address is, do these first four seals involve the wrath of God? Yes, they do.

How does the first seal involve the wrath of God?

We notice that, with the first seal, there is a rider on a white horse that comes forth with a bow and a crown on his head and his goal is to conquer; apparently to conquer the world. We have seen that this is a false messiah. In essence, he's trying to mimic what Christ will do at His Second Coming after the seven-year Tribulation period.

Can we identify this particular false messiah more specifically? Yes, we can. The Scriptures indicate that Satan is going to have a false messiah in the world, the Antichrist.

Remember when we were looking at Daniel 9:27. We know that the Antichrist, at the very beginning of this seven-year, 70th week of Daniel 9, will enforce or establish a covenant with the nation of Israel. We also saw that the Antichrist, during the first half of the 70th week, will appear to be Israel's friend and ally and defender. But then we saw that in the middle of the 70th week he will commit the abomination of desolation—he'll go into Israel's new temple, set himself up as God there, declare that he's God, then he'll turn against Israel and desolate it severely. It's very clear this is Satan's man and that he's a false messiah to the world, the Antichrist.

Question #45

Can it be said that Christ is the One who unleashes the Antichrist upon the world in Revelation 6:7?

N OW, SOME WOULD SAY, "But if this first rider that comes as a result of Christ's breaking the first seal is the Antichrist, then are you not saying that Christ is the one who is unleashing the Antichrist upon the world? How could that be? Wouldn't that be self-defeating? Why would Christ unleash upon the world the man who belongs to God's great enemy, Satan?" And they would say, "This is a war against yourself; and a kingdom divided against yourself could not stand. God would never do something like that."

Would God not do something like that? He would do something like that if it would suit His sovereign purposes. Consider this: According to Exodus 9 and Romans 9, who is it that raised up and put into power the Pharaoh, who is described in the opening part of Exodus 1? This Pharaoh "*knew not Joseph*," and passed that horrible decree that every boy baby born to a Jewess in the land of Egypt was to be put to death?

The Scriptures clearly state that it was God who raised up that particular Pharaoh. We read in Romans 9:17, "*For the scripture says unto Pharaoh* [quoting from Exodus 9], '*Even for this same purpose have I raised you up that I might show my power in you and that my name might be declared throughout all the earth.*'" God is clearly declaring that He's the one who raised up that fiendish ruler who would unleash a devilish attack against the nation of Israel. Satan, through him, tried to annihilate the nation so that the Redeemer couldn't come into the world through that nation.

But the Scriptures clearly declare—and God is the One saying it—that He raised up that devilish Pharaoh there in the land of Egypt for His sovereign purposes, to display His glory. And God did display His glory through that Pharaoh; because as a result of that Pharaoh decreeing these terrible things and stubbornly rebelling against God, God unleash His ten supernatural plagues upon the land of Egypt during that time and displayed His great glory through that. That brought about the exodus of the Jews from their slavery in Egypt. He miraculously parted the waters of the Red Sea, again displaying His glory. In the same way, God will have His sovereign purpose for raising up the Antichrist.

Question #46

Are there Old Testament passages that predict God will bring wrath upon the nations by raising up the Antichrist?

YOU HAVE A GREAT prophecy in the Old Testament in Zechariah 11 where God Himself declared that He is the One who would raise up the Antichrist upon the face of the earth. When you read the early part of Zechariah 11, God says that He would send a Good Shepherd to the people of Israel and then that Good Shepherd would say to the people of Israel, *"You give to me what you think I'm worth."* And it's foretold that the people of Israel would give their Good Shepherd 30 pieces of silver; and that 30 pieces of silver in turn would be cast into the potter in the house of the Lord.

This is a very clear prophecy of God giving Jesus Christ, the true Messiah, to Israel. But Israel is saying, "He's only worth 30 pieces of silver," which under the law in Israel was the value of a gored slave who was totally worthless to his master. God was foretelling here that He would give Israel its Good Shepherd, Jesus Christ the Messiah, but that Israel would reject Him and evaluate Him as being worth no more than a useless slave.

After that God says in Zechariah 11:15-16, *"And the Lord said unto me, 'Take unto you yet the instruments of a foolish shepherd, for, lo, I will raise up a shepherd in the land which shall not visit those that be cut off, neither shall seek the young one, nor heal that that is broken, nor feed that stands still....*" In other words, he's not going to do the work that a shepherd is supposed to do to its sheep, but here's what he will do: "*but he shall eat the flesh of the fat and tear their claws in pieces.*" This foolish shepherd is going to devastate the nation of Israel. He's going to tear it to shreds. And then God went on to say in verse 17, "*Woe to the idol shepherd,*" and the word "**idol**" here in the Hebrew is referring to one who is **not a god but is worshipped as a god**. "*Woe to the idol shepherd that leaves the flock. The sword shall be upon his arm and upon his right eye; his arm shall be clean dried up and his right eye shall be utterly darkened.*"

God is foretelling the future Antichrist. Notice, He's saying, "*I will raise up this foolish shepherd who will tear the nation of Israel to shreds.*" What He is saying is He is going to use the Antichrist as His tool to persecute the nation of Israel so severely during the second half of the 70th week of Daniel 9 that Israel will be backed so tightly into a corner that Israel will have no means of escape from total annihilation unless it repents of all its rebellion against God and willingly acknowledges God's Son, Jesus Christ, as its true Messiah and Savior.

God will use the Antichrist as His tool to break Israel's stubborn rebellion against Him and bring Israel into right relationship with God, by the end of the 70th week of Daniel 9, to repentance. So, yes, God would unleash the Antichrist upon the earth for the purpose of bringing Israel to repentance, and for other purposes as well. So the Antichrist will be an expression of God's wrath upon the nation of Israel, particularly during the second half of the 70th week of Daniel 9.

Question #47

Is warfare upon the face of the earth an expression of God's wrath on the nations?

WHEN WE READ THE passage in Revelation 6 about the second seal, we noted that the second seal removes peace from the earth, and people are killing one another; there is going to be warfare upon the face of the earth. When you go through the Old Testament, a number of times God declares that the removal of peace or the lack of peace in the world is an expression of His wrath or judgment upon the earth.

By contrast, He declares that the presence of peace is evidence of His blessing upon the earth. And so this removal of peace, again, will be an expression of God's wrath upon the world. Granted, that removal of peace will involve human instruments, as we saw with the beginning of birth pangs—wars, rumors of wars, nations rising against nations. But when you go to the Old Testament, God indicated He raised up the Assyrians to wage war against the northern Kingdom of Israel as the rod of His wrath against the northern Jews for rebelling against Him. God indicated that He raised up Babylon to wage war against the southern kingdom of Judah as an expression of His judgment or wrath upon the southern kingdom of Judah so that the wrath of God through human beings or nations waging war against each other it is often carried out through those kind of human instruments.

Question #48

Would God ever use famine as an instrument of His wrath upon the world?

WHEN WE COME TO the third seal (Revelation 6) the third seal brings famine upon the face of the earth. When you go through the Old Testament, a number of times God indicates that famine, lack of food, is a form of His wrath or judgment upon human beings here on the face of the earth. It's significant to note with the third seal in Revelation 6, that John said in verse 6, "*I heard a voice in the midst of the four beasts say, 'A measure of wheat for a penny and three measures of barley for a penny and see you hurt not the oil and the wine.'*" The implication is, whoever that speaker is, is the one who is authoritatively controlling that famine. He's determining how scarce food will be and therefore how much food will cost, and He's determining what is not to be harmed and what will be harmed.

Who is this person who is determining that? Well, the person has the voice that John heard from the midst of the four beasts. If you go back to Revelation 4 and 5, you'll find that God the Father is seated upon a throne in Heaven in the midst of the four beasts, and you also see that Christ the Messiah, the Lamb, is standing there before the throne in the midst of the four beasts. So, that the voice is either that of God the Father or of Christ the Lamb. They are in control of that famine, which would indicate again this is an expression of God's wrath or God's judgment upon human beings upon the face of the earth.

When we come to the fourth seal in Revelation 6:7-8, John said, "*I looked and, behold, a pale horse. His name that sat on him was Death, Hell followed with him and power was given unto them over the fourth part of the earth to kill with sword and with hunger and with death and with the beasts of the earth.*"

One fourth of the world's population is being annihilated through these four means:

- The **sword**—which is another way of saying war
- **hunger**—which is another way of saying famine
- **death**—literally pestilence
- **beasts** of the earth—wild beasts attacking and killing human beings.

Now, this is very intriguing. When you go to the Old Testament, there are places where God indicates that **war** and **famine** are expressions of His wrath; **pestilence** is an expression of His wrath; **wild beasts** killing human beings are an expression of His wrath; but even more intriguing is the fact that you sometimes have a number of those four items lumped together where God is indicating those are expressions of His wrath.

Perhaps the most significant passage along those lines is in Ezekiel 14:21. In the context of Ezekiel 14:21, God uses one of the Hebrew words for His *wrath* and it's one of the Hebrew words even used for the *Day of the Lord wrath* in other passages in the Old Testament. **Ezekiel 14:21** says: "*For thus says the Lord God, 'How much more when I send my four sore judgments upon Jerusalem: the* **sword** *and the* **famine** *and the noisome* **beast** *and the* **pestilence** *to cut off from it man and beast?'*" These are the same four things described for the fourth seal of Revelation 6, and God says that those are His four sore judgments.

It was fascinating to read while studying this that some very prominent, highly-regarded Greek scholars declared that when John recorded what will happen in the fourth seal, he was practically quoting Ezekiel 14:21 and really basing the fourth seal on Ezekiel 14:21. So the fourth seal is an expression of God's wrath upon the earth.

Question #49

Who is the One that breaks the seals in Revelation 5 and 6?

HO IS IT THAT is breaking those four individual seals that are expressions of God's wrath? This is very important to note. As we stated earlier, it's Jesus Christ (our Kinsman-Redeemer) who is breaking these seals; not Satan, not his Antichrist, not the false prophet, nor human beings, other human beings here on the face of the earth. It is Jesus Christ, the Lamb of God, the Lion of the Tribe of Judah, who is breaking these seals. This is indicating that He, with full authority, is the One who is unleashing these different forms of God's wrath upon the earth. Again, this is coming from Christ, this is not coming from Satan and his forces. So this is the work of God, the wrath of God, not the wrath of man that's being described here in the first four seals.

As we saw earlier, those first four seals are the same things as the beginning of birth pangs in Matthew 24; we saw that Jesus is placing the beginning of birth pangs before the abomination of desolation in the middle of the 70th week. The implication is that those beginning of birth pangs are in the first half of the 70th week; that means, therefore, that the first four seals are the first half of the 70th week, and since those first four seals are expressions of the wrath of God, that means the wrath of God is being poured out in certain respects during the first half of the 70th week.

Since the Church saints are to be raptured out of the world before the wrath of God begins on planet earth in that future period of trouble sometimes called the Day of the Lord, this indicates that the Church will be raptured out of the world before the 70th week of Daniel 9 begins—before that seven-year period that many scholars have called the Tribulation Period will begin. That forces me to conclude again that we're having inferred here a pre-tribulation Rapture of the Church from the earth before that seven-year Tribulation period.

Question #50

Doesn't Revelation 6:12 indicate that "the great day of God's wrath" begins at the breaking of the sixth seal, not before that?

YOU MAY SAY, "ALRIGHT, I've heard what you had to say but I've got some problems with what you're saying." For example, when the sixth seal is broken in Revelation 6, there are all different kinds of cosmic disturbances which will take place on the face of the earth and you will have unsaved people running to the mountains and the caves and asking them to fall upon them to hide them. Revelation 6, beginning with verse 12:

> And I beheld when he had opened the sixth seal, and, lo, there was a great earthquake, and the sun became black as sackcloth of hair and the moon became as blood, and the stars of heaven fell unto the earth even as a fig tree casts her untimely figs when she is shaken of a mighty wind. And the heaven departed as a scroll when it is rolled together and every mountain and island were moved out of their places. And the kings of the earth and the great men and the rich men and the chief captains and the mighty men and every bond man and every free man hid themselves

*in the dens and in the rocks of the mountains and said to the mountains
and rocks, "Fall on us and hide us from the face of him that sits on the
throne and from the wrath of the Lamb, for the great day of his wrath is
come, and who shall be able to stand?"*

Perhaps you are saying, "Look, isn't this indicating that this is where the
great day of God's wrath begins and up to this point there is no wrath of
God?" Or some would even say, "Well, this is saying that the great day of His
wrath is about to come." And they would say that God's wrath begins with
the breaking of the seventh seal over in Revelation 8:1, and that therefore
you don't have the great day of God's wrath in the first four seals whatsoever.

What do we do with this? First, let me take you to 1 Thessalonians 5 where
the apostle Paul gives some very specific revelation as to how the future
Day of the Lord with its wrath will begin. He says in 1 Thessalonians 5: 2,
"*For yourselves know perfectly* [accurately] *that the Day of the Lord so comes as a
thief in the night.*" The idea here is that the Day of the Lord is going to catch
the unsaved people totally off guard. There will be no forewarning of any
kind at all that the Day of the Lord is coming upon them. It will catch them
totally by surprise. No thief who is worth his salt will send a forewarning
ahead of time to his intended victim and inform him that he intends to
break into his home on such and such a day at such and such an hour to
rob him of his possessions. Good thieves rely upon the element of surprise
to catch their intended victims totally off guard. So the point here is, no
forewarnings of the Day of the Lord coming upon the unsaved.

Those who say that with the breaking of the sixth seal and the unsaved
calling for the mountains and the rocks to fall upon them because the great

day of His wrath has come say, "Well, this is saying that His wrath is **about to** come." They claim that the sixth seal is a forewarning, a precursor to them that the wrath of God is about to come. But that contradicts what Paul says in 1 Thessalonians 5 concerning the beginning of the Day of the Lord with its wrath. He's indicating there, there will be no forewarnings, no precursors to the unsaved that the Day of the Lord is about to come. It's going to hit them without any forewarning, catch them totally by surprise, just like a thief who comes in the night when you're not expecting him to rob you of your possessions. In addition, Paul says in 1 Thessalonians 5:3, *"For when they shall say, 'Peace and safety,' then sudden destruction comes upon them as travail* [literally as the birth pang] *upon a woman with child and they shall not escape."*

Paul is saying that the Day of the Lord will come, and the Greek indicates at the same time that they are saying, "We have peace; we have safety," when they are convinced that they have finally established peace and safety in the world, that's when the Day of the Lord is going to break in upon them and give them just the opposite of what they think they have. They're going to receive incredible destruction as the wrath of God begins to be poured out upon them.

We noted when we looked at the first seal in Revelation 6 that the rider on the white horse, the false messiah, goes out conquering to conquer. That implies warfare, lack of peace. We also noted with the second seal in Revelation 6 that with the breaking of the second seal peace is removed from the face of the earth. Notice, that's several seals before the sixth seal. And will peace be removed from the earth there. When you begin reading from the second seal and read on right up through the Second Coming of

Christ in Revelation 19, there is no peace, lasting peace and safety, upon the face of the earth through all the rest of the seals, the seven trumpet judgments, and through the seven bowl judgments.

We noted earlier that these first four seals are the same as the beginning of birth pangs so that Christ seemed to put the beginning of birth pangs in the first half of the 70th week. We have a **false messiah going out to wage war** with the **first seal**; we have **peace being removed** with the **second seal**; those are early in the beginning birth pangs. That puts them *early* in the first half of the 70th week, which indicates that the Day of the Lord actually begins at the beginning of the 70th week, not sometime later when the sixth seal is broken or at another time when there's a trumpet judgment or something to that effect. The Day of the Lord will be taking place even with the beginning of the first seal and certainly by the breaking of the second seal in the book of Revelation.

Question #51

Does the dreadful Day of the Lord come after the beginning of the seventieth week of Daniel, sometime after Elijah the prophet has come?

THERE'S ANOTHER OBJECTION THAT some people give to the view that we've been presenting, and they base this on a prophecy that's in the book of Malachi. In **Malachi 4:5** God said, "*And behold, I will send you Elijah the prophet before the coming of the great and dreadful Day of the Lord.*" They say that God is stating here, very clearly, that **Elijah** the prophet must come before the coming of the great and dreadful Day of the Lord. Some who object to the view that we've been presenting would say the **Elijah** here obviously has to be one of the two witnesses in Revelation 11.

When we read Revelation 11 we are told about two rather unique men who are going to be here in the world for one half of the seven-year 70th week of Daniel 9. We're clearly told here that they will minister for 1260 days (three and a half years).

And when you read the description of the two witnesses, you will find that one of them will have the kind of miraculous powers that Elijah had; and in light of that, some have concluded that one of those two witnesses will be Elijah brought from Heaven back to the earth for one half the Tribulation Period. And if it's one half the Tribulation Period it has to be at least the first half, maybe even the second half, but if it's one half it has to be at least the first half.

And they would say, "Well, since Malachi says that Elijah the prophet must come before the great and terrible Day of the Lord and if, let's say Elijah is one of the two witnesses during the first half of the 70th week, then you're not going to have the Day of the Lord beginning at the very beginning of the 70th week. It has to begin sometime into the 70th week after Elijah has been here ministering." What do we do with this? It's very important to note that when you study everything the Scriptures teach about the future Day of the Lord that the Bible teaches both a **broad** sense of the Day of the Lord and a **narrow** sense of the Day of the Lord.

Question #52

Who are the two witnesses in Revelation 11?

W̶E READ ABOUT THE two witnesses that will preach during the first three and a half years of the seven-year Tribulation period in Revelation 11:3-13:

And I will give power unto my two witnesses, and they shall prophesy a thousand two hundred and three score days, clothed in sackcloth. These are the two olive trees, and the two lampstands standing before the God of the earth. And if any man will hurt them, fire proceeds out of their mouth, and devours their enemies: and if any man will hurt them, he must in this manner be killed. These have power to shut heaven, that it rain not in the days of their prophecy: and have power over waters to turn them to blood, and to smite the earth with all plagues, as often as they will. And when they shall have finished their testimony, the beast that ascends out of the bottomless pit shall make war against them, and shall overcome them, and kill them. And their dead bodies shall lie in the street of the great city, which spiritually is called Sodom and Egypt, where also our Lord was crucified. And they of the people and tribes and tongues and nations shall see their dead bodies three days and a half, and shall not allow their dead bodies to be put in graves. And they that dwell upon the earth shall rejoice over them, and make merry, and shall send gifts one to another; because these two prophets tormented them that dwelt on the earth. And after three days and a half the Spirit of life from God entered into them, and they stood upon their feet; and great fear fell upon them who saw them. And they heard a great voice from heaven saying unto them, Come up here. And they ascended up to heaven in a cloud; and their enemies beheld them. And the same hour there was a great earthquake, and the tenth part of the city fell, and in the earthquake were slain of men seven thousand: and the rest were frightened, and gave glory to the God of heaven.

As we have mentioned, most people believe that one of the witnesses is Elijah. We believe the two witnesses are Elijah and Enoch because both of them have never died. They were both translated into heaven and they will come back. As Hebrews 9:27 says, "*It is appointed unto man, once to die, and after this, the judgment.*" These two men will die and lay in the streets of Jerusalem for three and a half days; then they will miraculously be raised from the dead and enter into heaven.

Question #53

Does the Bible teach that there is a "broad" and "narrow" sense of the Day of the Lord?

WHAT DO WE MEAN by those two terms? In the broad sense of the Day of the Lord, the Scriptures indicate that the Day of the Lord will cover an extensive period of time. It will begin with the seven-year Tribulation period (the 70th week of Daniel 9), this time of tremendous trouble here on the face of the earth. And that's why some descriptions of the Day of the Lord describe it as a time of darkness. But then it will be followed by a period of light; a time of God's great blessing upon the earth which is referring to the thousand year Millennium after the seven-year Tribulation period.

In **Amos 5** we have the Day of the Lord described as a time of darkness; it'll be a time of darkness for those who are unbelievers and rebelling against God. But in **Zechariah 14** where the Day of the Lord is talked about within the first couple of verses of that chapter, we're told that the Day of the Lord will involve the armies of all the nations of the world surrounding Jerusalem. They begin to destroy the city and to ravish people in that city. We read in Zechariah **14:1-2**: "*Behold, the Day of the Lord comes and your spoils* *shall be divided in the midst of you; for I will gather all nations against Jerusalem to battle and the city shall be taken and the houses rifled and the women ravished, and half of the city shall go forth into captivity and the residue of the people shall not be cut off from the city."* This will happen right at the end of the seven-year Tribulation period.

Then we read in **Zechariah 14:3**: *"Then shall the Lord go forth."* Here's the Second Coming of the Messiah. In Israel's darkest hour, when all the nations are gathered there and they have Israel's capital city Jerusalem surrounded and they're destroying it, the Messiah, the Lord, is going to come forth out of Heaven at this Day of the Lord. And we're told He's going to fight against those nations (verse 3) as when He fought in the day of battle. *"His feet shall stand in that day upon the Mount of Olives."* That's where His feet will touch down in His glorious Second Coming. And then when you continue reading in Zechariah 14, it describes how the Lord will destroy these godless armies that were gathered there.

We're told then in verse 9, *"And the Lord shall be King over all the earth in **that day**."* What day? The Day of the Lord that was introduced in Zechariah 14:: *"In that day shall there be one Lord and his name one."* And then he goes on to describe the great blessings that will come through the Millennial kingdom as the Lord rules the world on behalf of God, indicating that the Day of the Lord will also include the thousand year reign of Jesus Christ as King over the entire earth. So the Day of the Lord will begin with a period of darkness, the seven-year Tribulation period or 70th week of Daniel 9. It will also include the thousand year Millennial reign of Messiah upon the face of the earth.

So there's a **broad** "Day of the Lord" covering *at least a 1,007 year span* of time. On the other hand, the Bible presents a **narrow** concept of the Day of the Lord, referring to one specific literal day, namely, *the day that Jesus Christ will come out of Heaven* immediately after the seven-year Tribulation Period in His glorious Second Coming to take the rule of the earth back on behalf of God.

Question #54

Where does the Bible teach that there is going to be a "narrow" Day of the Lord? How do you know that the "narrow" Day of the Lord is the Second Coming of Christ?

Now, HOW DO WE know there's going to be a narrow Day of the Lord, namely, the Second Coming of Christ? When we go over to the prophet Joel, in Joel 3, again we have a description of the armies of the nations coming there to the land of Israel. Joel 3:1, "*For, behold, in those days and in that time when I shall bring again the captivity of Judah and Jerusalem, I will also gather all nations and will bring them down into the valley of Jehoshaphat and will plead with them there for my people and for my heritage Israel whom they have scattered among the nations and parted my land.*"

God continues on with that theme in Joel 3:9-14: "*Proclaiming this among the Gentiles, 'Prepare war. Wake up the mighty men. Let all the men of war draw near. Let them come up. Beat your plowshares into swords and your pruning hooks into spears. Let the weak say, "I am strong." Assemble yourselves and come all ye heathen and gather yourselves together round about. There cause your mighty ones to come down, O Lord. Let the heathen be wakened and come up to the valley* of Jehoshaphat, for there will I sit to judge all the heathen round about. Put you in the sickle, for the harvest is ripe. Come, get you down for the press is full. The vats overflow for the wickedness is great. Multitudes, multitudes in the valley of decision [now notice this next statement], for the Day of the Lord is near in the valley of decision.'"

God's describing the time when the armies of all the nations of the world will be gathered in the land of Israel, God playing a role in bringing them there so that He can judge them in the valley of Jehoshaphat. Jehoshaphat means "Jehovah judges." And he says that when the armies are there, the Day of the Lord is near. In other words, there's a Day of the Lord that is about to come when the armies of all the nations are gathered there for judgment in the land of Israel.

And then He goes on to say that there will be cosmic disturbances in conjunction with that Day of the Lord when the armies are there. Joel 3:15-16: "The sun and the moon shall be darkened; the stars shall withdraw their shining. The Lord also shall roar out of Zion;" God's going to go to war. The Lord's going to go to war against these godless forces, "and utter his voice from Jerusalem. The heavens and the earth shall shake but the Lord will be the hope of his people and the strength of the children is Israel." That's when He's going to deliver Israel in its darkest hour.

There's going to be a Day of the Lord that's going to come with cosmic disturbances when the armies of all the nations of the world are gathered there. It's about to come when they're gathered there, and then it will come while they are there.

When will that take place? Is there anything in the Scriptures that indicate this? Yes. In Revelation 16, John is recording what will happen in the world when the sixth bowl is poured out. When you read Revelation 6-19 you will find that throughout the 70th week of Daniel 9, throughout that seven-year Tribulation period, there will be **three series of judgments** poured out: first, **seven seals**; then, **seven trumpets**; then **seven bowls**. So the bowls are the last series of judgments, and John is seeing here the sixth of those seven bowls.

So, this is the next to the last judgment of the 70th week of Daniel 9. What happens? Revelation 16:12-13, "*And the sixth angel poured out his vial upon the great river Euphrates and the water thereof was dried up that the way of the kings of the east might be prepared. And I saw three unclean spirits like frogs come out of the mouth of the **dragon*** [in Revelation the *dragon* is Satan], *out of the mouth of the **Beast*** [in Revelation the *beast* is the Antichrist], *out of the mouth of the false prophet, for they* [these unclean spirits] *are the spirits of devils* [literally of demons] *working miracles which go forth unto the kings of the earth and of the whole world to gather them to the battle of that great day of God Almighty.*"

Verse 16: "*And he gathered them together into a place called in the Hebrew tongue Armageddon.*" What John is witnessing here is this: The armies of all the nations of the world do not even begin to gather to the land of Israel for Armageddon until the **sixth bowl**. In other words, they don't even **begin** to gather until the **next to the last judgment**, almost at the very end of the seven-year Tribulation period.

We see in Revelation 16 the armies don't even begin to gather there until almost the end of the seven-year Tribulation Period. According to Joel 3, once they are gathered there, there's a Day of the Lord that is near that will have great cosmic disturbances tied in with it; meaning that there's another Day of the Lord coming with great cosmic disturbances.

When we read **Joel 2** (and in the context this is referring to the same type of thing as described in Joel 3), he talks about cosmic disturbances. **Joel 2:30-31**, *"I'll show wonders in the heavens and in the earth, blood, fire, pillars of smoke. The sun will be turned into darkness, the moon into blood, before the great and terrible Day of the Lord come."* It's referring to the same Day of the Lord with the same cosmic disturbances as in Joel 3, but here he calls that future Day of the Lord, *"the great and terrible Day of the Lord."*

What is this Day of the Lord? It's the day when Christ will come out of Heaven in His glorious Second Coming immediately after the seven-year Tribulation period, accompanied by great cosmic disturbances that Jesus describes in **Matthew 24:29-30**: *"Immediately after the Tribulation of those days shall the sun be darkened, the moon shall not give her light; the stars shall fall from heaven, the powers of the heavens shall be shaken. Then shall appear the sign of the Son of Man in heaven and then shall all the tribes of the earth mourn and they shall see the Son of Man coming in the clouds of heaven with power and great glory."*

This great and terrible Day of the Lord with its cosmic disturbances is the precise day that Jesus Christ will come out of Heaven in His glorious Second Coming immediately after the seven-year Tribulation period. And according to Revelation 19, when He does that, here will be all the rulers and armies of the nations of the world gathered together against Him under Antichrist and the false prophet. And Jesus unleashes the wrath of God upon them and destroys them.

Now, what's the point of all this? The point is this: We've seen evidence that there's a broad "Day of the Lord" that will begin at the beginning of the seven-year Tribulation Period and will go right through the thousand year reign of Christ, the Millennium. But now we've seen evidence that there is another Day of the Lord which will be part of the broad day but in a sense is distinct in its own, namely, the day the Christ comes out of Heaven in His glorious Second Coming to judge the armies that are gathered there against Israel by the end of the seven-year Tribulation period, and Joel calls that *"the great and terrible Day of the Lord."* It's the Day of the Lord when Christ comes out of Heaven in His glorious Second Coming—that's the great and terrible Day of the Lord. Malachi was saying that Elijah will come before the great and terrible Day of the Lord—exactly the same Hebrew construction as in Joel 2.

The Day of the Lord that Elijah must come before is the Second Coming of Christ, immediately after the Tribulation Period. In other words, Elijah must come before the **narrow** Day of the Lord, *"the great and terrible Day of the Lord"*, but not before the **broad** Day of the Lord, which will begin at the very beginning of the seven-year Tribulation period.

So the objection that the Day of the Lord can't begin until Elijah comes and—since they believe Elijah won't be here until at least the first half of the 70th week—that therefore the Day of the Lord cannot begin at the beginning of the 70th week, is really not valid. Because the Day of the Lord before Elijah must come is the *"great and terrible"* Day of the Lord, which is the Second Coming of Christ, the day He comes out of Heaven after the 70th week. It's **not** the **broad** Day of the Lord, which will cover the entire 70th week of Daniel chapter 9.

Question #55

Doesn't the Day of the Lord have to begin in conjunction with Christ's Second Coming described in Matthew 24 at the breaking of the sixth seal?

ANOTHER OBJECTION THAT COULD be leveled against the view that we've been advocating is this: When the sixth seal was broken (as we noted earlier) there are incredible cosmic disturbances that take place. The moon, the sun being darkened, stars falling from the heavens, etc. When you look at Matthew 24 where we have the description of Christ's Second Coming, you have the same type of cosmic disturbances being described again: sun and moon being darkened; stars being affected, etc.

In light of that, some have concluded that therefore these have to be the same cosmic disturbances and that the Second Coming of Christ must take place in conjunction then with the breaking of the sixth seal, and that this is where the Day of the Lord's wrath begins.

But there's a problem with that approach, and that's the fact that the cosmic disturbances described with the sixth seal are **not** the **only cosmic disturbances** described for the future in the Word of God.

In fact, when you read further in the book of Revelation, you will find that there will be other cosmic disturbances **after** the sixth seal. For example, when you have the fourth trumpet being sounded and its judgment unleashed upon the world, we read in Revelation 8:12, "*And the fourth angel sounded and the third part of the sun was smitten and the third part of the moon and the third part of the stars so as the third part of them was darkened and the day shone not for a third part of it and the night likewise.*" Here are more cosmic disturbances affecting the sun, the moon and the stars.

The fact that this will happen one seal and four trumpets after the sixth seal indicates this is not the same set of cosmic disturbances as with the sixth seal. This also implies that the cosmic disturbances of the sixth seal were temporary; that they don't continue on indefinitely. Otherwise, you couldn't have this separate set of cosmic disturbances one seal and four trumpets after the sixth seal. And there's at least one other place in the book of Revelation where later on you have cosmic disturbances again.

Then we saw that according to Joel 3 there will be more cosmic disturbances very similar to those described at the sixth seal, more cosmic disturbances when the armies of all the nations of the world are gathered in the land of Israel. But we saw from Revelation 16 that those armies don't even begin to gather there until the sixth bowl, which would be one seal, seven trumpets and six bowls after the sixth seal.

So those cosmic disturbances: sun and moon being darkened; stars falling from heaven, etc., when the armies of the nations are all together there in Israel, cannot be the same cosmic disturbances as those that take place with the sixth seal. So you cannot conclude therefore that since the cosmic disturbances when Christ comes in the Second Coming, when the armies are in Israel, are basically the same as those at the sixth seal, that it's the same set of cosmic disturbances. They can't be, because they're separated by many other events in between. And therefore, they are not the same; and so therefore the Second Coming is not taking place with the breaking of the sixth seal.

Question #56

Why is the trumpet that sounds at the Rapture in 1 Thessalonians 4 not the same as "the last trump" in Matthew 24?

NOTHER OBJECTION SOME PEOPLE give to this view is the fact that when the Rapture takes place, according to 1 Thessalonians 4, the trump of God will be sounded. According to 1 Corinthians 15, "the last trump" will be sounded and then, according to Matthew 24, there will be the sound of a great trumpet when the Lord Jesus comes out of Heaven in His glorious Second Coming.

Some say—you obviously have a trumpet blown at the Rapture—it's the trump of God—it's the "last trump." And you obviously have a trumpet being blown at the Second Coming of Christ after the Tribulation Period—therefore, the Rapture and the Second Coming must take place at the same time. And if it's the *last* trump at the Rapture, which is what 1 Corinthians 15 says—then this **has** to be at the Second Coming of Christ. It couldn't be before, because if the Rapture is taking place before the Second Coming, and there's a trumpet there which is supposedly the "last" trump, but then later on, maybe seven years later, you have a trumpet at the Second Coming of Christ, then how could the trumpet at the Rapture be the **last** trump when you've got a trump supposedly seven years later at the Second Coming of Christ?

Let me point something out to you with regard to this. Even the trumpet that will be blown at the Second Coming of Christ will not be the absolute last trumpet blown here on planet Earth.

When you go to Zechariah 14, we are clearly told there that during the Lord's reign upon the earth—this would be during the future Millennial Reign—that the Feast of Tabernacles is going to be observed every year here on the earth. And we're told in verses 16-17: "*It shall come to pass that everyone that is left of all the nations which came against Jerusalem shall go up from year to year to worship the King, the Lord of Hosts, and to keep the feast of tabernacles. It shall be that whoso shall not come up of all the families of the earth unto Jerusalem to worship the King, the Lord of Hosts, even upon them shall be no rain.*" And He goes on to indicate in verse 18, "*if the family of Egypt go not up and come not that have no rain, there shall be the plague wherewith the Lord shall smite the heathen that will not come up to keep the feast of tabernacles,*" indicating that every year throughout the Thousand Year Reign of Messiah upon the earth the people of the world will be required to observe the Feast of Tabernacles.

Now, when you study what's involved with the Feast of Tabernacles, you have the blowing of trumpets in the Feast of Tabernacles. This means therefore you will have the blowing of trumpets every year throughout the Thousand Year Reign of Christ.

So even the trumpet that's blown at the Second Coming of the Lord will not be the absolute last trumpet that's blown on planet Earth. Therefore, you cannot equate, automatically, the trumpet at the Rapture with the trumpet of the Second Coming of Christ.

Then, why is the trump of the Rapture called "the last trump"? Well, it's not indicating the absolute last trump; it has another significance to it and there are several possibilities with regard to this.

For one thing, it's interesting that Paul refers to the last trump in 1 Corinthians 15. In the immediately preceding chapter, 1 Corinthians 14, he refers to the blowing of a trumpet, and there he's referring to a military trumpet. And in light of that, it would appear that he has military trumpets in mind when he's writing 1 Corinthians 15. So it could very well be that when he refers to the last trump, which will be blown at the Rapture, he has a military trumpet in mind.

What's the significance of that? When you study the Roman army and some of the Greek armies and even the Jewish army back in Bible times, when they went into war, they had a "last trump" that would be blown that would tell the fighting men, "Your time of fighting is over. It is time for you to go home and rest"—a last trump that ended their time in the warfare.

By analogy, the Scriptures teach that Christians today are involved in a spiritual war while they live out their lives in this present age, in this present world. When the Rapture takes place and the trumpet is blown at that time—that will be a signal to them that their part in the warfare is over; their fighting in this present age is done in this spiritual war. It is time for them to go home to be with the Lord and rest together with Him in Heaven.

In addition, when you read the use of trumpets in the military of the ancient world, particularly with the Romans, they had a first trump that signaled when a man was to start his watch on guard duty. But then they had a "last trump" which signaled that his time on guard duty was over and again it was time for him to go home. In other words, before that last trump he's on watch; he's watching, watching, watching to be on guard. But when the last trump is sounded, that tells him his watching is done, he can go home.

Scriptures also teach that while Christians are living in the world in this present age, we are to continually be watching, watching, watching and the idea again could be that when the Rapture takes place and that trumpet is sounded, it's a signal to them, "This is the last trump signaling that your tour of duty on the watch is completed and now it's time for you to go home."

So the expression "the last trump" there in 1 Corinthians 15, in conjunction with the Rapture, does not mean the absolute last trump in a sequence, but it is tied in apparently with military terminology back in Paul's day. And the fact that Paul, when he mentions the last trump, doesn't explain to the Corinthians what he meant by that indicates that they understood what he meant by "the last trump."

And they were very familiar, being part of the Roman empire, with that terminology of "the last trump" as signals used for Roman soldiers, whether their fighting is done or their tour of duty on the watch is over for that day and so that would have a tremendous significance to them in light of those military uses of the day.

Question #57

Why is the trumpet at the Rapture not the same as the trumpet at the Second Coming of Christ after the Tribulation Period?

To summarize what we've been saying about these different trumpets, we have previously given some solid evidence to the effect that the Rapture of the Church and the Second Coming of Christ after the Tribulation Period will be separated by a seven-year period of time. That evidence would rule out the trumpet at the Rapture being the same as the trumpet at the Second Coming of Christ after the Tribulation Period.

In addition, we noted that the expression *"the last trumpet"* tied in with the Rapture of the Church does not mean the absolute last trumpet in a sequence of trumpets after which there would be no more. And so therefore you don't have to conclude that it will be the trumpet that's sounded at the Second Coming of Christ and as we noted earlier, there will be other trumpets sounded throughout the Millennium in observance of the Feast of Tabernacles even after that of the Second Coming of Christ.

But then what about that trumpet at the Second Coming of Christ? Previously we noted that that trumpet is sounded as Christ sends forth His angels to gather together His elect from the four winds of heaven and that trumpet literally we're told, it is the sound of a great trumpet. We also noted that *the elect* in Matthew 24 (based on Old Testament passages) are Jews. We also saw in Isaiah 27:12 and 13 that God promised that in the future He would regather scattered Jews from nations around the world in conjunction with the sounding of a great trumpet.

And so, therefore, the trumpet that is sounded at the Rapture is a trumpet for the Church—it's involving the Rapture of the Church. But the sound of a great trumpet at the Second Coming of Christ in Matthew 24:30-31, is the sounding of a trumpet for *Israel* and the signal of the angels of Christ to regather the scattered Jews back to their homeland.

Question #58

Is the trumpet of the Rapture in 1 Thessalonians 4 one of the seven trumpets mentioned in the Book of Revelation? If not, why not?

ONE FINAL THING WITH regard to the trumpets. There are some who try to make the trumpet of the Rapture or even the trumpet of Matthew 24 one of the seven trumpets that you have in the book of Revelation, or some even group all seven trumpets together and make them one and say that's the trumpet at the Rapture and Second Coming of Christ. But there's a problem with that approach.

When Paul referred to the last trumpet in conjunction with the Rapture in 1 Corinthians 15, he was writing that to the Corinthians during his lifetime. The Revelation that John recorded, the book of Revelation, wasn't even given until several decades after Paul wrote his epistle to the Corinthians. We noted earlier that when Paul referred to the last trumpet in 1 Corinthians 15, he gave no description or explanation of that to the Corinthians because he knew they already understood what was meant by that *last trump.*

In light of the fact he already understood what was meant by *"the last trump,"* together with the fact that the seven trumpets were not even revealed for the book of Revelation until **decades** after Paul wrote 1 Corinthians, the Corinthians wouldn't have known a thing about the seven trumpets that are in the book of Revelation because it hadn't been revealed to anyone yet. John received that revelation around 95 or 94 A.D. when he wrote the book of the Revelation; Paul died in the 60's A.D. so that John didn't receive that revelation until at least approximately three decades after Paul had died. Paul certainly wrote 1 Corinthians before he died. So that revelation about the seven trumpets would not have been available to the Corinthians when Paul wrote to them about the last trump; and the fact that Paul didn't explain what he meant indicates that the Corinthians understood what he meant by the last trump, but they could not have understood that if by that Paul was referring to one of the seven trumpets of Revelation or all seven collectively together. So, therefore, *"the last trump"* could not be referring to any of the seven trumpets of the book of Revelation.

Question #59

The Rapture: which position is right and which is wrong?

SOMETIMES YOU READ SOMETHING by a pre-tribulationist and you say, "*That really sounds convincing.*" Then you pick up something by a mid-tribulationist and you say, "*Well, that sounds good, too.*" And then a little while later, you hear a post-tribulationist give a sermon and you say, "*He really sounds like he's on target, too.*" How do you make up your mind as to which position is right and which position is wrong?

First of all, you must figure out what each position must prove biblically in order to demonstrate that its position is the correct one. For example, post-tribulationists say that the Rapture and the Second Advent are described in almost exactly the same way; therefore, they're really talking about the exact same time and the exact same event. And since the Second Advent will occur at the end of the Tribulation, then the Rapture must also occur at the end of the Tribulation. Anyone who hears this will recognize the logical place to begin.

Pre, mid, and post-tribulationists need to go to those biblical passages that speak about the Second Advent and about the Rapture and try to show the following: 1.) Pre-tribulationists must show that there are enough differences between the biblical passages to show that the Bible is teaching that the Rapture is a completely different event from the Second Advent. 2.) Mid-tribulationists must show the same thing, and also show there are at least three and a half years between the Rapture and the Second Advent. 3.) Post-tribulationists must show that the biblical passages that speak about the Rapture and the ones about the Second Advent are so similar in what they are saying, that they are really talking about the exact same time and the exact same event. If the post-tribulationists can do this, then they have proved that the Rapture must occur at the Second Advent and it will occur after the Tribulation.

I believe that a careful study of the biblical passages will show that there are some significant differences between the clear Rapture passages and the clear Second Advent passages, thus demonstrating that there are two different events happening at two different times. For example, **1 Thessalonians 4**, joined with **John 14**, teaches that when the Rapture takes place, believers will be **removed** from the earth in blessing to meet the Lord in the air and then taken by Jesus to the Father's house in Heaven. Believers are removed from the earth and unbelievers are left behind. On the other hand, when you go to Matthew 24, which describes the Second Coming of Christ following the Tribulation, you have just the reverse order taught. Namely, at the Second Coming of Christ, the unbelievers are the ones removed from the earth in judgment and the believers are the ones **left behind** alive on the earth, who go into the Millennial Kingdom. This same order is taught in Matt**hew 13, 29** and **30**.

Second, at the Rapture, believers are caught up to meet Christ in the air; Christ does not come all the way down to earth. But, according to **Zechariah 14:4**, there will be a time (the Second Coming of Christ) when His feet shall touch down upon the Mount of Olives.

Third, according to **1 Thessalonians 4:16**, it is the Lord Himself who descends from Heaven and gathers believers to Himself, not the angels; whereas, in Matthew **13:49,50**, Jesus plainly states, *"the angels shall come forth, and take out the wicked from among the righteous, and will cast them into the furnace of fire; there shall be weeping and gnashing of teeth."*

Fourth, the Rapture is an imminent event, that is, it could happen at any moment; whereas, the Second Coming of Christ is not imminent but preceded by the Tribulation period, the "Abomination of Desolation" at the three and a half year point of Daniel's Seventieth Week, and great cosmological signs which take place (according to **Matthew 24:29**) just before Christ visibly descends to planet Earth.

If the Rapture and the Second Coming are not two different events, then how could **1 Thessalonians 1:10** be true? There Paul said about the Thessalonian Christians, *"...they had turned to God from idols to serve the living and true God and to wait for His Son from heaven, whom He raised from the dead, that is, Jesus, who delivers us from the wrath to come."* They were waiting expectantly for Christ to come at any moment.

In **1 Corinthians 16:22**, Paul interjected the expression, *"Maranatha,"* which means, *"Our Lord, Come."* Post-tribulationists should ask, "Why was Paul petitioning the Lord to come if He couldn't come until after the

Tribulation?" According to **James 5:9**, Christians should be careful not to complain against each other, because "Jesus the judge is standing right at the door" and could come at any moment. These and other passages reveal that Paul, the other apostles, and the early Christians all believed that Christ could come back at any moment. This shows that the Rapture must be a separate event from the Second Coming of Christ, which has definite signs that must take place before it can occur.

Other biblical truths also apply to end-time events, and these also must be explained by those who hold to a pre-tribulation rapture, a mid-tribulation rapture, or a post-tribulation rapture view.

One such biblical truth that needs to be addressed is how human beings go into the Millennial Kingdom in non-glorified bodies. Let me explain. In **Revelation 20:1-10**, the thousand year reign of Christ on earth is described. In verses 7-10, Satan is released at the end of that Millennial Kingdom; he's been bound for a thousand years. At that time he goes out and deceives a number of people and leads them in one last rebellion against God.

But we need to ask, "Where did Satan get anybody to follow him?" According to **1 Thessalonians 4** and **1 Corinthians 15**, at the Rapture the dead in Christ are raised and Christians who are living on earth are transformed, that is, given glorified bodies, and caught up to meet the Lord with whom they remain forever.

This presents a real problem for some of the positions. **Revelation 20** says there are going to be some sinners at the end of the Millennial Kingdom. These people had to come from human parents who entered the Millennial

Kingdom in natural, physical bodies, just like yours and mine, so that they could have children. Where did these people come from?

The pre-tribulation rapture view holds that the Church is raptured before Daniel's Seventieth Week—that is, before the Tribulation; yet the gospel will still be proclaimed throughout the seven years of the Tribulation and many people will respond to Christ and be saved. Some of them are going to lose their lives during that seven-year period, but others will make it through that time. Those who make it all the way through the Tribulation period will enter the Millennial Kingdom in their non-glorified, natural, physical bodies.

There is also evidence from passages such as **Zechariah 12:10** that when the Lord returns at the Second Advent, there will be a large number of Jewish people who will turn to Jesus Christ as personal Savior. They, too, will go into the Kingdom in natural bodies. They will have children who will then have other children who may not accept Christ as personal Savior and could be the ones available to follow Satan at the end of the Millennial Kingdom.

The mid-tribulation rapture position holds that the Church is raptured 3½ years into the Tribulation period, which leaves another 3½ years for other people in the Tribulation to get saved, not die, and go into the Kingdom in natural bodies.

The position that has the most trouble with this issue is the post-tribulation rapture view. It says that everyone who is saved during the Tribulation and lives to the end of it is part of the Church and will be raptured just prior to the Second Advent. But if all believers at the end of the Tribulation will be raptured and given glorified bodies, and if all unbelievers are swept away and brought to judgment by God, then no believers will be left on earth. So who will be left to go into the Millennial Kingdom in natural bodies to produce children who someday will rebel and follow Satan at the end of the Millennial Kingdom? In other words, post-tribulationists have a real problem in finding people who exist in non-glorified bodies to go into the Millennial Kingdom.

Another biblical truth that must be dealt with by all positions is the **Marriage Supper of the Lamb. Revelation 19:7-9** describes Christians in Heaven engaged in the Marriage Supper of the Lamb. Immediately after that event is described, **Revelation 19:11** reveals the Lord riding out of Heaven with His saints at the end of the Tribulation to destroy His enemies.

Post-tribulationists say the Church goes through the Tribulation. But if **Revelation 19:7** describes the Church being in Heaven before the end of the Tribulation, how did it get there? It must have been raptured. Of course, if the Church is on earth throughout the whole Tribulation period, then when was it raptured to allow enough time for the Church to be caught up into Heaven, attend the Marriage Supper of the Lamb, and then return with Christ at His Second Advent?

Mid-tribulationists have 3½ years for the Church to be in Heaven, attend the marriage feast, and then return with Christ at the Second Advent.

The pre-tribulationists have 7 years for the events surrounding the Marriage Supper of the Lamb to occur before Christians return with

Christ at the end of the Tribulation, to defeat His enemies and to establish His Millennial Kingdom. But the point is that each of the different views must show that their position best fits the events described.

A third biblical truth that all sides must deal with is the **Judgment Seat of Christ**. This is spoken of in **1 Corinthians 3** and **2 Corinthians 5**. The question is, When does this event occur and where does it occur? Does it occur during the Tribulation period? Or, does it occur during the Millennial Kingdom? The pre-tribulationist has 7 years between the Rapture and the Second Advent for the Church to be in Heaven, to be brought before the Judgment Seat of Christ, and take part in the Marriage Supper of the Lamb. The mid-tribulation rapture position has 3½ years for these events.

The position that seems to have the most trouble with this issue is, again, the post-tribulationist. The reason is, they are saying that the Church is present on earth and experiences the Tribulation for 7 years. Then the Church is raptured at the very end, and believers are caught up to meet the Lord in the air, but immediately turn around and come back to Earth with Christ as He descends at the Second Advent. Post-tribulationists thus must show that the Judgment Seat of Christ occurs in the Millennial Kingdom period. But there seems to be no evidence for that.

Question #60

When are the Marriage Supper of the Lamb and the Judgment Seat of Christ?

S THERE EVIDENCE THAT shows the Judgment Seat of Christ happens in Heaven before the Second Advent (at the end of the Tribulation)? The answer is, "Yes." When we come to the Marriage Supper of the Lamb in **Revelation 19**, we find that the bride (the Church) is adorned with her wedding gown. She is dressed in linen, white and clean. And we're told that the wedding gown represents the righteous deeds of the saints, which suggests that by the time the Church gets to the marriage feast, she has already received her recognition and her rewards for the things she has done in the flesh. This suggests the Church has already stood before the Lord at the Judgment Seat of Christ.

The sequencing seems to be very clear. The Second Advent occurs at the end of the Tribulation; the Marriage Supper occurs before that; and then, before the Marriage Supper occurs, the Judgment Seat of Christ occurs so that the Church gets her rewards which she is seen wearing at the Marriage Supper of the Lamb.

Finally, all positions teach that the Church is promised exemption from God's judgmental wrath. But when one examines **Revelation 4, 5 and 6**, it is apparent that the seals on the scroll, once broken, begin the sequence of judgments that runs throughout the whole Tribulation period. These "seal judgments" parallel the beginning of "birth pangs" mentioned by Jesus in **Matthew 24**. They run throughout the Tribulation time period and they are all God's judgmental wrath.

If this is so, and the Church is promised deliverance from God's judgmental wrath, it seems that the most likely way that this deliverance will occur is that the Church is not present in the Tribulation at all. As **Revelation 3:10** says, *"Because you have kept the word of my perseverance, I also will keep you from the hour of testing, that hour which is about to come upon the whole world, to test those who dwell upon the earth."* Believers will not only be kept from the testing, but the whole time period of the testing. How? 1 **Thessalonians 4** says believers will be *"caught up," "snatched,"* or *"raptured,"* from the earth to meet Christ in the clouds. That is why we *"wait for God's Son from heaven whom He raised from the dead, that is, Jesus, who delivers us from the wrath to come"* (1 **Thessalonians 1:10**). In brief, the Rapture and the Second Advent are described as containing events that can only be explained by realizing they are two separate events. Also, the evidence indicates the pre-tribulational viewpoint is necessary to conclude that the Rapture must occur at least 7 years before the Second Advent in order for Christians to escape the judgmental wrath of God poured out during the entire Tribulation time period.

Question #61

Why is the Pre-tribulation Rapture view the only view fully consistent with the concept of imminency?

A S I BEGAN TO examine the teaching of the pre-wrath rapture view, I began to find real problems with this view in light of biblical teaching concerning the Rapture.

So I began doing even more extensive research over a period of a number of years. Why is it important that we deal with this? Because of the false views concerning the Rapture of the Church that are floating around in Christian circles today, and some of these false views have very persuasive arguments on the surface. But the important thing is to go below the surface and see what is the foundation for these arguments and see in depth what the Scriptures teach about this.

It's important for people to be taken more in depth in the Scriptures on what it says about the Rapture. It's important for Christians to really know what each of the views teach so we will have a better insight against views that really do not correspond with what the Scriptures teach.

But even more significantly, the imminency concept of the return of the Lord according to the Bible is to be the greatest motivating factor for holy living in a practical way. The other views of the Rapture of the Church are not consistent with that imminency concept in the Word of God. Only the Pre-Tribulation Rapture view is fully consistent with it and therefore really preserves the teaching of the imminency of the Lord's return which is so critical a motivator for believers to be living holy, godly lives—moment by moment, day by day, in the world and age in which we live.

Question #62

What are some of the basic teachings of the Pre-wrath Rapture view and the problems with those teachings?

N 1990 A NEW view concerning the Rapture of the Church began to be published. It was called The Pre-Wrath Rapture View. According to this view the Second Coming of Christ and the Rapture of the Church will take place between the sixth and seventh seals of Revelation, approximately three-fourths of the way through the seven-year 70th week of Daniel 9. The Church will go through the first half of the 70th week of Daniel 9 and the Great Tribulation, but will be raptured before the Day of the Lord begins prior to the end of the 70th week. This present article will present some of the basic teachings of the view and problems with those teachings.

Teaching 1

The Great Tribulation and the Day of the Lord will be totally distinct entities. They will not overlap with each other.

Problem

The Bible indicates that the Great Tribulation and The Day of the Lord will have several things in common.

A. Both are associated with the concept of "trouble" or "tribulation."

1. The Great Tribulation—Daniel 12:1 (described by Jesus as "great tribulation")

2. The Day of the Lord—Zephaniah 1:14-17 (v. 15)

Note—The Septuagint used the Greek word for "*tribulation*" to translate the Hebrew word for "*trouble*" in Daniel 12:1 and Zephaniah 1:15. Thus, both the Great Tribulation and the Day of the Lord will be characterized by "*trouble*" or "*tribulation*."

B. The concept of an unparalleled time of trouble.

1. The Great Tribulation—Daniel 12:1; Matthew 24:21

2. The Day of the Lord—Joel 2:1-2

Note—There can be only one unparalleled time of trouble. Thus, the Great Tribulation and the Day of the Lord must cover the same unparalleled time of trouble. The Great Tribulation will be included within the Day of the Lord, but the Day of the Lord will last longer than the Great Tribulation.

Teaching 2

The Great Tribulation will begin in the middle of the seven-year 70th week of Daniel 9, but it will not continue throughout the entire second half (three and one-half years) of the 70th week. It will end before the Day of the Lord will begin with the seventh seal in the latter part of the 70th week.

Problem

Several things indicate that the Great Tribulation will last throughout the entire second half of the 70th week of Daniel 9.

A. Matthew 24:15-21

Jesus indicated that the Great Tribulation will begin with the abomination of desolation and will be characterized by severe persecution of the Jews and their hiding in a wilderness area to escape the persecution. **Daniel 9:27** reveals that the abomination of desolation will begin in the middle of the 70th week. According to **Revelation 12**, Israel will hide in a wilderness to escape persecution for 1260 days (v. 6) or three and one-half years (v. 14). Thus, the Great Tribulation will last throughout the entire second half of the 70th week.

B. Daniel 12:6

After the Great Tribulation was introduced in **Daniel 12:1**, an angel asked how long it would last to its end. The answer to the angel's question was three and one-half years (v. 7). Since the Great Tribulation will begin in the middle of the 70th week, this means that it will last throughout the entire second half of the seven-year 70th week.

Note—The being who answered the angel's question raised both hands toward heaven and swore an oath by God. He thereby affirmed the absolute certainty of the Great Tribulation lasting for three and one-half years.

But—What about Jesus' statement about the days of the Great Tribulation being "*shortened*" (Matthew 24:22)? According to the Pre-Wrath view, that indicates that the Great Tribulation will be shortened to less than three and one-half years.

Problem

1. The verb translated "*shortened*" means "*to cut off*."
2. The verb is aorist tense, indicative mood, with the augment. Unless the context clearly indicates otherwise, verbs in that tense and form express action in the past. In eternity past God shortened the days of the Great Tribulation in the sense that He determined to cut it off at a specific time of three and one-half years rather than let it run its own course indefinitely (see Mark 13:20).

Teaching 3

The sixth seal will be a precursor or forewarning of the coming of the Day of the Lord.

Problem

1 Thessalonians 5:2 indicates that the Day of the Lord will come like a thief in the night. Thus, the unsaved will be given no precursor or forewarning of the coming of the Day of the Lord.

Teaching 4

The Day of the Lord will not begin until the seventh seal is broken in the latter part of the 70th week.

Problem

Several things indicate that the Day of the Lord will begin at the beginning of the 70th week.

1. **1 Thessalonians 5:2-3**—The Day of the Lord will begin at the same time that the unsaved are claiming that the world has "peace and safety." A study of the first, second, third, fourth and sixth seals of Revelation 6 indicates that, once the seals begin to be broken at the beginning of the 70th week, there will be no peace and safety for the world. Thus, peace and safety will be removed long before the seventh seal is broken.

2. **1 Thessalonians 5:2-3**—In his description of how the Day of the Lord will begin, Paul said, "then sudden destruction cometh upon them, as the birth pang upon a woman (literal translation of the Greek text). Since it is the very first birth pang that comes suddenly upon a woman, Paul was referring to the very first birth pang of the Day of the Lord. He thereby indicated that the Day of the Lord will begin with the very first birth pang.

Jesus talked about "the beginning of birth pangs" in **Matthew 24:5-8**. Surely the first birth pang would be the start of the beginning of birth pangs. The Day of the Lord will start at the very beginning of the beginning of birth pangs and will include the entire beginning of birth pangs.

Jesus placed the beginning of birth pangs (**Mathew 24:5-8**) before the abomination of desolation (**Matthew 24:15**) that begins in the middle of the 70th week (**Daniel 9:27**). He thereby indicated that the beginning of birth pangs will be in the first half of the 70th week. Thus, the Day of the Lord will start at the beginning of the 70th week with the very first birth pang.

Teaching 5

The Great Multitude of **Revelation 7:9-17** is the Church which has just been raptured to Heaven between the sixth and seventh seals.

Problem

If it is the Church that has just been raptured, then this was a partial rapture of the Church.

1. Every person in this great multitude comes out of "the Great Tribu-lation" (Greek has the definite article) (**Revelation 7:13-14**). Where is the rest of the Church which has lived and died for many centuries and will never be in the Great Tribulation? **1 Thessalonians 4:13-18** indicates that the entire Church (dead and live alike) will be rap-tured together at the same time.

2. The verb "came" in the statement "These are they who came out of the great tribulation" is in the present tense which normally indi-cates continuous action. The people of *The Great Multitude* come out of the Great Tribulation one-by-one through death, not all at once as in the Rapture of the Church.

Teaching 6

There is only one future coming of Christ, not two. The Rapture and Second Coming of Christ take place at the same time between the sixth and seventh seals. The Pre-tribulation Rapture View is wrong to teach two future comings of Christ.

Problem

The Pre-Wrath View teaches **four** future comings of Christ within the boundaries of the one Second Coming. They are as follows:

First

Between the sixth and seventh seals immediately after the Great Tribulation has ended but before the Day of the Lord begins and the 70th week ends. Christ comes to Rapture the Church and take it to Heaven. He remains in Heaven for the rest of the 70th week.

Second

Immediately after the end of the 70th week and at the beginning of a 30-day reclamation period. Christ descends to the earth to save Israel and to reclaim the rule of the earth for God. Sometime after the sixth day of the reclamation period Christ returns to Heaven and remains there for about 24 days.

Third

After the seventh vial judgment at the end of the 30-day reclamation period. Christ returns to earth with His angels to defeat Antichrist and his forces at Armageddon. Then there is a 45 day restoration period. At the close of these 45 days Christ returns to Heaven to deliver the kingdom of earth to God and to receive the rule of the whole earth from God.

Fourth

Several days after Christ receives the rule of the earth from God, on the first day of the Millennium, He descends permanently to the earth with the Church to rule the world for 1,000 years.

Teaching 7

In **Matthew 24:31** Jesus taught that the Church will be raptured at His Second Coming after the Great Tribulation (see vv. 21, 29-30). At that time His angels will "gather together His elect from the four winds, from one end of heaven to the other" with "a great sound of a trumpet." Since the Church is God's elect, and since it *will* be raptured to Heaven with the sound of "the trump of God" (1 **Thessalonians** 4:16-17), this must be a reference to the Rapture of the Church.

Problem

Each part of Jesus' **Matthew 24:31** statement is derived from Old Testament passages that relate exclusively to the nation of Israel, not to the Church.

1. The Old Testament calls Israel God's "elect" (**Isaiah 45:4**) or "chosen" (**Deuteronomy 7:6**). These passages use the same Hebrew word for "elect" or "chosen. "

2. Because of Israel's persistent rebellion, God said that He would scatter them "into all the winds" (**Ezekiel 5:10**). Later He said that He had spread them abroad "as the four winds of heaven" (**Zechariah 2:6**).

3. God promised that He would gather together the scattered of Israel and of Judah "from the four corners of the earth" (**Isaiah 11:12**). He also promised that they would be brought from the east, west, north, and south, from far, and from the ends of the earth" (**Isaiah 43:5-6**).

4. God promised that in the future He would gather the people of Israel from all the nations where He had scattered them. He said to them, "*If any of thine be driven out unto the outmost parts of heaven, from there will the Lord thy God gather thee, and from there will he fetch thee*" (**Deut. 30:3-4**). "

5. God indicated that the people of Israel will be gathered when "*the great trumpet shall be blown*" (**Isaiah 27:12-13**).

Question #63

Where does the Bible teach that Christians will be removed from the earth before the Day of the Lord ever begins?

I N 2 **THESSALONIANS** 2 the apostle Paul gives some teaching that relates to the Rapture issue. In verse 1, he says, "*Now we beseech you brethren by the coming of our Lord Jesus Christ and by our gathering together unto Him, that you be not soon shaken in mind or be troubled neither by spirit nor by word nor by letter as from us as that the day of Christ* (literally as that the Day of the Lord) *is at hand. Let no man deceive you by any means. For that day, namely the Day of the Lord shall not come except there come a falling away first and that man of sin be revealed the son of perdition who opposes and exalts himself above all that is called God or that is worshipped so that he as God sits in the temple of God showing himself that is God.*"

In verse 1, where Paul says "*We beseech you brethren by the coming of our Lord Jesus Christ and by our gathering together unto Him,*" it's obvious he's talking here about the Rapture of the Church. In **John 14**, a Rapture passage, Jesus talks about His coming and receiving the believers unto Himself so that they may be with Him. And the implication is the believers will be transported from the earth to meet the Lord so that they can be with Him. There is a gathering of the believers together with the Lord.

In **1 Thessalonians 4**, the most extensive passage on the Rapture of the Church in the Bible, he talks about Jesus coming and the Church saints being caught up from the earth to meet the Lord in the air. There again is the gathering of the Church saints to be with the Lord. The language is basically the same. And so here in **2 Thessalonians 2:1**, Paul is clearly talking about the Rapture of the Church to meet the Lord.

A significant thing about this statement of Paul in verse 1 is this, the preposition translated *by* in the statement "**by** *the coming of our Lord Jesus Christ and our gathering together unto Him*," has the force of *on behalf of* or *in defense of*. A number of Greek scholars point out that Paul is writing here to defend his teaching that he had given to the Thessalonians earlier about the Rapture of the Church. Why was it necessary for him to defend this teaching? Verses 2 and 3 give us the reason why. Someone had come to the Thessalonians after Paul had already taught them about the doctrine of the Rapture and had said to them—I know that the apostle Paul has either received a revelation from God through the Spirit; or I also know that he has given some official teaching; or I know that he has written a letter in which he has declared that you are already in the Day of the Lord with the wrath of God to be poured out.

Now, Paul indicates here in verses 2 and 3 that that teaching by false reporters was really shaking up or disturbing the Thessalonian Christians. The language he uses here he says verse 2, "*you're not to be soon **shaken** in mind or be **troubled** neither by spirit nor by word nor by letter as from us as that* *the Day of the Lord is at hand.*" The words translated here as ***shaken*** and ***troubled*** carry the implication of being **shaken loose from your mooring from your anchor and thereby departing from a view that you had taught and that you had held in the past.**

The idea was that the fact that they were told that the Day of the Lord had already come and that they were in it was beginning to shake them loose from the teaching about the Rapture that Paul had given them before. The statement at the end of verse 2 that "*the Day of the Lord is at hand*"—there's a perfect tense involved in the verb form here so they were really being told that the Day of the Lord had already begun before Paul wrote this second epistle to them—and therefore they were already in it.

It's not that the Day of the Lord is **about** to come, the perfect tense indicates that what they'd been told falsely contrary to Paul's teaching is that the Day of the Lord **had already started in the past** before Paul wrote this letter and that therefore they as church saints were already in it. But why would that teaching that the Day of the Lord had already begun and that they were in it shake them up so badly to the point that some of them were ready to depart from the teaching that Paul had given earlier about the Rapture of the Church?

It seems to me you're forced to conclude the reason they were shaken up is because Paul earlier had taught them that the Rapture of the Church would take place **before** the Day of the Lord would begin and that therefore by rapture they would be **removed from the earth** before the Day of the Lord would begin and as result of the Rapture that they as Christians would never be **in** the Day of the Lord. But now this false report that Paul later on had changed his mind and had taught that the Day of the Lord had **already begun** and that **they were in it** really shook them up because that seemed to contradict what Paul had taught them earlier about the Rapture of the Church.

So Paul's teaching in 2 Thessalonians 2 very strongly infers that he had taught them that the Rapture of the church will take place **before** the Day of the Lord will begin; be a totally separate event even from the beginning of that Day of the Lord; and that therefore by Rapture the church saints would never go into the Day of the Lord. And then to demonstrate even more so that this report that they'd been given was false, he says in verse 3, *"Let no man deceive you by any means for that day* (referring to the Day of the Lord) *shall not come except there come a falling away first and that man of sin be revealed the son of perdition."* Paul is teaching that two things must take place **before** the Day of the Lord had begun and obviously his point is neither one of those had taken place yet—and since they had not taken place— therefore the Day of the Lord had not begun and they were not in it.

Question #64

When will the Antichrist be revealed? When will the "man of sin" be revealed?

ET ME DEAL WITH one of these events, the one that Paul expresses closer to the concept of the Day of the Lord coming and that is the man of sin being revealed.

The man of sin here is a reference to the future Antichrist, Satan's political ruler of the future Tribulation period here on planet earth. What does he mean by the *"man of sin being revealed?"* It means that the man of sin is being identified for who he is.

When will the man of sin be revealed? When you go back to Daniel 7 we have revealed there the fact that toward the end times there will be a revived form of the Roman Empire that will be established in the world. That revived Roman Empire initially will consist of ten divisions confederated together under ten equal rulers.

The language indicates that after that ten unit revived Roman Empire has been present and functioning for a period of time there will be an eleventh ruler who will begin to rise to power from within that future revived Roman Empire. That eleventh ruler when you compare Scripture with Scripture will be the future Antichrist. So the fact that he will be an eleventh ruler, not an eighth one, not a ninth one, not a tenth one, but the eleventh ruler who rises to power from within this revived Roman Empire will be one thing which will identify who the Antichrist is.

But in addition we are told in Daniel 7, that as this eleventh ruler, the Antichrist, rises to power he will overthrow three of the original ten rulers of this revived Roman Empire. That action of overthrowing three of those rulers will be a second identification mark concerning who the Antichrist is.

But then when you go to Daniel 9:27, we have indicated to us that at the very beginning of the 70th week of Daniel 9 or if you choose to call it, the very beginning of the seven-year tribulation period, the Antichrist will enforce or establish a covenant with the majority of people of Israel in the Middle East. This passage indicates that he will do that as the starting point of the seven-year tribulation period. Please note that it is the establishment of this covenant between Antichrist and Israel that starts the seven-year tribulation period, it's not the Rapture of the Church that starts the seven-year tribulation period. But that act of establishing a seven-year covenant with Israel at the beginning of the tribulation period will be a third item that will identify who the Antichrist is. So there are at least three things there from the book of Daniel that will identify the Antichrist. I am convinced that's what Paul is referring to in 2 Thessalonians 2:3 concerning the man of sin being revealed.

Paul is saying that the Day of the Lord will not come until the Antichrist, the man of sin, is revealed. And I'm convinced that at least the first two identification marks: First, his rising as an eleventh ruler within the revived Roman Empire and then second, his overthrowing three of the original ten rulers of that revived Roman Empire—will reveal who he is before the Day of the Lord begins at the beginning of the 70th week of Daniel 9. So Paul offers this as proof to the Thessalonian Christians that they are not in the day of Lord. It has not begun yet and one reason so is because the man of sin, the Antichrist, had not yet been revealed.

Question #65

What is the sequence
of future prophetic events
as spelled out in the Word of God?

WHAT WILL BE THE sequence of events of the future as spelled out in the Word of God? Our understanding of the Scriptures is that the next major prophetic event that God has scheduled for the world is the Rapture of the Church out of the world. As we have previously discussed, the Bible teaches that's an **imminent** event. It could happen at any moment. And some things may happen before this takes place but nothing must happen before it takes place.

But then the Scriptures indicate that there will be a **revived Roman Empire** formed of a ten unit division with ten equal rulers ruling over that revived Roman Empire and after that revived Roman Empire has been here for an undisclosed period of time, an eleventh ruler will rise to power from within it. That eleventh ruler, according to the Scriptures, is **the Antichrist**. As he rises to power he will overthrow three of the original ten rulers of that revived Roman Empire and thereby gain controlling authority over that empire.

Once he's in a position of authority, he will now be able to make political agreements with other nations on the face of the earth. And according to Daniel 9:27 at the very beginning of the 70th week of Daniel 9 or the seven-year tribulation period, **Antichrist** will establish or **enforce a covenant** with the nation of Israel. It's our understanding that through that covenant he will guarantee Israel's national security and thereby will appear to be Israel's great friend and protector and benefactor. In the middle of the 70th week according to Daniel 9:27, Antichrist will commit the **abomination of desolation**. He will enter into a new temple that the people of Israel will have in Jerusalem by that time. There he will set himself up as God. Will declare boldly that he is God and require all of his subjects to worship him as God and those who refuse to do so he will try to put to death.

At that time he will **break his covenant** with Israel and will turn against that nation and begin desolating it throughout the entire second half of the 70th week of Daniel 9, the second 3 ½ years, desolate Israel more than it's ever been persecuted in all of past history, at least in scope even worse than the Holocaust of World War II.

This will culminate with **Jesus Christ** coming out of heaven in His glorious **Second Coming** immediately after this 3 ½ years of tribulation— the Scriptures refer to that second 3 ½ years from the abomination of desolation up until the Second Coming of Christ as the **great tribulation** but also the time of Jacob's trouble. And the reason it's called the time of Jacob's trouble is because this will be the unparalleled time of trouble for Israel and the world as Antichrist and Satan will go after that nation with a vengeance.

But as we've indicated that will culminate with **Jesus Christ** coming out of heaven in His glorious Second Coming immediately after the end of that 70th week of Daniel 9 and Jesus at that time **will crush the forces of Satan**. We read about this in Revelation 19. He will destroy all the godless armies and the rulers of the nations that have gathered there in the land of Israel by the end of the 70th week of Daniel 9 from Armageddon.

Antichrist and the **false prophet**—at that point of the Second Coming of Christ—will be removed from the earth and **cast into the eternal lake of fire** where they will be tormented forever. And then Jesus will have **Satan bound**, according to Revelation 20:1-3, bound and imprisoned in the abyss for the next **1,000 years**. And then according to Revelation 20:4-7 **Jesus and His saints will rule the earth on behalf of God for 1,000 years**.

After the 1,000 years **Satan will be loose from the abyss** and will return to earth to lead one **final revolt against the rule of Christ** and God—but Revelation 20 makes it very clear that revolt will be crushed very quickly by God and **Satan** then will be **cast forever into the eternal lake of fire** where he will be tormented day and night forever and ever.

Then John saw in Revelation 20 a Great White Throne appear. And when that happens the present **heavens and earth disappear** or are destroyed and all the **unsaved** of all ages of history will be resurrected from the dead to **appear before the Lord at the great white throne judgment** and there they will receive their eternal judgment. They will be **cast forever into the eternal lake of fire together with Satan, his Antichrist and false prophet**, and Satan's angels will be put there in that eternal lake of fire as well and there Satan and his whole kingdom will be tormented throughout all of eternity.

Then in Revelation 21 after the Great White Throne judgment has been completed, John saw a **new heaven** and a **new earth**—which God creates for the future eternal state. And there in the new heaven and new earth **God, Christ, the Holy Spirit, the holy angels of God, and all the believers**—all the saints of God—of all ages of history will **live together in blessing forever** and ever and ever for the glory of God.

Question #66

What is the order of the different resurrections mentioned in the Bible?

THE BIBLE TEACHES THAT there are different orders of resurrection of human beings from the dead. In 1 Corinthians 15, which is the great resurrection chapter in the New Testament, Paul says in verse 22, *"For as in Adam all die, even so in Christ shall all be made alive but every man in his own order. Christ the first fruits, afterward they that are Christ's at His coming."* Paul is teaching here that there are several orders of resurrection. And human beings will be resurrected from the dead in their own order. The *first order* was the resurrection of Jesus Christ—that's why Paul calls Him the first fruits—the first one who is permanently resurrected from the dead with an immortal body which can never die again.

But then he says the **next resurrection** will be *"those who are Christ's at His coming."* This is referring to the resurrection of Church saints who have died. Their resurrection will take place at the Rapture of the Church when the Lord Jesus will come out of heaven from the Father's house down to the air, not the whole way down to the surface of the earth, but to the air, and then will catch up His Church saints from the earth to meet Him in the air.

We're told in 1 Thessalonians 4 that those church saints who've already died before the Rapture of the Church will be resurrected from the dead and then will be caught up to meet the Lord in the air.

So first, there was the *resurrection of Christ* and then the *resurrection of church saints* at the Rapture of the Church.

Question #67

When will Old Testament saints be raised from the dead?

WHEN YOU LOOK AT Daniel 12:1-2, we are taught here that the Old Testament saints will be resurrected from the dead **after the great tribulation**. Now the great tribulation will be the second half of the 70th week of Daniel 9—or if you prefer to call it—the second half of the seven-year tribulation period. Jesus taught in Matthew 24 that He will return the whole way down to the earth in His glorious Second Coming immediately after that great tribulation—so this is indicating that the Old Testament saints will be **resurrected from the dead immediately after the great tribulation** in conjunction with the Second Coming of Jesus Christ back to the earth to rule the earth.

So, Christ was raised from the dead first, then at the Rapture Church saints are resurrected from the dead, and then seven years later at the glorious Second Coming of Christ—immediately after the great tribulation—Old Testament saints will be raised from the dead.

In addition, in Revelation 20, we have another group of saints we're told will be resurrected at the Second Coming of Christ. These are Tribulation saints. Tribulation saints are people who will get saved during the Tribulation period, and of those who become saints during the Tribulation period, but then die during the Tribulation period, those dead **Tribulation saints** will be **resurrected** from the dead together **with Old Testament saints** resurrected from the dead, **at the Second Coming of Christ** back to the earth immediately after the great tribulation.

Question #68

Who is in the first resurrection in Revelation 20?

WE ARE TOLD IN **Revelation 20** that this is the **first resurrection**. The first resurrection is a broad term that covers all the resurrections of the saints—whether Church saints at the Rapture or Old Testament saints and Tribulation saints at the Second Coming. The term **first resurrection** is referring to the **resurrection of all believers** from the dead regardless of what order or time that they are resurrected from the dead.

Now the expression **first resurrection** clearly **implies** there is a **second resurrection** and Revelation 20 teaches that—and it's the **resurrection of the unsaved**—no believers in the second resurrection. The resurrection of the unsaved—all of them from all ages of past history at the Great White Throne judgment which will take place after the 1,000 reign of the Lord Jesus and before the future eternal state. There all the unsaved of all ages of history will be resurrected from the dead to appear before the Lord and receive the sentence of their final judgment to be cast forever into the eternal lake of fire where they will be tormented forever.

So the first resurrection has several different orders of resurrection within it. First the resurrection of Christ; then the resurrection of church saints at the Rapture; seven years later the resurrection of Old Testament saints and dead tribulation saints at the glorious Second Coming of Christ after the Tribulation period—different orders of saints being raised from the dead—different orders within the first resurrection. The Bible says, *"blessed are those who take part in the first resurrection"* making it obvious these are all saints resurrected in that resurrection.

But then the second resurrection, after the 1,000 year reign of Christ—all unbelievers of all ages of history—and they're not blessed in that resurrection. They end up under eternal judgment in the eternal lake of fire forever.

Question #69

Who are the parties of the New Covenant according to the Old Testament?

A SIGNIFICANT BIBLICAL COVENANT WHICH will determine important issues related to Israel and the future Kingdom of God is the New Covenant. According to the Old Testament, the parties of this covenant are God and the nation of Israel.

Three things in the Old Testament indicated that God would establish the New Covenant with the people of Israel.

First, the Old Testament made clear statements to that effect. For example, Jeremiah 31:31 states, *"Behold, the days come, saith the Lord, that I will make a new covenant with the house of Israel, and with the house of Judah."* Similar clear statements were made in Isaiah 59:20-21; Jeremiah 50:4-5; Ezekiel 34:25-30, and 37:21-28.

Second, God declared that He would establish the New Covenant with the descendants of those people with whom He established the Mosaic Covenant (the Law). Having promised that He would establish a new covenant with the houses of Israel and Judah, God stated, "Not according to the covenant that I made with their fathers in the day that I took them by the hand to bring them out of the land of Egypt" (Jeremiah 31:32). Since God gave the Mosaic Law only to the people of Israel (Leviticus 26:46: Deuteronomy 4:8) and not to the Gentiles (Romans 2:14), and since He promised to establish the New Covenant with the descendants of those to whom He gave the Mosaic Law Covenant, then the New Covenant must also be established with the people of Israel, the physical descendants of Jacob.

Third, the Old Testament associated the establishment of the New Covenant with the endless existence of the nation of Israel (the physical descendants of Jacob) and with the rebuilding and permanent standing of the city of Jerusalem (Jeremiah 31:31-40).

In light of these three items in the Old Testament, it is evident that God intended to establish the New Covenant with the literal people of Israel.

The Promises of the New Covenant

God promised many things to the people of Israel in the New Covenant.

First, He promised regeneration. This would involve the giving of a new heart (a new inner control center where the issues and direction of life are determined) and the new nature (a new favorable disposition toward God consisting of the law of God in the heart)(Jeremiah 31:33; 32:39-40; Ezekiel 36:26).

Second, God promised forgiveness of sin (Jeremiah 31:34; Ezekiel 36:25).

Third, He pledged the indwelling of the Holy Spirit (Ezekiel 36:27). Fourth, He guaranteed a universal knowledge of Jehovah among the people of Israel (Jeremiah 31:34).

The context of this **fourth** promise indicated that God was referring to a personal experiential knowledge of Himself (the kind of knowledge which comes through a genuine salvation experience), not just a "head knowledge" of His existence.

Fifth, God promised that Israel would obey Him and have a right attitude toward Him forever (Jeremiah 32:39-40; Ezekiel 36:27; 37:23-24).

Sixth, God promised many national blessings to the people of Israel. He pledged that His Spirit and words would never depart from them (Isaiah 59:21), that the nation would have a great reputation because of God's special blessing (Isaiah 61:8-9), that Israel would have a unique relationship with Him as His special people (Jeremiah 31:33; Ezekiel 36:28), that God would do them good (Jeremiah 32:40-42), that wild beasts would be eliminated from their land (Ezekiel 34:25, 28), that Israel would enjoy complete security in its land (Ezekiel 34:25-28), that the nation would receive no more threats and insults from other nations (Ezekiel 34:28-29), that great abundance of food would eliminate famine (Ezekiel 34:27, 29; 36:29-30), that Israel's land would be so luxurious that it would have the reputation of being like the Garden of Eden (Ezekiel 34:29; 36:34-35), that rainfall would be controlled perfectly (Ezekiel 34:26), that Israel's cities would be rebuilt and inhabited (Ezekiel 36:33), that the nation would enjoy a population explosion (Ezekiel 36:37-38; 37:26), that the nation would be completely unified (Ezekiel 37:21-22), that the people of Israel would live in their own land forever (Ezekiel 37:25), that once again God would have His sanctuary in Israel and would dwell in the midst of the nation forever (Ezekiel 37:26- 28), and that God would never turn away from the people of Israel (Jeremiah 32:40).

It should be noted that some of the promises of the New Covenant were purely spiritual in nature, but others were material and national in nature.

The Nature of the New Covenant

Two things can be said concerning the nature of the New Covenant. First, God intended it to be an unconditional covenant. God stated no conditions in the passages that deal with the covenant. This meant that the fulfillment of the promises of the New Covenant would not depend upon the obedience of Israel. In fact, God indicated that He would fulfill the New Covenant's promises, not because Israel would deserve it, but because of Israel's disobedience. In Ezekiel 36:22 God declared, "Therefore, say unto the house of Israel, Thus saith the Lord GOD: I do not do this for your sakes, O house of Israel, but for mine holy name's sake, which ye have profaned among the nations, to which ye went."

In addition, in the New Covenant God promised that He would cause the people of Israel to have a right attitude toward Him and to obey Him (Jeremiah 32:39-40; Ezekiel 36:27; 37:23-24). Thus, instead of the New Covenant being dependent upon Israel's obedience for its fulfillment, it would cause Israel's obedience.

When God presented the promises of the New Covenant, instead of stating conditions for Israel, He continually said, "I will" (Jeremiah 31:31-34; 32:37-

42; Ezekiel 36:24-37). This meant that the fulfillment of the promises of the New Covenant would be dependent totally upon God's faithfulness to His word. God emphasized this fact when He said, "I, the Lord, have spoken it, and I will do it" (Ezekiel 36:36).

The second thing that can be said concerning the nature of the New Covenant is that God intended it to be an everlasting covenant. He specifically declared it to be everlasting in nature (Isaiah 61:8-9; Jeremiah 32:40; Ezekiel 16:60; 37:26). The fact that God intended the New Covenant to be everlasting, together with the fact it would be unconditional in nature, meant that the New Covenant would never be abolished or annulled with or by Israel. Once it would be established, its promises would have to be fulfilled. Once Israel would enter into that covenant relationship with God, it would continue in that relationship forever.

The relationship of the Church to the New Covenant

As noted in our previous article, the Old Testament clearly indicated that God would establish the New Covenant with the literal people of Israel, the physical descendants of Jacob. The Old Testament said nothing concerning a relationship of the Church to the New Covenant. This silence should not be a surprise for at least two reasons.

First, the apostle Paul indicated that no revelation concerning the Church was given before the time of the apostles and New Testament prophets (Ephesians 3:2-9). Thus, the Old Testament contained no information concerning the Church.

Second, the Old Testament prophets who presented God's revelation concerning the New Covenant were Israelite prophets. It was their responsibility to declare God's message specifically to the people of Israel. Thus, they described how the nation of Israel would be related to the New Covenant, not how others possibly would be related to it. Since the Old Testament contains their declaration of God's message to Israel, one would expect the Old Testament to present only that nation's relationship to the New Covenant.

In spite of the Old Testament's silence concerning the relationship of the Church to the New Covenant, the New Testament seems to indicate that the Church does have some relationship to it. There are at least three lines of evidence for this conclusion.

First, the Church partakes of the communion service, which Christ instituted on the night before He went to the cross (1 Corinthians 10:21; 11:23-30). When Jesus instituted the communion service, He stated the following concerning the cup of that service: "This cup is the new covenant in my blood" (1 Corinthians 11:25; Luke 22:20—literal translation). Two things should be noted concerning Jesus' statement.

First, since Jesus used the word the in the expression the new covenant, and since God had promised only one New Covenant (the one promised to Israel in Jeremiah 31) prior to Jesus' statement, it seems evident that Jesus was referring to that New Covenant. Thus, Jesus was saying that the cup of the communion service represented the New Covenant, which God had promised to literal Israel in Jeremiah 31 and other Old Testament prophetic passages.

Second, Jesus made His statement to Jewish men. They would have been aware of only one New Covenant—the one God had promised to Israel in Jeremiah 31. Since Jesus did not tell them to think otherwise, they would have understood Him to be referring to that specific New Covenant.

It seems obvious that Jesus was stating that the communion cup represents the New Covenant, which God promised to Israel in the Old Testament. The fact that the Church partakes of the communion cup, which represents the New Covenant promised by God to Israel, seems to indicate that the Church has a relationship to that covenant.

The second line of evidence for concluding that the Church is related to the New Covenant is the fact that believers who make up the Church partake of the spiritual blessings, which God promised as part of the New Covenant in the Old Testament. Church believers have been regenerated (Titus 3:5), received forgiveness of sin (Ephesians 1:7; 4:32; Colossians 1:14; 1 John 2:12), been indwelt by the Holy Spirit (1 Corinthians 6:19), and received the new nature (a new favorable disposition toward God consisting of the law of God written in the heart—Romans 7:22; 2 Corinthians 3:3; 2 Peter 1:4).

The third line of evidence that the Church is related to the New Covenant is the apostle Paul's indication that the apostles of the Church functioned as ministers of a New Covenant (2 Corinthians 3:6).

It seems evident that, although the Old Testament promised the New Covenant specifically to the literal nation of Israel, the Church also has a relationship to that covenant. This prompts an issue.

The Statement of the Issue

The issue can be stated in the form of a question. Since the Church has a relationship to the New Covenant, partaking of its spiritual blessings, what is the relationship of the nation of Israel to the fulfillment of that covenant?

Theologians disagree with each other in their answers to this question. Many Covenant Theologians claim that the New Covenant is being fulfilled totally in the Church today. According to this view, the literal nation of Israel forfeited any relationship to the New Covenant because of its unbelief and rebellion against God. The New Testament Church has replaced literal Israel in that relationship. Thus, the promises of the New Covenant that were presented in the Old Testament are to be fulfilled in a spiritualized Israel (the Church) now. They are not to be fulfilled in the literal nation of Israel in the future. According to this view, there never will be a fulfillment of the New Covenant for national Israel.

By contrast, Dispensational Theologians claim that, since God promised to establish the New Covenant with the literal people of Israel (Jeremiah 31:31), since He intended the New Covenant to be unconditional in nature (totally dependent for the fulfillment of its promises upon God's faithfulness to His word—Ezekiel 36:36), and since God declared that He would fulfill the promises of the New Covenant with Israel, not because the nation would deserve it, but because of its disobedience (Ezekiel 36:21-36), then the literal nation of Israel has not forfeited its relationship to the New Covenant because of its unbelief and rebellion against God. According to this view, the Church has not replaced literal Israel in its relationship to the New Covenant, and the New Covenant is not being fulfilled totally in the Church today. The fact that the Church has a relationship to the

New Covenant does not rule out the fulfillment of all the promises of the New Covenant with national Israel in the future. Thus, according to the Dispensational view, there will be a fulfillment of the New Covenant for literal Israel in the future.

In light of this disagreement between Covenant and Dispensational Theologians, a conclusion can be drawn. The major issue related to the New Covenant is if there will be a complete fulfillment of the New Covenant with literal, national Israel in the future.

Evidences for The Future Fulfillment of The New Covenant With National Israel

We will examine several biblical evidences to the effect that God will fulfill the New Covenant with literal, national Israel in the future.

First, in one of the major Old Testament passages in which God presented promises of the New Covenant (Ezekiel 36:21-38), He clearly indicated that He would fulfill those promises with the same national people who profaned His holy name among the Gentiles. The context (Ezekiel 36:16-20) and language ("house of Israel," vv. 22, 32, 37) of this passage signify that those people were the literal people of Israel. Because of its unbelief, national Israel has not yet received the fulfillment of the New Covenant promises of Ezekiel 36 since the time Jesus established that covenant when He shed His blood on the cross. Since God indicated that He would fulfill the New Covenant promises with literal Israel, and since that nation has not yet received the fulfillment of those promises, one must conclude that they will be fulfilled with national Israel in the future.

Second, God's declaration that He would fulfill the promises of the New Covenant because of Israel's profaning of His holy name among the Gentiles (Ezekiel 36:20-23) indicates that literal, national Israel does not forfeit its relationship to the New Covenant. Instead of the nation's disobedience preventing its receiving the fulfillment of the New Covenant promises, it actually causes it.

Third, an earlier article noted that some of the New Covenant promises were spiritual in nature, but others were material and national in nature. In addition, it was noted that the Church today partakes of the spiritual blessings which God promised as part of the New Covenant, such as regeneration, the indwelling of the Holy Spirit, and possession of the new nature. The apostle Paul declared that Church believers have been blessed "with all spiritual blessings" (Ephesians 1:3).

It should be noted, however, that although the Church partakes of the spiritual blessings of the New Covenant, the material and national promises of that covenant are not being fulfilled with the Church. For example, one of the national promises was that once Israel would enter into the New Covenant relationship with God, that nation would receive no more threats and insults from other nations (Ezekiel 34:28-29). By contrast, in spite of the fact that the Church has had a relationship to the New Covenant throughout its history, it has been threatened, insulted, and persecuted many times by different nations.

Since the material and national promises of the New Covenant are not being fulfilled with the Church—that means that those promises have not yet been fulfilled. Since God has declared His determination to perform all His promises (including the material and national ones) of the New Covenant (Ezekiel 36:26), one must conclude that those promises will be fulfilled with the nation of Israel in the future.

Fourth, after the Church came into existence and began to partake of the spiritual blessings of the New Covenant, the Apostle Paul declared that the nation of Israel would experience the fulfillment of the New Covenant when the Messiah would come in His Second Coming (Romans 11:25-29). Paul was not original in this declaration, for the Old Testament taught that God would fulfill the New Covenant with Israel when the Messiah would come in conjunction with Israel's final regathering from its dispersion and permanent restoration to the land of Israel (Isaiah 59:20-21; Jeremiah 32:37-44; 50:4-5; Ezekiel 36:22-28; 37:21-28).

Paul stated that God would not repent (change His mind) concerning this future calling for Israel, which He announced in the Old Testament (Romans 11:29). In other words, God's calling for Israel to enter into New Covenant relationship with Him in the future is irrevocable. It must happen. Paul signified, when Israel enters into that relationship with God, the Isaiah 59:20-21 New Covenant prophecy will be fulfilled.

The fact that Paul had the literal nation of Israel in mind when he made these statements in Roman 11 is evident from at least three things. **First,** in verse one he clearly indicated that he was talking about the people of God who were as much literal Israelites, physical descendants of Abraham, and members of Israelite tribes as he was. **Second,** in verse 14 Paul declared that the Israel to which he referred was his flesh (his own countrymen). **Third,** Paul contrasted the Israel of this chapter with the Gentiles (vv. 11-14, 25). It is evident that in Romans 11 Paul was teaching that literal, national Israel will enter into New Covenant relationship with God in conjunction with the Second Coming of the Messiah.

The fact that Paul taught this after the Church had come into existence and had begun to partake of the spiritual blessings of the New Covenant indicates two things. **First**, the literal nation of Israel has not forfeited its promised relationship to the New Covenant because of its unbelief and rebellion against God. **Second**, although the Church is partaking of the spiritual blessings of the New Covenant, it has not replaced literal Israel in its promised relationship to that covenant. Thus, Paul clearly stated that God has not cast away His people of Israel (Romans 11:1-2).

Concluding Considerations for the New Covenant

It is apparent that Jesus established the New Covenant when He shed His blood on the cross (Luke 22:20; 1 Corinthians 11:25; Hebrews 8:6-13; 9:15; 12:24). The Church, which began shortly after Christ's death (Acts 2:1-4; 11:15), has partaken of the spiritual blessings of the New Covenant. According to the Apostle Paul's teaching in Romans 11, during the time of the Church, a remnant of literal, national Israel is being saved by the grace of God through faith in Christ. Those Israelites become members of the Church through salvation. They thereby partake of the spiritual blessings of the New Covenant, as do the other members of the Church. But they do not partake of the material and national blessings of the New Covenant, as the rest of the Church does not.

By contrast with this remnant of Israel, the majority of literal, national Israel during the time of the Church does not become saved because of its hardened unbelief. As a result, that majority does not obtain any of the promised blessings of the New Covenant, even though it seeks many of those blessings during that time. Because of their unbelief, the majority of the nations have been removed by God from the place of covenant blessing which the nation of Israel enjoyed with Him in the past. This means, then, that national Israel failed to enter the New Covenant relationship with God in conjunction with the Messiah's First Coming.

While the majority of national Israel remains in unbelief outside the place of covenant blessing, many Gentiles, who originally were not in that place of blessing, are being grafted into it by God's grace through faith in Christ. These saved Gentiles are members of the Church. They are grafted into the place of covenant blessing in the sense that they partake of the spiritual blessings of the New Covenant, as do the remnant Israelite members of the Church.

Although believing Gentiles are grafted into the place of covenant blessing in place of the unbelieving majority of national Israel, that does not mean that the fulfillment of the New Covenant with literal, national Israel has been nullified. Paul made it very clear that the majority of national Israel will not be removed from the place of covenant blessing forever. That removal is only temporary. When the great harvest of Gentile souls has been gathered and the Messiah returns, national Israel will be saved and placed back into the place of covenant blessing (Romans 11:23-27). At that time literal, national Israel will enter fully into the New Covenant relationship with God, and all the promises (spiritual, material, and national) of that covenant will be fulfilled completely with that nation. Thus, although national Israel failed to enter the New Covenant relationship with God in conjunction with the Messiah's First Coming, it will enter it in conjunction with His Second Coming.

In Romans 11, therefore, Paul explained how the Church now partakes of the spiritual blessings of the New Covenant. The complete fulfillment of that covenant with national Israel, however, has not been and never will be nullified.

Why does the Bible forbid the setting of dates for the Lord's return?

I N LIGHT OF THE biblical teaching that the return of the Lord is imminent, in other words, there is nothing that has to take place before the Lord returns—it's always hanging overhead, it could happen at any moment—this really rules out the setting of dates for the Lord's return. But tragically there have been some prophetic teachers that have set dates and said that the Lord will return on this particular month and day or particular year and really that's contrary to the Word of God. And its tragic that some sincere souls feel compelled to set dates because when that date comes and goes and the Lord has not returned that really causes the unsaved world to kind of laugh up its sleeve at these Bible teachers and the whole concept that the Bible foretells what's going to happen in the future. And that's sad.

So that we must avoid the setting of dates, the Bible does not permit us to do that. Now on the other hand, the Bible does though clearly spell out many significant things that will happen in the future and we as students of the Word of God are to be constantly with what the Bible teaches in mind watching world events and looking at it from that perspective comparing what's happening in the world, in light of the Scriptures, to try to discern without violating the Word of God, trying to be faithful with our God, trying to discern trends that are taking place. And to discern, are things in the world moving in the direction that the Bible indicates they will move as the world comes closer and closer and closer to end time events.

We as Christians should be looking at what's going on in the world and general directions in the world from the perspective of the prophetic Word of God. That gives the believer a tool to gain insight into why things are happening the way they are and where things are headed for the future.

Question #71

Will Israel be invaded by a six nation confederation led by Russia?

W E READ IN EZEKIEL 38 and 39 that in the future there will be a massive military invasion consisting of the armies of six confederated nations against the tiny state of Israel in the Middle East. The leader of the six nation confederation is identified for us in a number of different ways and those identifications appear to point in the same direction that that leader will come from the southern part of what we have known historically as Russia or the Soviet Union.

When will this invasion take place against Israel? Ezekiel 38 indicates it will be a time when Israel feels very safe and secure to the point that it's let down its own guard militarily as far as defenses are concerned. It's my understanding that that will be the situation with Israel during the first half of the 70th week of Daniel 9, that it will feel safe and secure as a result of the covenant that Antichrist, the head of the revived Roman Empire will make with Israel at the very beginning at the seven-year tribulation period. Through that covenant I'm convinced that Antichrist will guarantee the security of Israel and therefore Israel will feel very safe and secure.

I believe that that future invasion against Israel by that six nation confederation will take place just shortly before the middle of the seven-year tribulation period when Israel is feeling so safe and so secure.

Question #72

What will happen to Israel in the future when the six nation confederation comes against them?

A CCORDING TO EZEKIEL 38 and 39 when that six nation confederation comes against Israel, God Himself is going to intervene supernaturally in the course of human events and God will supernaturally destroy this massive invading military force against Israel and thereby glorify Himself not only before the people of Israel but before the nations of the world. I'm convinced by the things that are taught in Daniel 11—that the destruction of that force will then give the Antichrist a free hand to do what he wants to do in the Middle East. And I believe that that's when you come to the middle point of the 70th week of Daniel 9 where Antichrist now seeing he has an unopposed freehand to do what he wants in the Middle East, will become very bold, walk into Israel's new temple, declare that he's God, break his covenant, and then begin to turn against the people of Israel with a vengeance.

The Scriptures indicate that some of the nations that will be part of that six nation confederation that will come against Israel before the middle of the tribulation period will involve some of the Islamic nations of the world. For example, Libya is named there and today that's an Islamic nation. There's a force there that at least in ancient times was located in the northern part of what we've known today as the nation of Turkey. Turkey today is an Islamic nation. Israel will have problems with Islamic nations in the future. There's a prophecy in Daniel 11 which seems to indicate that Syria and Egypt will also at a certain time in the future attack Israel jointly. Both of those nations today are Islamic nations.

What about China and other Asiatic nations? The book of Revelation indicates that there is a period in the future—my understanding is this will be part of Armageddon toward the end of the tribulation period—when the kings of the East, which are the kings of the Orient, will march their armies westward across the Euphrates River apparently heading toward the nation of Israel to be part of the combined military might of the whole human race which will come against Israel there toward the very end of the tribulation period.

Question #73

What will take place at Armageddon?

A SUMMARY OF WHAT WE are saying is that Russia will lead a six nation military attack against Israel shortly before the middle of the seven-year tribulation period. That will then enable the Antichrist to take complete control there of the land of Israel and other parts of the Middle East and begin exercising his will in that part of the world. But then we find that almost at the end of the seven-year tribulation period, all the nations of the world without exception will send their combined military armies against the tiny state of Israel in the Middle East.

Why all these attacks against Israel? There's a reason. The Scriptures indicate that God will not finally crush Satan and get rid of him and his kingdom rule from planet earth until the nation of Israel repents and believes in Jesus Christ as His promised Messiah and Savior. Now Satan knows the Scriptures quite well. He quoted them verbatim to Jesus when he tempted Him in the wilderness. And so to Satan's way of thinking, since Israel must repent first before God will crush him, if he can annihilate Israel before it repents, then God will never crush him.

So in Revelation 16 when the sixth bowl will be poured out, Satan, his Antichrist and his false prophet will use demonic spirits to persuade the rulers of all the nations of the world to march their armies against the tiny state of Israel in the Middle East. Satan wants the combined military might of the whole human race gathered there against Israel to be his tool to annihilate Israel—he hopes to do this before Israel can repent. But Israel will repent in its darkest hour and that's when Christ will go to war against these godless forces and destroy them.

Question #74

What are the different millennial views?

DURING THE HISTORY OF the Church, three major views have been held concerning the future Kingdom of God foretold in such biblical passages as **Daniel 2** and **7**. Today those views are called Premillennialism, Amillennialism, and Postmillennialism. The names of these views all contain the term *millennialism* (a form of the word *millennium*). They use this common form as a synonym for the expression *the Kingdom of God*.

Premillennialism

The prefix *pre* means *before*. Thus, Premillennialism is the view which states that Christ will return to the earth *before* the Millennium or Kingdom of God. He will return in His Second Coming for the purpose of establishing the Kingdom of God on earth. This kingdom will last for 1,000 years on this present earth (**Revelation 20:1-7**), and it will be a literal, political kingdom with Christ ruling worldwide as King together with the saints of God. The word *millennium* was derived from the concept of 1,000 years. It is the combination of two Latin words: *mille* (1,000) and *annum* (year). In the early days of the Church, the Premillennial View was called *chiliasm* (derived from the Greek word meaning 1,000).

Amillennialism

The prefix *a* means *no*. Thus, Amillennialism is the view which states that there will be *no* literal, political Kingdom of God on earth. The future

Kingdom of God foretold in such passages as **Daniel 2** and **7** is totally spiritual in nature. It consists either of the Church of this age, or of Christ's present rule from Heaven over the hearts of believing human beings, or the future eternal state. When Christ returns to the earth in His Second Coming, there will be a general resurrection of all the dead, a general judgment, the end of this present earth, and the immediate beginning of the future eternal state.

Postmillennialism

The prefix *post* means *after*. Thus, Postmillennialism is the view that states that Christ will return to this earth *after* the Millennium or Kingdom of God. There will be a literal Kingdom of God on this earth, but it will not be established through the supernatural intervention of Christ into history at His Second Coming. Instead, it will be established through human efforts, such as man's expanding knowledge, new discoveries and inventions, increasing ability to exercise dominion over nature, and the expanding influence of the Church. The Church has the responsibility to help bring in the Kingdom. Christ's Second Coming will occur at the close of the Millennium as the crowning event of that golden age.

The Earliest Millennial View

Numerous historians declare that Premillennialism (initially called chiliasm) was the first major millennial view of the Church, and that it was the predominant view of orthodox believers from the first to the third centuries. A sampling of historians will be quoted as evidence for this declaration.

Edward Gibbon (1737-1794), the noted English historian who wrote the classic work *The History of the Decline and Fall of the Roman Empire*, stated the following:

The ancient and popular doctrine of the Millennium was intimately connected with the Second Coming of Christ. As the works of the creation had been finished in six days, their duration in their present state, according to a tradition which was attributed to the prophet Elijah, was fixed to six thousand years. By the same analogy it was inferred, that this long period of labor and contention, which was now almost elapsed, would be succeeded by a joyful Sabbath of a thousand years; and that Christ, with the triumphant band of the saints and the elect who had escaped death, or who had been miraculously revived, would reign upon earth till the time appointed for the last and general resurrection... The assurance of such a Millennium was carefully inculcated by a succession of fathers from Justin Martyr and Irenaeus, who conversed with the immediate disciples of the apostle, down to Lactantius, who was preceptor to the son of Constantine. Though it might not be universally received, it appears to have been the reigning sentiment of the orthodox believers.[13]

It should be noted that Gibbon had an unfriendly attitude toward Christianity. Therefore, he was not biased in favor of Premillennialism. His comments have added significance in light of that fact.

J. C. I. Gieseler, Professor of Theology at the University of Gottingen, Germany, in the early 19th century, a highly acclaimed historian in his time and himself not a premillennialist, wrote the following when referring to some early Christian literature which was produced between 117 and 193 A.D.: "In all these works the belief in the Millennium is so evident, that no one can hesitate to consider it as universal in an age, when such motives as it offered were not unnecessary to animate men to suffer for Christianity."[14]

Henry C. Sheldon, Professor of Historical Theology at Boston University in the late 19th century, said that chiliasm "was entertained in the second century not only by the Ebionites, and by writers who, like Cerinthus, mixed with their Gnosticism a large element of Judaism, but by many (very likely a majority) of those of the Catholic Church."[15] It should be noted that Sheldon used the term *Catholic* (which means *universal*) to refer to the entire organized Church. This was the sense of that term during the early centuries before the Roman Catholic system was formed.

Philip Schaff, prominent German Reformed theologian and Church historian in America during the major part of the 19th century, stated the following concerning the early Church (100-325 A.D.) in his monumental eight volume *History of the Christian Church:*

> The most striking point in the eschatology of the ante-Nicene age is the prominent chiliasm, or millennarianism, that is the belief of a visible reign of Christ in glory on earth with the risen saints for a thousand years, before the general resurrection and judgment. It was indeed not the doctrine of the church embodied in any creed or form of devotion, but a widely current opinion of distinguished teachers, such as Barnabas, Papias, Justin Martyr, Irenaeus, Tertullian, Methodius, and Lactantius.[16]

Adolph Harnack, Lutheran theologian and Church historian in Germany during the late 19th and early 20th centuries and recognized authority on Ante-Nicene Church history (100-325 A.D.), wrote the following:

> First in point of time came the faith in the nearness of Christ's second advent and the establishing of His reign of glory on the earth. Indeed it appears so early that it might be questioned whether it ought not to be regarded as an essential part of the Christian religion.[17]

> ...it must be admitted that this expectation was a prominent feature in the earliest proclamation of the gospel, and materially contributed to its success. If the primitive churches had been under the necessity of framing a "Confession of Faith," it would certainly have embraced those pictures by means of which the near future was distinctly realized.[18]

Harnack also stated that "In the anticipations of the future prevalent amongst the early Christians (c. 50-150) it is necessary to distinguish a fixed... element." He indicated that the following items were included in that fixed element: "(1) the notion that a last terrible battle with the enemies of God was impending; (2) the faith in the speedy return of Christ; (3) the conviction that Christ will judge all men, and (4) will set up a kingdom of glory on earth."[19]

Harnack declared that among other early Christian beliefs concerning the future "was the expectation that the future Kingdom of Christ on earth should have a fixed duration,—according to the most prevalent opinion, a duration of one thousand years. From this fact the whole ancient Christian eschatology was known in later times as 'chiliasm.'"[20]

Harnack claimed that in their eschatology the early Christians preserved the Jewish hopes for the future presented in ancient Jewish literature.[21]

He also asserted that Justin Martyr, a prominent early Christian writer (100-165 A.D.) who had been saved out of pagan Greek philosophy, "speaks of chiliasm as a necessary part of complete orthodoxy, although he knows Christians who do not accept it."[22]

Harnack made this significant observation: "That a philosopher like Justin, with a bias towards an Hellenic construction of the Christian religion, should nevertheless have accepted its chiliastic elements is the strongest proof that these enthusiastic expectations were inseparably bound up with the Christian faith down to the middle of the 2nd century."[23]

It should be noted that Harnack was strongly liberal in his theology; therefore, he was not biased in favor of Premillennialism. In light of this fact, his comments take on added significance.

Will Durant, the 20th-century historian who produced the multi-volume set entitled *The Story of Civilization*, wrote the following concerning Jesus Christ's view of the Kingdom of God:

> What did he mean by the Kingdom? A supernatural heaven? Apparently not, for the apostles and the early Christians unanimously expected an earthly Kingdom. This was the Jewish tradi-

tion that Christ inherited; and he taught his followers to pray to the Father, "Thy Kingdom come, thy will be done on earth as it is in heaven."[24]

Durant further declared that "The apostles were apparently unanimous in believing that Christ would soon return to establish the Kingdom of Heaven on earth."[25] Then he stated that, "One faith united the scattered congregations: that Christ was the son of God, that he would return to establish his Kingdom on earth, and that all who believed in him would at the Last Judgment be rewarded with eternal bliss."[26]

Just a few historians have been quoted who have claimed that Premillennialism was the first and predominant millennial view of the Church. Others who have made the same claim could be cited. Research indicates that a good number of such historians were not premillennialists themselves.

In fact, a number were opposed to the premillennial view personally. The fact that scholars who were not biased in favor of Premillennialism would assert that it was the first and predominant millennial view of the Church is quite significant. It indicates that they based their assertion upon evidence which they were convinced was too strong to be denied.

We have noted the claim of historians to the effect that Premillennialism (initially called Chiliasm) was the first major millennial view of the Church, and that it was the predominant view of orthodox believers from the first to the third centuries. Much of the evidence which these historians use to substantiate their claim is found in the writings of early Church leaders. Now we will begin to examine some of those writings.

The Millennial View of Early Church Leaders

Papias

Papias lived from approximately 60 to 130 A.D. It is believed that he was taught directly by the apostle John. He was a friend of Polycarp, another prominent Church leader who was a disciple of John. Papias served as Bishop of Hierapolis in Phrygia, Asia Minor. His writings have not been preserved to the present day; however, Irenaeus and Eusebius, two other Church leaders, referred to his writings.[27]

Irenaeus, after relating Christ's teaching concerning the dramatic changes which the earth will experience in the future Millennium, wrote, "And these things are borne witness to in the writings by Papias, the hearer of John, and a companion of Polycarp, in his fourth book."[28]

Eusebius, Bishop of Caesarea and "The Father of Church History",[29] wrote the following concerning Papias in his work *Ecclesiastical History*,[30] "Among other things he says that a thousand years will elapse after the resurrection of the dead and there will be a corporal establishment of Christ's Kingdom on this earth."[31]

The Epistle of Barnabas

Scholars have concluded that this piece of early Christian literature was written between 120 and 150 A.D. by a Christian in Alexandria, Egypt, not by the Barnabas of the New Testament.[32]

The epistle presented the septamillennial view that appears to have been rather popular among ancient Jews and Christians. It declared that just as God labored for six days in creation, so the present earth will labor in its turmoil for 6,000 years. Then it asserted that just as God rested on the seventh day after His six days of labor, so the present earth will enjoy 1,000 years of rest after its 6,000 years of labor. This thousand years of rest will begin "When His Son, coming [again], shall destroy the time of the wicked man, and judge the ungodly, and change the sun, and the moon, and the stars."[33] In other words, the thousand years of rest will begin in conjunction with the Second Coming of Christ.

The epistle further stated that after the earth's seventh day (thousand years of rest), there will be an "eighth day, that is, a beginning of another world."[34] It would appear that this "eighth day" is a reference to the future eternal state with the new eternal earth after the thousand-year Millennium.

Justin Martyr

Justin Martyr lived from approximately 100 to 165 A.D. He was well-educated. He held no regular church office but served as a traveling evangelist and defender of Christianity. In his writings he argued for the superiority of Christianity to paganism and Judaism. On his second journey to Rome he was arrested, lashed, and beheaded because of his testimony for Christ.[35]

In his writing entitled *Dialogue With Trypho* Justin stated, "But I and others, who are right-minded Christians on all points, are assured that there will be a resurrection of the dead, and a thousand years in Jerusalem, which will then be built, adorned, and enlarged, [as] the prophets Ezekiel and Isaiah and others declare."[36] His use of the expression *"right-minded*

Christians on all points" was his way of asserting that Premillennialism was the orthodox view of his day.

Again Justin said, "And further, there was a certain man with us, whose name was John, one of the apostles of Christ, who prophesied by revelation that was made to him, that those who believed in our Christ would dwell a thousand years in Jerusalem; and that thereafter the general, and, in short, the eternal resurrection and judgment of all men would likewise take place."[37]

In his statement Justin referred to John's declarations in Revelation 20. In that passage John asserted that Christ and His saints will reign for 1,000 years. Justin's statement indicates that he understood John to be referring to 1,000 *literal* years.

Irenaeus

Irenaeus received his early Christian training from Polycarp, Bishop of Smyrna in western Asia Minor. Polycarp had been a disciple of the apostle John. Irenaeus may have served under Polycarp for several years before being sent to Gaul (France) as a missionary. Around 178 A.D. Irenaeus became Bishop of Lyons in Gaul. There he continued to serve effectively during the last quarter of the second century.[38]

Irenaeus wrote the following concerning the blessings of the future Kingdom of God foretold in the Scriptures:

The predicted blessing, therefore, belongs unquestionably to the times of the kingdom, when the righteous shall bear rule upon their rising from the dead; when also the creation, having been renovated and set free, shall fructify with an abundance of all kinds of food, from the dew of heaven, and from the fertility of the earth: as the elders who saw John, the disciple of the Lord, related that they had heard from him how the Lord used to teach in regard to these times.[39]

Irenaeus declared that in conjunction with the future Kingdom and its renovation of nature, the Lord promised great fruitage of vines, abundance of grain, large productivity of fruit-bearing trees, seeds, and grass, "and that all animals feeding [only] on the productions of the earth, should [in those days] become peaceful and harmonious among each other, and be in perfect subjection to man."[40]

According to Irenaeus, in **Isaiah 11:6-9** Isaiah prophesied concerning this *future* time when all animals will be tame and vegetarian in diet as they were before the fall of man. Commenting on this prophecy, he said, "And it is right that when the creation is restored, all the animals should obey and be in subjection to man, and revert to the food originally given by God (for they had been originally subjected in obedience to Adam), that is, the productions of the earth."[41]

Irenaeus warned against any attempts to allegorize the Kingdom prophecies: "If, however, any shall endeavor to allegorize [prophecies] of this kind, they shall not be found consistent with themselves in all points and shall be confuted by the teaching of the very expression [in question]."[42]

With regard to prophecies concerning the resurrection of saints, Irenaeus wrote:

> For all these and other words were unquestionably spoken in reference to the resurrection of the just, which takes place after the coming of Antichrist, and the destruction of all nations under his rule; in [the times of] which [resurrection] the righteous shall reign in the earth, waxing stronger by the sight of the Lord; and through Him they shall become accustomed to partake in the glory of God the Father, and shall enjoy in the kingdom intercourse and communion with the holy angels.[43]

Along the same lines he said the following concerning John's comments in Revelation 20: "John, therefore, did distinctly foresee the first 'resurrection of the just,' and the inheritance in the kingdom of the earth; and what the prophets have prophesied concerning it harmonize [with his vision]."[44]

These statements indicate that Irenaeus was convinced that saints will be resurrected from the dead to reign with Christ in His Kingdom on this earth. Concerning conditions on the earth during the Kingdom he said, "But in the times of the kingdom, the earth has been called again by Christ [to its pristine condition], and Jerusalem rebuilt after the pattern of the Jerusalem above."[45]

Irenaeus stated that after the times of the Kingdom, the Great White Throne will appear, the present heavens and earth will flee away, the unjust will be resurrected and judged, the new heaven and earth will come into existence, and the new Jerusalem will descend from heaven to earth.[46]

Tertullian

Tertullian lived from approximately 160 to 220 A.D. He was thoroughly trained for politics, the practice of law, and public debate. After he was converted around 195 A.D. he devoted his life to the defense of Christianity against paganism, Judaism, and heresy. He opposed infant baptism, promoted the Traducian theory of the origin of the human soul, and developed the term *trinity* to describe the Godhead. In the later years of his life he became associated with Montanism, a movement which some regarded to be a heretical sect.[47]

In a work which he wrote before his association with Montanism, Tertullian stated, "But we do confess that a kingdom is promised to us upon the earth, although before heaven, only in another state of existence; inasmuch as it will be after the resurrection for a thousand years."[48]

Then he wrote, "After its thousand years are over... there will ensue the destruction of the world and the conflagration of all things at the judgments."[49]

Lactantius

Lactantius lived from approximately 240 to 320 A.D. He was trained in rhetoric (the effective use of language in literature and oratory).[50] By 290 he had been appointed by Emperor Diocletian to teach rhetoric at a school in Nicomedia. He became a Christian around 300 A.D. and suffered greatly under the persecution by Emperor Galerius. After Emperor Constantine granted freedom to the Church and declared himself a Christian, he appointed Lactantius to be the personal teacher of his son.[51] Through his writings in defense of Christianity he became known as "the Christian

Cicero."[52] Jerome designated him the most learned man of his time.[53] Eusebius and Augustine honored him.[54]

Lactantius wrote,

> And as God labored six days in building such great works, so His religion and the truth must labor during these six thousand years, while malice prevails and dominates. And again, since He rested on the seventh day from His completed labors and blessed that day, so it is necessary that, at the end of the six thousandth year, all evil be abolished from the earth, and that justice reign for a thousand years, and that there be tranquility and rest from the labors which the world is now enduring for so long.[55]

Lactantius understood that the end of this present age will be characterized by a time of unprecedented tribulation: "As the end of this age is drawing near, therefore, it is necessary that the state of human affairs be changed and fall to a worse one, evil growing stronger, so that these present times of ours, in which iniquity and malice have advanced to a very high peak, can be judged, however, happy and almost golden in comparison with that irremediable evil."[56] He followed this statement with an amazing description of the future Tribulation period.[57]

Although he lived while Rome was the great world power, Lactantius was convinced from the prophetic Scriptures that Rome would be destroyed and that then the rule of the world would shift from the west to the east: "This will be the cause of the destruction and confusion, that the Roman name, by which the world is now ruled—the mind shudders to say it, but

I will say it, because it is going to be—will be taken from the earth, and power will be returned to Asia, and again the Orient will dominate and the West will serve."[58]

Lactantius believed that at His Second Coming Christ will war against and judge Antichrist and his godless forces.[59] Then "the dead will rise again... so that they may reign with God for a thousand years after being again restored to life." [60]

He said of Jesus, "When He shall have destroyed injustice and made the great judgment and restored to life those who were just from the beginning, He will stay among men for a thousand years and will rule them with just dominion."[61]

Lactantius described conditions of the future Kingdom:

> Then, those who will be living in bodies will not die, but will generate an infinite multitude during those same thousand years,... Those who will be raised from the dead will be in charge of the living as judges.[62]

> At this time, also, the prince of demons who is the contriver of all evils will be bound in chains, and he will be in custody for the thousand years of the heavenly power whereby justice will reign on earth, lest any evil be exerted against the people of God... the holy city will be set up in the center of the earth in which the Founder Himself may abide with the just who are its rulers.[63]

Lactantius claimed that the earth will be transformed; the sun will be more effective; fertility will be great; crops will be abundant, and animals will be tame.[64]

In light of these changes he said:

> Men will enjoy, therefore, the most tranquil and most abundant life, and they will reign together with God. Kings of the nations will come from the ends of the earth with gifts and presents to adore and honor the great King, whose name will be famous and venerable to all peoples which will be under heaven and to the kings who will rule on the earth.[65]

Lactantius asserted that at the end of the thousand years Satan will be set loose to lead a final revolt. God will crush the revolt and judge Satan forever. The unjust will be resurrected to everlasting sufferings. Heaven and earth will change drastically.[66]

The Rejection of Premillennialism in the East

Although Premillennialism was the predominant view of orthodox believers from the first to the third centuries, eventually it was superseded by a new millennial view—Amillennialism (also called allegorical Millennialism by some).[67] By the fifth century Amillennialism had been developed to replace early Premillennialism.

The rejection of Premillennialism began with some leaders of the Greek Church in the east during the second century. As early as 170 A.D. a church group (known as the Alogi) in Asia Minor rejected the prophetic writings from which the premillennial view was derived. This group "denounced the Apocalypse of John as a book of fables."[68]

Several factors contributed to this rejection of the premillennial view in the east.

First, was the Montanistic controversy which raged from 160 to 220 A.D.[69] The Montanists were a church group which, because of certain beliefs which it emphasized, became controversial. Christians who did not hold to the Montanists' views came to regard them as extremists and even heretics. Since the Montanists were premillennial by conviction, and because some carried their Premillennialism to extremes not supported by the Scriptures, some leaders of the Greek Church became suspicious of the entire premillennial view.

They began to associate Premillennialism with extremism and heresy because it was advocated by a group that they considered extremist and heretical. Thus, Premillennialsim began to be discredited through guilt by association.

Second, some Church leaders feared the Premillennial teaching that Christ at His Second Coming would crush the Roman power and take over the rule of the world. They were afraid that this teaching would be "a source of political danger," that it would prompt greater persecution of the Church from the Roman Empire.[70] They concluded that it was expedient to sacrifice the premillennial view for the sake of avoiding more intense persecution.

Third, some churches were convinced that the premillennial emphasis upon the glorious Kingdom reign of Christ in the future drew attention away from the organizational structure and programs which they had developed. This caused them to fear that Premillennialism posed a threat to the very existence and function of the Church in the present.[71]

Fourth, a strong anti-Semitic spirit developed in the Eastern Church. Because the majority of first century Jews had rejected Christ, and since so many of their descendants refused to believe in Him, Gentiles who professed to be Christians increasingly called Jews "Christ-killers" and developed a strong bias against anything Jewish. Because the premillennial belief in the earthly, political Kingdom rule of the Messiah in the future was the same hope that had motivated the Jews for centuries, that belief was increasingly "stigmatized as '*Jewish*' and consequently as '*heretical*'" by eastern Gentile Christians.[72] Once again Premillennialism was discredited through guilt by association.

Fifth, a new theology, known as Alexandrian theology, developed in the Greek Church.[73] This new theology was formed by Origen (185-253 A.D.) and other Church scholars in Alexandria, Egypt. Because of his intellectual abilities, Origen became president of the influential theology school of Alexandria at the young age of eighteen years.[74] Because of that position and his exceptional abilities, Origen had extensive influence.

Origen and his associates had intense interest in pagan Greek philosophy. They pursued it extensively. Origen studied under "*the heathen Ammonius Saccas, the celebrated founder of Neo-Platonism.*"[75] Through time Origen and other Alexandrian Church scholars tried to integrate Greek philosophy with Christian doctrine. This attempted integration played a significant role in the development of the new Alexandrian theology.

Much of Greek philosophy advocated that anything which is physical or material is evil by nature, and only what is totally spiritual or nonphysical is good. Through this influence the Alexandrian scholars developed the idea that an earthly, political Kingdom with physical or material blessings would be an evil thing, and that only a totally spiritual, nonphysical Kingdom would be good. That idea prompted the Alexandrian theology to reject the premillennial belief in an earthly, political Kingdom of God with physical blessings. The impact of the Alexandrian theology and Origen's new method of interpreting the Bible.

Historian Earnest R. Sandeen described one result of the attempt to integrate Greek philosophy with Christian doctrine as follows:

> The influence of Greek thought upon Christian theology undermined the millennarian world view in another, possibly more significant, manner. In the theology of the great 3rd-century Alexandrian Christian thinker Origen, the focus was not upon the manifestation of the kingdom within this world but within the soul of the believer, a significant shift of interest away from the historical toward the metaphysical, or the spiritual.[76]

Because of the great influence of the Alexandrian scholars, most of the Greek Church followed their lead in rejecting Premillennialism. Concerning this rejection of the premillennial views in the east, Adolph Harnack wrote, "*It was the Alexandrian theology that superseded them; that is to say, Neo-Platonic mysticism triumphed over the early Christian hope of the future.*"[77] Again he stated that "*mysticism*" played a significant role in giving "*the death-blow to chiliasm in the Greek Church.*"[78]

The **sixth** factor in the demise of Premillennialism in the Greek Church was the development by Origen of a new method of interpreting the Bible. This method has been called the allegorical or spiritualizing method, and it stands in contrast to the literal, historical-grammatical method. This new method of interpretation permitted Origen to read almost any meaning he desired into the Bible, and it led him into heresy in certain areas of doctrine (for example, he rejected the idea of physical resurrection and believed in universal salvation for all human beings and fallen angels).[79]

Concerning this approach by Origen to the interpretation of the Scriptures, Philip Schaff wrote,

> His great defect is the neglect of the grammatical and historical sense and his constant desire to find a hidden mystic meaning. He even goes further in this direction than the Gnostics, who everywhere saw transcendental, unfathomable mysteries.... His allegorical interpretation is ingenious, but often runs far away from the text and degenerates into the merest caprice.[80]

Premillennialism is strongly based upon the literal, historical-grammatical interpretation of those Old Testament passages which the prophets wrote concerning the future Kingdom of God. In his opposition to Premillennialism, Origen spiritualized the language of the prophets.[81]

Once again, because of Origen's great influence, this allegorical method of interpreting the prophets was widely accepted by the Greek Church.

Seventh, the Greek Church rejected the Book of Revelation from the canon of Scripture. Around 260 A.D. Nepos, an Egyptian Church bishop, tried "to overthrow the Origenistic Theology and vindicate chiliasm by exegetical methods."[82] Although several churches supported his endeavor, Nepos' efforts eventually were defeated by Dionysius, who had been trained by Origen. Dionysius succeeded in "asserting the allegorical interpretation of the prophets as the only legitimate exegesis."[83]

Harnack related the following information concerning the controversy between Dionysius and Nepos:

> During this controversy Dionysius became convinced that the victory of mystical theology over "Jewish" chiliasm would never be secure so long as the Apocalypse of John passed for an apostolic writing and kept its place among the homologoumena of the canon. He accordingly raised the question of the apostolic origin of the Apocalypse; and by reviving old difficulties, with ingenious arguments of his own, he carried his point.[84]

Dionysius so prejudiced the Greek Church against the Book of Revelation and its canonicity that during the fourth century that church removed it from its canon of Scripture, "and thus the troublesome foundation on which chiliasm might have continued to build was got rid of."[85] The Greek Church kept the Book of Revelation out of its canon for several centuries, "and consequently chiliasm remained in its grave."[86] The Greek Church restored the book to its canon late in the Middle Ages, but by that time the damage to the premillennial view could not be remedied.[87]

It should be noted that, although the Greek Church rejected Premillennialism, other church groups in the east, such as the Armenian Church and the Semitic churches of Syria, Arabia, and Ethiopia, held on to Premillennialism for a considerably longer time.[88]

The Western or Latin Church remained strongly premillennial longer than the Greek Church in the east. Adolph Harnack stated that "in the west millennarianism was still a point of 'orthodoxy' in the 4th century."[89] The reason for this longer duration of premillennial belief in the west was twofold. First, through the fourth century many western theologians "escaped the influence of Greek speculation."[90] Second, the western church always recognized the apostolic authorship and canonicity of the Book of Revelation.[91]

A change began to develop, however. After the fourth century the western church began to join the revolt against premillennial belief. Two major factors contributed to this change. First, Alexandrian theology was brought to the west by such influential church leaders as Jerome and Ambrose. As a result of being taught by Greek theologians in the east for several years, Jerome (345-420 A.D.) declared that he had been delivered from "Jewish opinions," and he ridiculed the early premillennial beliefs.[92] Concerning those early beliefs, Harnack declared that Jerome "and other disciples of the Greeks did a great deal to rob them of their vitality."[93]

The second major factor which prompted the rejection of Premillennialism in the west was the teaching of Augustine (354-430 A.D.), the Bishop of Hippo, concerning the Church. Augustine himself had been a premillennialist in the early days of his Christian faith. However, through time he rejected that view in favor of a new one which he developed.[94] That new view became known as Amillennialism.

Several things prompted this change in Augustine. **First**, the political situation of the Church in the Roman Empire had changed radically around the period of his life. By his time the Roman persecution of the Church had stopped, and the state had made itself the servant of the Church. As the Roman Empire crumbled, the Church stood fast, ready to rule in place of the empire. It looked as if Gentile world dominion was being crushed and that the Church was becoming victorious over it.[95]

Under these circumstances Augustine concluded that Premillennialism was obsolete, and that it did not fit the changed situation. In place of it he developed the idea that the Church is the Kingdom of the Messiah foretold in such Scriptures as Daniel 2 and 7 and Revelation 20. In his book, *The City of God*, he became the first person to teach the idea that the organized Catholic (universal) Church is the promised Messianic Kingdom and that the Millennium began with the first coming of Christ.[96] Augustine wrote, "The saints reign with Christ during the same thousand years, understood in the same way, that is, of the time of His first coming,"[97] and, "Therefore the Church even now is the kingdom of Christ, and the kingdom of heaven. Accordingly, even now His saints reign with Him."[98]

The **second** factor that prompted Augustine to reject Premillennialism was his negative reaction to his own pleasure-seeking, self-indulgent, immoral lifestyle in his preconversion days. "After his conversion to Christianity, Augustine, a former **bon vivant**, consistently favoured a world-denying and ascetic style of life."[99] This led him to reject "as carnal any expectations of a renewed and purified world that the believers could expect to enjoy."[100]

The **third** factor in his change of view was the influence of Greek philosophy upon his thinking. Before his conversion Augustine was deeply immersed in the study of this philosophy, much of which asserted the inherent evil of the physical or material and the inherent goodness of the totally spiritual. This philosophy continued to leave its mark upon him even after his conversion. It prompted him to reject as carnal the premillennial idea of an earthly, political Kingdom of God with great material blessings. He believed that, in order for the Kingdom of God to be good, it must be spiritual in nature. Thus, "for him the millennium had become a spiritual state into which the Church collectively had entered at Pentecost... and which the individual Christian might already enjoy through mystical communion with God."[101]

Concerning the premillennial opinion Augustine wrote,

> And this opinion would not be objectionable, if it were believed that the joys of the saints in that Sabbath shall be spiritual, and consequent on the presence of God; for I myself, too, once held this opinion. But, as they assert that those who then rise again shall enjoy the leisure of immoderate carnal banquets, furnished with an amount of meat and drink such as not only to shock the

feeling of the temperate, but even to surpass the measure of cre-
dulity itself, such assertions can be believed only by the carnal.
They who do believe them are called by the spiritual Chiliasts,
which we may literally reproduce by the name Millennarians.[102]

In order to avoid the implications of some of the millennial passages in
the Bible, Augustine applied Origen's allegorical method of interpretation
to the prophets and the Book of Revelation. For example, according to
Augustine the abyss in which Satan is imprisoned during the millennial
reign of Christ (Revelation 20:1-3) is not a literal location or place. Instead,
he said, "*By the **abyss** is meant the countless multitude of the wicked whose
hearts are unfathomably deep in malignity against the Church of God.*"[103] His
interpretation of Satan being cast into the abyss was as follows: "*He is said
to be cast in thither, because, when prevented from harming believers, he takes more
complete possession of the ungodly.*"[104] He said that the binding and shutting
up of Satan in the abyss "*means his being more unable to seduce the Church.*"[105]
Augustine was convinced that this binding of Satan in the abyss is a reality
during this present Church age.[106]

Augustine interpreted the first resurrection (referred to by John in
conjunction with the establishment of the millennial reign of Christ,
Revelation 20:4-6)) as being, not the future bodily resurrection of believers,
but the present spiritual resurrection of the soul which takes place at the
new birth.[107]

"Augustine's allegorical millennialism became the official doctrine of the
church," and Premillennialism went underground.[108] Some aspects of
Premillennialism were even branded as heretical.[109] The Roman Catholic

Church strongly advocated and maintained Augustine's amillennial view throughout the Middle Ages. During that span of time occasional premillennial groups formed to challenge the doctrine and political power of the major part of organized Christendom, but they were not able to restore Premillennialism to its original position as the accepted, orthodox view of the Church. Many Anabaptists were premillennial by conviction during the Reformation era. Some of these were quite radical in their Premillennialism, but many were not.[110] The Lutheran, Reformed, and Anglican reformers rejected Premillennialism as being "Jewish opinions."[111] They maintained the amillennial view which the Roman Catholic Church had adopted from Augustine.[112]

The Revolt Against Amillennialism

Augustine's Amillennialism remained the dominant view of organized Christendom until the seventeenth century. During that century a major change in western thought took place. This change developed into an intellectual revolution. It caused many to reject Augustine's amillennial interpretation of the universe and history.[113]

Two aspects of the intellectual revolution prompted this rejection. First, a new interest in science focused mankind's attention upon the material universe and mankind's ability to control nature. This clashed with Augustine's view that interest in the material universe was carnal. For example, Francis Bacon attacked the Augustinian conviction that any attempt to control or understand nature was prompted by Satan.[114]

Second, European intellectuals became intensely interested in a **literal** understanding of the universe. They focused attention upon literal measurements, literal quantities, and literal calculations. This clashed with the allegorical interpretation of the universe which characterized the Augustinian approach. The allegorical approach was seriously discredited when its interpretation of the nature of the heavens was proved to be mistaken by discoveries made through the use of the telescope.[115]

Through time this new concern with literalism as opposed to allegory spread to biblical scholars. Joseph Mede (1586-1638), a prominent Anglican Church Bible scholar, pioneered the return to the literal interpretation of the Kingdom of God passages in the Bible. As a result, he "concluded that the Scriptures held the promise of a literal Kingdom of God,"[116] and that this Kingdom would come in the future. This conclusion prompted him to adopt the premillennial view of the early Church.[117] Other scholars began to follow his example.[118]

The Development of Postmillennialism

Some seventeenth century Bible scholars who became convinced that the Bible promises a literal, future Kingdom of God did not adopt the premillennial view of the early Church. Instead, they developed the third major view concerning the Kingdom of God which has been held during the history of the Church.[119] That view has been called Postmillennialism (also called progressive Millennialism by some).[120]

The person credited with pioneering the development of the postmillennial view is Daniel Whitby (1638-1726) of England.[121] In spite of the fact that as a liberal Unitarian he was condemned for heresy, his view concerning the Kingdom of God became popular.

John Walvoord explained the reason as follows:

> His views on the millennium would probably have never been per-
> petuated if they had not been so well keyed to the thinking of the
> times. The rising tide of intellectual freedom, science, and philos-
> ophy, coupled with humanism, had enlarged the concept of hu-
> man progress and painted a bright picture of the future. Whitby's
> view of a coming golden age for the church was just what people
> wanted to hear.[122]

Postmillennialists were optimistic concerning the course of history. They
believed that, in spite of periodic conflicts and struggles, the ultimate
progress of history is upward, eventually all problems will be solved, and
time will be climaxed with a golden, utopian age.[123] This future time of
blessing will not occur through the supernatural intervention of Christ
into world history at His Second Coming. Instead, it will come by a gradual
process through human effort.[124]

Two Kinds of Postmillennialism

Through time two major kinds of Postmillennialism developed. The **first**
could be called **conservative** Postmillennialism. It was advocated by people
who believed the Scriptures to be the inspired Word of God. They were
convinced that the Old Testament prophecies concerning a future age of
peace and righteousness must be fulfilled literally during the course of this
earth's history. As God's people spread the gospel, eventually the whole
world will be Christianized and brought into subjection to that message.
Thus, society will be transformed primarily through the efforts of the

Church ministering in the power of the Holy Spirit. However, civilization, science, and political agencies will play a role in this transformation as well.

This means that the Church will play the key role in bringing in the future Kingdom of God foretold in the Bible. Christ will not be physically present on earth to rule from a literal, earthly throne. Instead, He will rule from Heaven while seated at the right hand of God. Thus, the throne promised to Him in the Scriptures is the Father's throne in Heaven. Christ's Second Coming will occur at the close of the Millennium as the crowning event of that golden age. In conjunction with the Second Coming there will be a general resurrection of all the dead, a general judgment of all human beings, the end of the world, and then the future eternal state will begin.[125]

Jonathan Edwards (1703-58), a major leader of the Great Awakening in America during the eighteenth century, and Charles Hodge (1797-1878), the great Princeton theologian during the nineteenth century, were advocates of conservative Postmillennialism.[126]

Edwards was convinced that the discovery and settlement of the New World was significant with regard to the establishment of the Millennium. During the nineteenth century many Protestant pastors expressed the belief that America would play the key role in leading the rest of the world in ushering in the Kingdom of God on earth.[127]

In a typical utterance, a leading Presbyterian minister of the 1840s, Samuel H. Cox, told an English audience, "in America, the state of society is without parallel in universal history.... I really believe that God has got

America within anchorage, and that upon that arena, He intends to display his prodigies for the millennium."[128]

This kind of postmillennial thinking aided the spread of America's nineteenth century doctrine of Manifest Destiny.[129] Preachers declared that America obviously had been given a divine mandate to bring the entire continent from shore to shore under its jurisdiction so that from that base it could lead the world into the Millennium.

Postmillennialism also gave great impetus to the nineteenth century American movement to abolish slavery. Many Christians regarded the Civil War as a battle of righteousness against this evil of slavery in society and, therefore, as an instrument to bring the world one step closer to the establishment of the Kingdom of God on earth. This was evidenced by the fact that the postmillennial hymn written by the Christian abolitionist, Julia Ward Howe, was called "The Battle Hymn of the Republic" (the Republic of America) and declared that God, His day, and His truth were marching on while men died to make men free.[130]

The **second** kind of Postmillennialism that developed could be called **liberal** Postmillennialism. It was very prevalent during the late nineteenth and early twentieth centuries. In common with conservative Postmillennialism, it shared great optimism concerning the upward progress of history. It too was convinced that a future golden age (the Kingdom of God) would be established on earth.[131]

In spite of this common bond, liberal Postmillennialism differed radically from conservative Postmillennialism in several areas. It rejected the idea of the sinfulness of mankind and asserted that mankind is inherently good (not perfect, but good). It was convinced that mankind is perfectible and that human perfection will be attained through proper education, the improvement of mankind's environment, and the natural process of evolution. Liberal Postmillennialism had total confidence in the ability of mankind and science to correct all problems through the course of time.

This form of Postmillennialism rejected the deity of Jesus Christ. It declared that He was the greatest human being who ever lived, perhaps even the first perfect man, but certainly not God incarnated in human flesh. According to liberalism, Jesus was the example that all humans should follow in their move toward perfection.

Liberal Postmillennialism rejected the substitutionary atonement of Jesus Christ. Based on its assumption that mankind is not sinful by nature, it concluded that mankind does not need a substitute to pay its penalty for sin. According to this view, instead of Jesus being a Savior from sin, He was the greatest teacher and example of ethics who ever lived.

Because liberalism rejected the substitutionary atonement of Christ, it also rejected the gospel of personal redemption from sin. In place of this gospel, which is revealed in the Bible, it substituted another message, which it called the **social gospel**.[132] According to this message, personal redemption from sin has nothing to do with the establishment of the Millennium. The social gospel declared that the total mission of the Church is the redemption of society from all of its social evils (such as war, poverty, racism, injustice, disease, inequality, etc.). The Church is to do this by bringing society into conformity with the ethical teachings of Christ by teaching the universal Fatherhood of God and universal brotherhood of mankind and by cooperating with science and the governmental, educational, charitable, labor, and other institutions of mankind.

Contrary to conservative Postmillennialism, which taught that society will be transformed primarily through the efforts of the Church spreading the gospel of personal redemption from sin in the power of the Holy Spirit, liberal Postmillennialism asserted that the Kingdom of God will be established on earth through the Church and other human institutions using totally natural, humanly devised means.[133]

Prominent advocates of the liberal postmillennial view in America were Walter Rauschenbusch (1861-1918), a German Baptist minister who served as Professor of New Testament and Professor of Church History at Rochester Theological Seminary and wrote such books as *Christianizing the Social Order* and *The Theology for the Social Gospel*, and Shirley Jackson Case (1872-1947), an American Baptist theologian who held the positions of Professor of New Testament Interpretation, Professor of History of Early Christianity, and Dean of the Divinity School at the University of Chicago and authored such books as *The Millennial Hope* and *The Christian Philosophy of History*.[134]

The gift of the Statue of Liberty to the United States in 1886 was, in essence, an expression of liberal Postmillennialism. The men of the Third Republic of France who conceived, designed, built, and presented the statue were liberal in their political outlook. They were convinced of several things: that the monarchies of Europe had oppressed their peoples for many centuries, that the American and French Revolutions were indicators that this oppressive yoke was about to be thrown off by the peoples of many nations, that personal liberty through governments of democracy was the wave of the future, and that America in particular was leading the rest of the world toward the future golden age of liberty through democracy. The fact that they were convinced that personal liberty was the wave of the future is indicated by the full title that they assigned to the statue: Liberty Enlightening The World. The fact that they determined to give the statue to the United States is evidence that they considered America to be the leader of the rest of the world toward the age of liberty through democracy.[135]

The Popularity and Decline of Postmillennialism

From the time of its early development in the seventeenth century until the twentieth century, Postmillennialism increased in popularity until it became "one of the most important and influential millennial theories. It was probably the dominant Protestant eschatology of the nineteenth century and was embraced by Unitarian, Arminian, and Calvinist alike."[136] It seemed to fit the optimistic spirit of the times. The rise of new democracies, the greater abundance of material goods and rising standard of living made possible by the industrial revolution in the west, the major discoveries in the fields of medicine, transportation, and communication, the rise of many new colleges and universities, and the relative peace maintained by Great Britain around the world for almost one hundred years during the nineteenth century all made it appear that man was, indeed, on the verge of entering an unprecedented golden age of history. On the surface it appeared that Postmillennialism was the correct view of eschatology.

The optimism of Postmillennialism was dealt a severe blow, however, with the outbreak of World War I in 1914. Never before had the world witnessed a war of such magnitude involving so many nations. Science, which was supposed to help man usher in the age of peace and righteousness, now provided him with tools with which to destroy great masses of humanity and thereby demonstrate his depraved nature more vividly than in the past. As a result, some theologians, such as Karl Barth, began to reject the liberal concept of the inherent goodness of mankind, which they had been taught by liberal theologians. Barth began to declare that mankind is sinful by nature and that the liberal view does not fit reality.

Postmillennialism recovered somewhat from the blow of World War I by asserting that this conflict would teach mankind an unforgettable lesson concerning the futility of war. Many pastors urged the men of their congregations to fight in this war that would end all wars and thereby play a role in permanently saving Christian civilizations from destruction. In line with this thinking, President Woodrow Wilson worked to enter the United States into this conflict in order "to make the world 'safe for democracy.'"[137]

After the end of World War I, President Wilson tried to make the postmillennial dream of permanent peace a reality by laboring hard to establish the League of Nations. The purpose of the League was to provide the nations of the world with the means of settling differences peaceably without going to war with each other. This was to be accomplished by the representatives of the nations discussing and settling differences in the League meetings.

In spite of what appeared to be a decent recovery by Postmillennialism from the blow of World War I, further events of the twentieth century proved to be very unkind to that optimistic millennial view. The League of Nations failed to accomplish its purpose and collapsed after a few years. Much of the world suffered a difficult economic depression during the 1930s. Nazi power tried to annihilate an entire nation of people through the practice of genocide. World War II, which proved to be even more horrible and of greater magnitude than World War I, began in the late 1930s. Mankind was catapulted into the atomic age with the development of weapons which had the potential of blowing mankind and all of civilization into oblivion. The outlook on life expressed through western music, art, literature, philosophy, and some theology became increasingly pessimistic in the years after World War I.

For many people the optimistic view of the future, which characterized much of the western world through World War I, did not fit the harsh realities of the world. As a result, most people rejected Postmillennialism, and it almost died. In the years immediately following the end of World War II, almost no people, including students of the Bible, advocated that view of the Millennium. During that time one of the few proponents of the conservative postmillennial view was Loraine Boettner (his postmillennial book, *The Millennium*, was published in 1958).[138]

Appendix A:

What is the significance of the four blood moons?

We have had many people asking us this question. Recently, books have been written about the four "blood moons" (lunar eclipses) taking place in 2014 and 2015. Their significance was discovered by Mark Blitz in 2007 and made popular by John Hagee in his book, *Four Blood Moons*.

Mark Hitchcock in his book *Blood Moons Rising*[139] notes that the blood moon theory is built upon four main ideas.

1. God uses the heavens to give signs to humanity

2. The scientific fact of four blood moons in 2014-2015 falling on the Jewish feasts of Passover and Tabernacles

3. Scripture mentions the moon turning to blood in conjunction with the end times

4. When the four blood moons fell on Jewish feasts in the last 500 years (three times), something significant happened regarding the Jews.

He looks at what prophetic signs are and their significance. He takes us through the feasts in Leviticus 23, reviews where the eclipses are visible and the significance of that, looks at each of the Bible passages mentioning signs in the heavens and the end times, and finds problems with Hagee's conclusions.

He then looks at the past events associated with previous tetrads, noting that in two cases the historical events *preceded* the tetrads and in the third case *preceded* all eclipses but the first one.

Hitchcock reminds us of the detrimental effects resulting from previous declarations of dates for Christ's return (such as William Miller—1844, Jehovah's Witness founder Charles Taze Russell—1914 and eight more dates, Edgar Whisenant—1988, Harold Camping—1994 and 2011). He notes the danger of assigning "significant" events to particular years (one can find an event of significant for practically every year).[140]

We asked astronomer Dr. Hugh Ross and this was his response:

Recently there's been a lot of speculation by Christian leaders about the four blood moons prefacing the soon return of Jesus Christ to planet earth. The blood moon refers to what happens to the moon during an eclipse where the earth's shadow covers the moon and you actually see the light refracted from the earth glowing on the moon. And it kind of looks likes the color of blood actually. And so that's what's referred to as a blood moon. You can get two to five lunar eclipses taking place in a year. So a four blood moon event is where you get four of these lunar eclipses happening in one year. And there have been some people saying four is some kind of magic number and it's prefacing the return of Christ. Well, I'm old enough to have seen that event happen more than once. I don't think there's anything significant at all.

Proponents of this biblical prophecy regard the recent blood moons significant because they coincide with two important Jewish holidays: Passover and the Feast of Tabernacles (also known as the Feast of Booths). Joel 2:31 says: *"The sun shall be turned into darkness, and the moon into blood, before the great and terrible day of the LORD come."* This verse is being misused in speculation of end time events that are not doctrinally correct.

Appendix B:

What is the Judgment of the Sheep and the Goats in Matthew 25?

This chapter is from

Dr. Thomas O. Figart's article "In the Fulness of Time"[141]

When the Son of man shall come in his glory, and all the holy angels with him, then shall he sit upon the throne of his glory. (Matthew 25:31)

The time-sequence indications of the Olivet Discourse, which point to the coming of the Son of man are all at the *end* of the seven years of Tribulation. Here in verse 31 three specific indications are given: He shall come in His glory, all the holy angels will come with Him and He will sit upon His own throne of glory. In Revelation 3:21 He said that He *was not yet on His throne, but is sitting with His Father in the Father's throne.* The Messianic Kingdom cannot begin until He returns to earth with the angels and sits on His throne of glory and completes the judgment of unbelievers.

The Separation of the Sheep from the Goats

And before him shall be gathered all nations: and he shall separate them one from another, as a shepherd divides his sheep from the goats: And he shall set the sheep on his right hand, but the goats on the left. (Matthew 25:32-33)

As Revelation 7:9 clearly demonstrates, a numberless multitude *"from all nations"* will survive the Tribulation and stand *"before the throne and before Lamb."* The term **panta ta ethna,** "all the nations" occurs in a number of contexts with various meanings. In Romans 16:26 it refers to the gospel being made known *"to all the nations."* In Revelation 15:4 *"all nations shall come and worship before the Lord."* Such usage includes the entire human race. In other passages the same phrase is used to contrast Gentiles from Jews. In Luke 21:24, the Jews *"shall be led away captive into all nations* (panta ta ethna) *and Jerusalem shall be trodden down by the Gentiles* (hupo ethna)." This same contrast can be noted in Romans 3:29; 9:27; Galatians 2:12.

These Gentiles will be separated *"one from another,"* as a shepherd divides his sheep from his goats. Obviously, therefore, it will not be one nation as distinguished from another nation, but will be on an individual basis. It is hardly possible that every person in a given nation will be saved, nor that every individual in another nation will be lost.

The Commendation of the Sheep

Then shall the King say unto them on his right hand, Come, you blessed of my Father, inherit the kingdom prepared for you from the foundation of the world: For I was hungry, and you gave me food: I was thirsty, and you gave me drink: I was a stranger, and you took me in: Naked, and you clothed me: I was sick, and you visited me: I was in prison, and you came unto me. Then shall the righteous answer him, saying, Lord, when saw we you hungry, and fed you? or thirsty, and gave you drink? When saw we you a stranger, and took you in? or naked, and clothed you? Or when saw we you sick, or in prison, and came unto you? And the King shall answer and say unto them, Verily I say unto you, Since you have done it unto one of the least of these my brethren, you have done it unto me. (Matthew 25:34-40)

The sheep are called "the righteous" (verse 37) and are assured of entrance into the kingdom prepared for them from the foundation of the world. The promise that all nations shall be blessed was traced through Genesis 12:1-3, "*Now the Lord had said unto Abram, Get you out of your country, and from your kindred, and from your father's house, unto a land that I will show you: And I will make of you a great nation, and I will bless you, and make your name great; and you shall be a blessing: And I will bless them that bless you, and curse him that curses you: and in you shall all families of the earth be blessed.*"

One question which remains is the identification of "*these my brethren*" (Matthew 25:40). The time and place mentioned in verse 31 eliminates any reference to the Church saints, since they will have been raptured before the Tribulation. Indeed, the Church saints will be part of the King's entourage when He returns "*with all His saints*" (1 Thessalonians 3:13). This will also be true of the Old Testament saints who will be raised after the Tribulation and appear with Him in their glorified bodies (Daniel 12:1-3).

The 144,000 who were sealed early in the Tribulation (Matthew 24:14) will doubtless be part of His "brethren" and possibly many other Jews saved through their testimony during those seven years. The "righteous" Gentiles will be concerned about such Jews who suffer all the persecutions and privations mentioned by the Lord, but because of their righteous character, will not consider these deeds of kindness as especially heroic or unusual. They will perform such acts out of the intrinsic goodness of their hearts. William Kelly has put it this way: "Their last lesson was the first that Paul learned on the road to Damascus—the truth that startled his soul: 'I am Jesus whom thou persecutest'" (Kelly, William, *Lectures on the Gospel of Matthew*. New York: Loizeaux Brothers, Inc. 1950, page 484). The only difference is that these saved Gentiles did not know that they were doing good toward (not persecuting) Christ when they aided His "brethren."

The Condemnation of the Goats

Then shall he say also unto them on the left hand, Depart from me, you cursed, into everlasting fire, prepared for the devil and his angels: For I was hungry, and you gave me no food: I was thirsty, and you gave me no drink: I was a stranger, and you took me not in: naked, and you clothed me not: sick, and in prison, and you visited me not. Then shall they also answer him, saying, Lord, when saw we you hungry, or thirsty or a stranger, or naked, or sick, or in prison, and did not minister unto you? Then shall he answer them, saying, Verily I say unto you, since you did it not to one of the least of these, you did it not to me. (Matthew 25:41-45)

At first it seems inconceivable that anyone could go through a period of Tribulation and witness the sufferings of believers without helping them, but when the apostle Paul is remembered, he thought he was doing God a favor by persecuting believers. In Acts 26:9-11 he said: "*I verily thought within myself, that I ought to do many things contrary to the name of Jesus of Nazareth, Which thing I also did in Jerusalem; and many of the saints did I shut up in prison, having received authority from the chief priests. And when they were put to death, I gave my voice against them. And I punished them often in every synagogue, and compelled them to blaspheme; and being exceedingly mad against them, I persecuted them even unto foreign cities.*" Fortunately for Saul of Tarsus, he was informed directly by Christ that he was persecuting Him, and Saul became Paul before it was eternally too late.

One significant thing about the punishment pronounced by the Lord; He said that the *"everlasting fire"* was not double predestination; rather, it was *"prepared for the devil and his angels,"* not for the unsaved. Jesus reminded us that man is condemned already, not because he was predestined to this, but: *"because he hath not believed in the name of the only begotten Son of God"* (John 3:18). The Apostle John made it clear that: *"This is his commandment that we should believe on the name of his Son, Jesus Christ"* (1 John 3:23). God can never be held responsible for the sin of man which results in eternal punishment.

The Destination of the Sheep and the Goats

> *And these shall go away into everlasting punishment: but the righteous into life eternal.* (Matthew 25:46)

Jesus closes His discourse with a brief summary statement of the two destinies; the goats go away into everlasting punishment, and the sheep into life eternal. This judgment is not a general judgment, as some suppose. After this there is the Millenial Kingdom, (Revelation 20:1-6) and there will be children born to those "righteous ones" who enter the kingdom in normal bodies, not yet glorified. They will bear children, build houses; they will live long lives, and enjoy the kingdom (Isaiah 65:20-23). But at the end, there will be another judgment, since those born during those thousand years will either believe in Christ or reject Him; and those who reject Him will either be killed during the kingdom, or will be judged after the kingdom *"in the fulness of time"* at the Great White Throne Judgment (Revelation 20:11-15).

Appendix C:

What happens when a person dies?

In the New Testament the Greek word for Sheol is the word Hades. Just like Sheol, the word Hades is never used solely of the grave, but always refers to the world of departed spirits. Before Jesus' death and resurrection, He described Sheol, or Hades, the realm of the dead, as having two compartments.

Dr. Thomas O. Figart explains the order of events when believers and unbelievers die:

> From the time of Adam until the last person on earth dies, their bodies are separated from their souls and spirits until the resurrection of their bodies occurs. In all cases from the time of Adam until the ascension of Christ, the souls and spirits of the dead went to Sheol (the Hebrew word), which is the same as Hades (the Greek word). According to Christ's own teaching in Luke 16:19-31, in the account of the rich man and Lazarus, the beggar, when Lazarus died, "he was carried by the angels into Abraham's bosom" (v. 22), but when the rich man died, "in hell (Hades) he was in torments" (v. 23). He could see Abraham "afar off" (v. 23), but there was "a great gulf fixed" between them (v. 26) and it was impossible to pass from the one part of Hades to the other. In

Luke 23:43, Jesus said to the thief who believed in Him, "Today [notice, not after three days] thou shalt be with me in paradise." Therefore, at that time, "Abraham's bosom" and "paradise" were the same place, namely, that part of Hades (Hell) where the spirits of believers went, until the ascension of Christ; for then, as Ephesians 4:8-10 reveals, Jesus "descended into the lower parts of the earth (Abraham's bosom) (v. 9) and "led captivity captive" (v. 8) when he ascended up on high" (v. 8), far above all heavens" (v. 10).

Thus, Christ took all those spirits of believers to heaven and emptied "Abraham's bosom," transferring "paradise" up to heaven. We can prove this from 2 Corinthians 12:2-4 where the Apostle Paul speaks of himself as "such an one caught up to the third heaven" (v. 2), "he was caught up into paradise" (v. 4). Paul was alive, of course, and came back to tell us about his being caught up into paradise.

So now, ever since Christ's ascension, every believer who dies is taken immediately into the third heaven, because 2 Corinthians 5:6-8, "while we are at home in the body we are absent from the Lord" (v. 6). "We are confident, I say, and willing rather to be absent from the body, and to be present with the Lord." (v. 8).

The souls of unbelievers, from Adam's time onward, remain in Hades (Hell) in torment.

There will be two resurrections; the resurrection of believers, when we will be caught up together with those believers who have died, to meet the Lord in the air (1 Thessalonians 4:13-18). "We know that when He shall appear, we shall be like Him [with glorified bodies] for we shall see Him as He is" (1 John 3:2). Those who live after the Church Age and accept Christ and die during the seven years of Great Tribulation will be raised right before the 1000 year earthly Kingdom of Christ begins (Revelation 20:4).

The resurrection of the unsaved will occur after the 1000 year Kingdom of Christ (Revelation 20:7-15) "and whosoever was not found written in the Book of Life, was cast into the Lake of Fire" (v. 15).[142]

Appendix D:

Does our soul sleep when we die?

This section is from our series

What Will Happen to you One Minute After You Die?

By Dr. Erwin Lutzer

There is a figure of speech in Scripture sometimes spoken of as a "restful sleep." In John 11 Jesus says regarding Lazarus, "Lazarus sleeps." [John 11:11-12] Now, I have to pause here for a moment, because you know there are some people who believe in what is known as "soul sleep." They believe that when you die your soul sleeps until the day of resurrection so no one who dies is conscious today. Now, I strongly disagree with that and let me give you a couple of reasons why.

First of all, we find that Moses did not sleep until the day of resurrection, did he? He was there on the Mount of Transfiguration. But furthermore, think of Stephen. You know, when he was being stoned and the heavens were opened and Jesus was standing on the right hand of God the Father, Stephen knew that when he died, Christ would be there to receive him.

Perhaps the most powerful information about this comes to us from the thief on the cross. Jesus said to him, *"Today you will be with me in paradise."* [Luke 23:43] Now, I have a question to ask you. If you had been that thief, how would you have interpreted that? Would you not have thought that Jesus was making you a promise that you were going to meet in paradise on that very day?

No, it is not true that the soul sleeps. *"To be absent from the body is to be present with the Lord."* [2 Cor. 5:8] You know, when Paul said in the Book of Philippians so very clearly, *"I desire to depart and be with Christ which is far better,"* [Phil. 1:23] why would he have desired to depart and to be with Christ if indeed he wouldn't be with Christ after he died, he'd have to wait until the day of resurrection?

My friend, I want you to know that when you die, you die without a break in consciousness. You slip from this life into the next.

Now, here is the good news. Why does the Bible talk about death as "sleep"? It's not because our soul sleeps, it's because **our body sleeps**. And the body sleeps until the day of resurrection and Jesus Christ is going to speak the word and we're going to be resurrected.[144]

Appendix E:

What is the purpose of The Judgment Seat of Christ?

Let's look specifically at what the Bible says will happen at the Judgment Seat of Christ. First, the apostle Paul says in **2 Corinthians 5:10**, "*We must all appear before the judgment seat of Christ.*" The "*we*" he is talking about here is all Christians, all who have believed on Christ. We must be very clear about this—the Judgment Seat of Christ is only for Christians.

There are two major judgments mentioned in the Bible: first, the Judgment Seat of Christ. The purpose of this judgment will be to evaluate each Christian so that he or she can be properly rewarded for the way they have faithfully or unfaithfully served Christ on earth. All those who appear at the Judgment Seat of Christ will be in Heaven.

The second major judgment mentioned in the Bible is called the Great White Throne Judgment where all unbelievers will be judged. According to Revelation 20, those who appear at this Judgment will afterwards be cast into the lake of fire, what the Bible calls hell. The purpose of the Great White Throne Judgment will be to assess the degree of punishment in hell that each unbeliever will experience as a result of how he or she has lived.

There's a popular notion today, depicted in television commercials, that when everyone dies, they will all appear before God at His Judgment, and God will determine whether each person's good works outweighed their bad works. If they do, the person will be rewarded with Heaven. If they have done too many bad things, God will send them to hell. But, in the Bible, there is no such judgment mentioned. Whether a person goes to Heaven or hell is determined in this life, not the next. It is during this life we are to choose whether or not we will place our faith in Christ. At death, those who know Christ as Savior go directly to Heaven where someday the Judgment Seat of Christ will take place. Those who have not believed in Christ will go directly to a place called Hades, where they will be held in constant punishment until the Great White Throne Judgment takes place. Either way, all men will stand before God. Nobody will get by or escape. The Bible says every one of us will give an account of himself to God (**Romans 14:12**).

Now, these are frightening statements. We should take them seriously. We should also cling to God's promises in the Bible that everyone who believes in Christ will certainly be in Heaven, free from the eternal punishment of our sins. You say, "Where does the Bible teach that?"

In **1 John 5:13** we read: "*These things I have written to you who believe in the name of the Son of God in order that you may know* [not guess, or hope you'll get there] *that you have eternal life.*" Jesus Himself said, "*I tell you the truth, whoever hears my word and believes him who sent me has eternal life and will not be condemned. He has passed over from death to life*" (**John 5:24**). This means that once we put our trust solely in Jesus to save us and to be our Lord and Savior, He forgives all of our sins. From that very moment we stand eternally justified, free from any punishment due our sins. Jesus said, *"For my Father's will is that everyone who looks to the Son and believes in Him shall have eternal life"* (**John 6:40**). This is great news. And it is on the basis of these verses that I say, salvation is guaranteed to all those who accept Christ by faith. If you have trusted solely in Christ, you can be certain that you will be in Heaven.

Entering Heaven is one thing; having a possession there is another. According to the Bible, all believers have been given the gift of eternal life, but not all believers will inherit the same things, or receive the same rewards. The Bible is a realistic book. It does not assume that all believers will live faithfully all through their lives. In fact, the Bible gives many examples of believers who have lived unfaithfully. Does it make any difference whether or not we live faithfully for Christ? Yes, it does! The Bible says, *"We must all appear before the judgment seat of Christ that each one may receive what is due him for the things done while in the body, whether good or bad"* (**2 Corinthians 5:10**).

Now, the word **appear** here tells us why it is important for us to live for Christ. It comes from the Greek word ***phaneroo*** and literally means *"turned inside out,"* *"to be laid bare."* It's like taking a pocket in your pants and pulling it out, so that you expose whatever is in your pocket. At the Judgment Seat of Christ, our lives will be literally turned inside out, exposing all that we are.

Let me give you another illustration of what ***phaneroo*** means. Down in the South, in the springtime we have some very violent tornadoes. I'm sure you have seen what happens to a house when a tornado hits it. The roof is blown off; the walls are pushed down; furniture, clothes, personal belongings are all scattered around. Anyone who comes to that house afterwards can see all of the personal, secret articles in that home, they are exposed. When the Bible says we must all appear, it means our lives will literally be laid bare before Christ. All of our hypocrisies and concealments, all of our secret, intimate sins of thought and deed will be open to the scrutiny of Christ. Christ will be able to look through the rubble of our lives and pick out anything that is of value. When Christ looks at the innermost areas of your life, what will He find? Most of us shrink back at the thought of Christ closely examining our lives.

Is there any encouragement? Well, not one of us has ever lived perfectly or come close to that. When Christ evaluates our life, most of us will not be at one extreme or the other but somewhere toward the middle. Dr. Erwin Lutzer encourages us in his book, *Your Eternal Reward*, when he says, *"Christians can take comfort in the fact that we will appear before Christ, the One who died for us and loves us in spite of ourselves. He is our Savior. But the One who died to save us, now stands to judge us. He wishes us well and He loves us. He is not anxious to condemn us. He is our Brother—we share the same Father. The Judgment Seat of Christ is 'family business.'"* Don't you love that?

Appendix F:

What can we expect at the Judgment Seat of Christ?

The Bible says that at Christ's Judgment Seat, each of us "*will receive what is due us for the things done while in the body, whether **good** or **bad**.*" What does the Bible mean when it says "*good* or *bad*"? We all want to be rewarded for the "*good*." The "*good*" here refers to those times when we let Christ live out His life through us: we obeyed Him, served Him, and worked for Him. All that you have done for the Lord that no one else saw, Christ says He will remember. In **Mark 9:41** Jesus talked about the smallest deeds we have done for Him when He says, "*Even those who give a cup of water in My name will not lose their reward.*" Every deed you have ever done for Christ will be looked for, remembered and rewarded. And, as we will see, God is going to be more generous in His rewards than we could ever imagine.

Jesus says, whatever we do will be rewarded a hundred times as much. It will be fantastic. But then, the Bible also says we will also receive what is due us for the things done in the body that are "*bad*." "*Bad*" refers to those deeds that are worthless, foul, wicked deeds. These will be brought up to show us the rewards we have forfeited. When we stand before Christ, we will realize the rewards God wanted us to have but are forever lost to us because of our sinful living. Look at **1 Corinthians 3:13-15** where we read that this Judgment will be like a fire which "*will test the quality of each man's* work. *If what he has built survives, he will receive his reward. If it is burned up, he will suffer loss.*" Notice, he will not lose Heaven, but what he will lose is *reward*. Paul says in **verse 10** that a Christian "*should be careful how he builds.*" He compares our daily Christian living to building a house. As we live for Christ, our deeds of service to Christ are likened to valuable materials—such as gold, silver and costly stones. When we live selfishly and commit sins, the Bible likens these deeds to shoddy materials—such as wood, hay and straw.

The apostle says someday our work "*will be shown for what it is, because the Day will bring it to light. It will be revealed with fire, and the fire will test the quality of each man's work.*

Do you remember **Ephesians 2:8,9**? It says, "*For it is by grace you have been saved, through faith—this not from yourselves; it is the gift of God—not by works, so that no one can boast.*"

But then, **Ephesians 2:10** says, "*For we are God's workmanship, created in Christ Jesus to do good works, which God prepared in advance for us to do.*" What does this mean? When God saved us, He created us in Christ Jesus to do good works. These works are opportunities and jobs He opens and brings to us and wants us to do. If we do them, God promises to reward us. If we live for Christ, take advantage of the opportunities that come our way, someday we can receive a full reward from God. But we don't always live for Christ. We leave God out. We don't read our Bible; we live selfishly, and commit sins. Such living will result in our forfeiting, losing, the rewards God intended for us to have. Again, please keep in mind, God is not speaking about your forfeiting salvation and Heaven. Those are totally gifts given by God. No one can earn them. But after we are saved, rewards are gained by our faithfully serving Christ.

Now, the next question people usually ask is, *"What if I die with unconfessed sin? Will He be angry?"* Well, again, we're not going to lose Heaven. We are not going to be punished. Why? Because all of God's anger and wrath was placed on Christ when He died on the cross and paid for our sins. But if we live with unconfessed sins, though Jesus paid for them on the cross and we stand forgiven, we run the risk of hearing His rebuke at the Judgment Seat. He disciplines Christians here on earth. I expect He will do so at His Judgment Seat. Such sins will cost us the loss of rewards we could have had. We will see our lives through the eyes of our loving Lord and He will know all. His judgment will take into account every circumstance, every motive, and He will judge fairly. At the Judgment Seat of Christ arguments, unresolved conflicts, unconfessed sins will be resolved by the Judge who knows everything. That's why Paul advises in Colossians 3:23, "Whatever you do, work at it with all your heart, as working for the Lord, not for men, since you know that you will receive an inheritance from the Lord as a reward. It is the Lord Christ you are serving. Anyone who does wrong will be repaid for his wrong and there is no favoritism." Our Lord's judgment of our lives will be absolutely impartial. There will be no favorites.

As Erwin Lutzer has said, *"This is one courtroom in which no one has an advantage. The Judge will fairly determine what we did with what He gave us."*

Appendix G:

What are some of the rewards Christians can gain or lose?

I would like to begin with a story. I first saw this in a book by Stephen Covey.

Imagine for a moment that it's a beautiful day and you're driving down a country road. You enter a small town and see a church by the side of the road. You park your car in the crowded parking lot and go up the steps and enter the church. Inside you see that it's standing room only. You walk down the aisle looking for a place to sit. You can't help but wonder, "Why are all these people here?" And then you notice that up at the front of the church there is a casket. It's a funeral. You wonder, "Who died?" As you continue walking down the aisle looking for a place to sit, you realize you know some of the people in the audience. You see your boss from work and some of your coworkers. You notice your cousins are there. Then you're surprised to see your brother, your sister; your mom and dad are present. As you reach the front of the church, you go by the coffin. Out of curiosity you look inside and you're startled to find out *you* are in the coffin. It is your funeral. You stand off to the side and watch the proceedings. The minister asks some people to say a word about what your life meant to them. You watch as some of your coworkers come to the front and give a little speech. You listen carefully. Your boss gets up to say a word, and one by one, your neighbors, your relatives, your own brother and sister speak. Finally, your mom and dad talk about you. What would you hope to hear people say about you?

Stephen Covey says, *"The things you want to hear them say about you are really the fundamental values that you hold to."* If someday you want people to say those things, then every day you ought to live in such a way that you are not violating your deepest values. In brief, you ought to live with the end in mind. According to the Bible, that's true. Christians are to live with the end in mind. We are to see life from the perspective of our final accountability before God.

Another way of saying this would be to ask, *"When your life is over, what do you hope to hear Jesus say about you?"* That is what I want to talk about. What will Jesus say about you at His Judgment Seat? The apostle Paul wrote, *"We make it our goal to please Him"*—talking about Christ—*"whether we are at home in the body or away from it"*—that is, whether we are alive in the body or we have died and are away from it and with Christ, *"For we must all appear before the judgment seat of Christ, that each one may receive what is due him for the things done while in the body, whether good or bad"* (2 **Corinthians 5:9-10**). According to the Bible, the purpose of this Judgment will be to evaluate our lives as Christians so that we can be properly rewarded for the way we have faithfully or unfaithfully served Christ on earth. And it does matter. There are tremendous rewards the Christian can win or lose.

Look at **1 Corinthians 3:13-15** where we read that this Judgment will be like a fire which *"will test the quality of each man's work. If what he has built survives, he will receive his reward. If it is burned up, he will suffer loss."* Notice, he will not lose Heaven, but what he will lose is reward. Paul says in **verse 10** that a Christian *"should be careful how he builds."* He compares our daily Christian living to building a house. As we live for Christ, our deeds of service to Christ are likened to valuable materials—such as gold, silver and costly stones. When we live selfishly and commit sins, the Bible likens these deeds to shoddy materials—such as wood, hay and straw.

The apostle says someday our work *"will be shown for what it is, because the Day will bring it to light. It will be revealed with fire, and the fire will test the quality of each man's work."* In a moment we will examine more about what the Bible says about Christians losing eternal rewards and privileges.

But **first**, what are the rewards Christians can gain or lose at Christ's Judgment Seat? Here are just a few. In **Revelation 3:21** Jesus says, *"He who overcomes, I will grant to him to sit down with Me on My throne, as I also overcame and sat down with My Father on His throne."* I'm not sure we can even fathom all that Jesus is implying with these words, but obviously He is saying that believers can in some marvelous sense reign with Him if we overcome our problems. Do you have a problem you're facing? Then rejoice, because you qualify for gaining the reward of ruling in some measure with Christ someday. You may be facing problems of sickness, finances, or temptations of various sorts. We all face problems. Jesus says if we overcome our problems with His strength, He will grant us the privilege of someday reigning with Him.

Paul teaches the same thing in **2 Timothy** 2:12. He says, *"If we endure, we shall also reign with Him."* In **Revelation 2:26** Jesus says, *"He who overcomes and he who keeps my deeds until the end, to him I will give authority over the* *nations.*" So, if you overcome your problems, they can result in your being granted the privilege of reigning with Jesus in some capacity for all eternity.

The **second** reward the Bible teaches we can gain or lose is the reward of praise and honor that will come from God. Jesus says in **John 12:26**, "*My Father will honor the one who serves Me.*" What is this honor that is mentioned? I like to think of it in this manner. Picture yourself walking up to the Judgment Seat of Christ to meet Jesus. Behind Christ's throne the Father's presence is manifested in some spectacular way. As you approach Christ's throne, walking in front of all the angels and people gathered around, suddenly the Father in a booming voice says, "This person faithfully served My Son. I want to honor him." At that moment all of Heaven knows you have honored, you have faithfully served Christ. Maybe that is more imagination than fact, but in some fashion Jesus says, "the Father *will* honor the one who serves Me."

At the same time, Jesus warns us in **Matthew 6:1**, "*Be careful not to do your acts of righteousness before men to be seen by them.*" Unfortunately, many of us do exactly that. We do our acts of righteousness before men to be seen by them. Is that you? Well, if it is, notice what else Jesus says. "*If you do your acts of righteousness before men to be seen by them, you will have no reward from your Father in heaven.*" What reward will you get? The only reward you will get is that you have been noticed by the people you were trying to impress—and you know how long that usually lasts. It is far better to serve the Lord who will not forget you and whose honors and privileges will last for all eternity.

The **third** category of rewards the Bible mentions are the honors and privileges that accompany the crowns that God will give out. The apostle Paul in **1 Corinthians 9:24-27** encourages Christians to live in such a way as to get a crown and a full reward. He says, *"Run in such a way as to get the prize. Everyone who competes in the games goes into strict training. They do it to get a crown that will not last, but we do it to get a crown that will last forever."* Here Paul uses the Olympic races of his own time to illustrate how we should live the Christian life. He says, if you're going to run the race—that is, live the Christian life—run it in such a way as to get the prize, to win.

Now, in the Olympics in Greece, any athlete who won the race received a prize, a crown. The crown was actually a wreath made out of celery leaves. It only lasted for a few hours and then faded away. In comparison, Paul said Christians are seeking to get a crown that will last *"forever."* Now, what is this crown all about? Athletes who won in the Olympics received a crown which entitled them to other ongoing rewards when they got home. Sometimes they would be given a new home, and their children's education would be provided free. Sometimes, a home would be built for the athlete's parents, and for the rest of his life and his family's lives, none of them would pay taxes. So the crown symbolized continuing honors and rewards that continued for the rest of the athlete's life.

I believe this is also true about the crowns God will give. Yes, we can throw our crowns at Christ's feet, but the privileges they represent will continue to be ours even then, for all eternity. In the Bible there are **five different crowns** mentioned that Christians can receive for service to Christ. **First,** in **1 Thessalonians 2:19-20** we read about the *crown of rejoicing*. This crown is actually symbolic of the people we have led to the Lord. Paul says about

WHAT ARE SOME OF THE REWARDS...

these people, "*You are our glory and joy*" (1 Thessalonians 2:20). Someday, someone in Heaven will thank you for bringing them the Gospel. You also will thank someone for leading you to the Lord. The Gospel message goes right back to Christ Himself who brought it to earth and made it possible.

Second, in **1 Peter 5:1-4** we are told about a crown of glory that will be given to church elders who have served well in the Church. Peter writes, "*To the elders among you, I appeal as a fellow elder, a witness of Christ's sufferings and one who also will share in the glory to be revealed: Be shepherds of God's flock that is under your care, serving as overseers—not because you must, but because you are willing, as God wants you to be; not greedy for money, but eager to serve; not lording it over those entrusted to you, but being examples to the flock. And when the Chief Shepherd appears, you will receive the crown of glory that will never fade away.*"

Third, in **2 Timothy 4:7-8** we see the crown of righteousness that will be given to those who eagerly await for Christ's appearing: "*I have fought the good fight, I have finished the race, I have kept the faith. Now there is in store for me the crown of righteousness, which the Lord, the righteous Judge, will award to me on that day—and not only to me, but also to all who have longed for His appearing*" (2 Timothy 4:7-8).

Fourth, in **James 1:12** we see the crown of life, which I believe is a heightened form of experiencing heaven and God, that will be given to those who endure the sufferings of temptation. James says, "*Blessed is the man who perseveres under trial, because when he has stood the test, he will receive the crown of life that God has promised to those who love Him*" (James 1:12).

Fifth, in **1 Corinthians 9:25** we see the crown of mastery that will be given to those who have mastered the sins of the body. Paul says, *"Everyone who competes in the games goes into strict training. They do it to get a crown that will not last; but we do it to get a crown that will last forever"* (1 Cor. 9:25).

If these are some of the rewards we, as Christians can gain, what are some of the rewards the Bible says we can lose if we live undisciplined, faithless lives? **First**, we can lose the approval of our Lord and receive His rebuke instead. Remember, the unfaithful servant who hid his talent in the ground in **Matthew 25**? That man received a stinging rebuke from his master instead of approval. In that parable the lord said to his servant, *"You wicked, lazy servant!"* I wonder if the Lord will say that to any of us? In **Colossians 3:23** we are told, *"It is the Lord Christ you are serving. Anyone who does wrong will be repaid for his wrong and there is no favoritism."* Pastors, missionaries, Sunday School teachers, we will all be judged impartially; there will be no favorites who get by.

That's why, when we sin, we should confess our sins as soon as the Lord reveals them to us. **1 Corinthians 11:31-32** says, *"But if we judged ourselves we would not come under judgment."* This means, if we judged ourselves and confessed our sin to the Lord, then we wouldn't experience the Lord's judgment and discipline on our lives. This is speaking of Christ's discipline of us in this life and also when we stand before His Judgment Seat. Maybe you ask, What if I can't remember every sin I've ever done? Don't worry. Confess those you know. Then ask God if there is anything He sees in your life that needs His forgiveness. Let the Holy Spirit guide you. As He reveals things, confess them and turn away from whatever it is. If nothing comes to mind, then be at peace. Keep in mind God's promise in **1 John 1:9** which says, "*If we confess our sins, he is faithful and just to forgive us our sins, and to cleanse us from all unrighteousness.*" The Greek word translated "*to cleanse*" means "*He will keep on cleansing us*" from all sin. That is, God graciously cleanses our lives from that which we know and that which we don't remember or aren't aware of. Just walk with Him daily and He promises to cleanse us from all sin.

The **second** reward we can lose at the Judgment Seat of Christ is—we risk seeing our reward given to another. In **Matthew 25** the Lord said concerning the unfaithful servant, "*Take the talent from him and give it to the one who has the ten talents. For everyone who has will be given more and he will have an abundance. Whoever does not have, even what he has will be taken from him.*"

In **Revelation 3:11** Christians are warned by Jesus: "*I am coming soon. Hold on to what you have so that no one will take your crown.*" Jesus isn't talking about losing heaven here; He is talking about our rewards. He says, Hold on, continue faithfully serving Me or another will be given your reward. The apostle John wrote to Christians and said, "*Watch out that you do not lose what you have worked for, but that you may be rewarded fully*" (**2 John 1:8**).

The **third** thing we can lose at the Judgment Seat of Christ is honor. The Bible says unfaithful Christians will be ashamed instead of honored. In **1 John 2:28** we read, "*Abide in him that when he shall appear, we may have confidence and not be ashamed before him at his coming.*" Will there be tears in heaven? Yes, I believe there will be tears at the Judgment Seat of Christ. Many Christians will be ashamed before Christ. In **Luke 9:26** Jesus said, "*For whoever is ashamed of me and my words, of him will the Son of man be ashamed when he comes in his glory, in the glory of the Father and of the holy angels.*"

Are you ashamed now to identify yourself with Jesus and with His words? If so, change now or Christ will be ashamed of you later. Someone might say, if this is what is going to happen at the Judgment Seat of Christ, Heaven sounds like a downer. That's not true. We need to hold what the Bible teaches in balance. At the Judgment Seat of Christ there will be tears and regrets. But shortly after the Judgment Seat of Christ the Bible says *"God shall wipe away all tears from their eyes; and there shall be no more death, neither sorrow, nor crying, neither shall there be any more pain; for the former things are passed away"* (**Revelation 21:4**). Also, everyone's cup will be full; it's just that the size cups will be different. Also, keep in mind that God will be very generous with His rewards. He promises to reward us a hundred times more than we deserve (**Matthew 19**).

In light of all that the Bible teaches about eternal rewards, how are you living your life for Christ now? If you really believe what the Bible teaches, it would be foolish to do anything else but say, *"Lord, help me live for you."* He will and it will be worth it.

Appendix H:

What was the length of a year in Daniel 9?

(This section is taken from our Book *The Case for Jesus the Messiah*.)

We have already seen that the "weeks" are "years." But what is the length of the year? How many days?

The calendar year used in the Scriptures must be determined from the Scriptures themselves. We will show why Daniel's figures were based on a year of 360 days.

In the Scriptures we find a historical example in Genesis 7. Comparing Genesis 7:11 with Genesis 8:4 and the two of these with Genesis 7:24 and Genesis 8:3, it is apparent that the flood began on the seventeenth day of the second month and came to an end on the seventeenth day of the seventh month, a period of exactly five months.

Then in Genesis 8:3, the length of the five-month period is given in days, and it is stated to be exactly "150 days." Dividing 150 days by five months leads to the conclusion that thirty days was the length of a month. Twelve such months would be a 360-day year.

The second example is found in the prophetical passages of Daniel and Revelation. As we have already seen, a "week" in Daniel 9 stood for a period of seven years. In Daniel 9:27 a future persecution is said to begin in the "middle" of the seventieth week. Obviously, the middle of a week (a seven-year period of time) is three and one-half years.

Two chapters earlier in Daniel 7:24-25, the same persecution is spoken of. There the duration of persecution is also given as "*a time, times, and half a time*," or three and a half years.

Then, Revelation 13:4-7 speaks of the same future persecution lasting "forty and two months." Forty-two months is exactly three and a half years.

Finally, Revelation 12:13,14 refers to the same event, and states the duration of time in the exact same words used in Daniel 7:25—"*a time, and times, and half a time.*" In Revelation 12:6 this period is given an exact number of days—one thousand two hundred and sixty days, which is exactly three and a half years or forty-two months.

Therefore, it is clear that the number of days in a year used by Daniel in the seventy-weeks prophecy is fixed by Scripture itself as exactly 360 days.

The Church Father Jerome, writing in 406-408 A.D., agreed. He acknowledged that "the Hebrews...did not number their months according to the movement of the sun [365 days], but rather according to the moon [360 days]."[144] (Israel had various methods of intercalating [adjusting] their 360 days so the year would come out correctly with a solar year. A 360-day year is strange to our ears, but it was the common calendar of those times.[145]

Thus, from the decree of Artaxerxes in 444 B.C. until after the 69th week, 483 years later, when Gabriel announced the Messiah would be killed in Jerusalem, we discover this turns out to be the very time in which Christ Himself lived.

Professor Harold W. Hoehner, in his *Chronological Aspects of the Life of Christ*[12] explains in detail the calculations:

Using the [accepted] 360-day [lunar] year the calculation would be as follows. Multiplying the 69 weeks by seven years for each week by 360 days gives a total of 173,880 days. The difference between 444 B.C. and A.D. 33, then, is 476 solar years. By multiplying 476 by 365.24219879 or by 365 days, 5 hours, 48 minutes, 45.975 seconds, one comes to 173,855.28662404 days or 173,855 days, 6 hours, 52 minutes, 44 seconds. This leaves only 25 days to be accounted for between 444 B.C. and A.D. 33. By adding the 25 days to March 5 (of 444 B.C.), one comes to March 30 (of A.D. 33) which was Nisan 10 [Jewish calendar] in A.D. 33. This is the triumphal entry of Jesus into Jerusalem.... As predicted in Zechariah 9:9, Christ presented himself to Israel as Messiah the King for the last time and the multitude of the disciples shouted loudly by quoting from a Messianic psalm: "Blessed is the King who comes in the name of the Lord" (Ps. 118:26; Mt. 21:9; Mk. 11:10; Lk. 19:38; Jn. 12:13). This occurred on Monday, Nisan 10 (March 30) and only four days later on Friday, Nisan 14, April 3rd, A.D. 33, Jesus was cut off or crucified.[146]

Notes

1. William F. Arndt and F. Wilbur Gingrich, *A Greek-English Lexicon of the New Testament*, p. 365

2. Wilhelm Michaelis, "kratos," *Theological Dictionary of the New Testament*, Vol. III, p. 907.

3. Ibid., p. 908.

4. Walter Grundmann, "dunamis," *Theological Dictionary of the New Testament*, Vol. II, p. 295.

5. Ibid., pp. 292, 306.

6. *Rational Apocalypticum*, Vol. I, p. 202.

7. Richard D. Patterson, "seper," *Theological Wordbook of the Old Testament*, Vol. II, p. 633.

8. "sphragis," *Theological Dictionary of the New Testament*, Vol. VII, p. 940.

9. C. F. Keil, *Biblical Commentary on The Book Of Daniel*, p. 505.

10. Ibid.

11. Leon Wood, *A Commentary on Daniel*, p. 319.

12. Harold W. Hoehner, *Chronological Aspects of the Life of Christ*

13. Edward Gibbon, *History of Christianity*. New York: Peter Eckler Publishing Company, 1916, pp. 141-4.

14. J. C. I. Gieseler, *Text-Book of Ecclesiastical History*, Vol. I, trans. from the third German Edition by Francis Cunningham. Philadelphia: Carey, Lea, and Blanchard, 1836, p. 100.

15. Henry C. Sheldon, *History of Christian Doctrine*, New York: Harper and Brothers, 1886, p. 145.

16. Eerdmans Publishing Company, 1973, p. 614.

17. Adolph Harnack, "Millennium," *The Encyclopedia Britannica*, Ninth Edition (New York: Charles Scribner's Sons, 1883, XVI, p. 314.

18. Ibid., XVI, p. 315.

19. Ibid.

20. Ibid.

21. Ibid.

22. Ibid., XVI, p. 316.

23. Ibid.

24. Will Durant, *Caesar and Christ*, New York: Simon and Schuster, 1944, pp. 564-565.

25. Ibid., p. 575.

26. Ibid., p. 603.

27. Elgin Moyer and Earle E. Cairns, *Wycliffe Biographical Dictionary of the Church*, Chicago: Moody Press, 1982, pp. 314-315.

28. Irenaeus, *Against Heresies*, Book V, chap. 33, section 4 in *The Ante-Nicene Fathers*, edited by Rev. Alexander Roberts and James Donaldson, Buffalo: The Christian Literature Publishing Company, 1885, I, p. 563.

29. Moyer and Cairns, *Biographical Dictionary*, p. 135

30. Eusebius Pamphilus, *Eusebius' Ecclesiastical History*, Book III, p. 39.

31. *The Apostolic Fathers* in *The Fathers of the Church*, edited by Ludwig Schopp, et al., translated by Francis X. Glimm, Joseph M. F. Marique, and Gerald G. Walsh, Washington, D.C.: The Catholic University of America Press, 1962, I, p. 378.

32. *The Epistle of Barnabas* in *The Ante-Nicene Fathers*, edited by Rev. Alexander Roberts and James Donaldson, Buffalo: The Christian Literature Publishing Company, 1885, I, pp. 133, 135.

33. *The Epistle of Barnabas*, chap. 15, in *The Ante-Nicene Fathers*, I, p. 146.

34. Ibid.

35. Moyer and Cairns, *Biographical Dictionary*, pp. 220-221.

36. Justin Martyr, *Dialogue With Trypho*, chap. 80, in *The Ante-Nicene Christian Library*, edited by Rev. Alexander Roberts and James Donaldson, Edinburgh: T. & T. Clark, 1867, II, p. 200.

37. Ibid., chap. 81, II, p. 201.

38. Elgin Moyer and Earle E. Cairns, *Wycliffe Biographical Dictionary of the Church*, Chicago: Moody Press, 1982, p. 204.

39. Irenaeus, *Against Heresies*, Book V, chap. 33, section 3, in *The Ante-Nicene Fathers*, edited by Alexander Roberts and James Donaldson, Buffalo: The Christian Literature Publishing Company, 1885, I, pp. 562-563.

40. Ibid., p. 563.

41. Ibid., section 4, I, p. 563.

42. Ibid., chap. 35, section 1, I, p. 565.

43. Ibid., p. 565.

44. Ibid., chap. 36, section 3, I, p. 567.

45. Ibid., chap. 35, section 2, I, p. 565.

46. Ibid., p. 566.

47. Moyer and Cairns, *Biographical Dictionary*, p. 396.

48. Tertullian, *Against Marcion*, Book III, chap. 25, in *The Ante-Nicene Fathers*, edited by Rev. Alexander Roberts and James Donaldson, Buffalo: The Christian Literature Publishing Company, 1885, III, p. 342.

49. Ibid., p. 343.

50. Elgin Moyer and Earle E. Cairns, *Wycliffe Biographical Dictionary of the Church*, Chicago: Moody Press, 1982, p. 233.

51. *The Fathers of the Church*, edited by Roy Joseph Defarrari, et. al., translated by Mary Francis McDonald, Washington, D.C.: The Catholic University Of America Press, 1964, p. 49, xii-xiii.

52. Ibid., xvi.

53. Moyer and Cairns, *Biographical Dictionary*, p. 233.

54. *The Fathers of the Church*, p. 49, xvi).

55. Lactantius, *The Divine Institutes*, Book VII, chap. 14, in *The Fathers of the Church*, edited by Roy Joseph Defarrari, et al., translated by Mary Francis McDonald, Washington, D.C.: The Catholic University of America Press, 1964, pp. 49, 510.

56. Ibid., chap. 15, pp. 49, 512.

57. Ibid.

58. Ibid., p. 513.

59. Ibid., chap. 19, pp. 49, 521.

60. Ibid., chap. 22, pp. 49, 527.

61. Ibid., chap. 24, pp. 49, 530.

62. Ibid.

63. Ibid., p. 531.

64. Ibid.

65. Ibid., p. 533.

66. Ibid., chap. 26, pp. 49, 535-536.

67. Ernest R. Sandeen, "Millennialism," *The Encyclopaedia Britannica*, Fifteenth Edition (Chicago: Encyclopaedia Britannica, Inc., 1974), pp. 12, 201.

68. Adolph Harnack, "Millennium," *The Encyclopaedia Britannica*, Ninth Edition (New York: Charles Schribner's Sons, 1882), XVI, p. 316.

69. Ibid.

70. Ibid.

71. Ibid.

72. Ibid.

73. Ibid.

74. Philip Schaff, *History of the Church*, Vol. II (Grand Rapids: Wm. B. Eerdmans Publishing Company, 1973), p. 787.

75. Ibid.

76. Earnest R. Sandeen, "Millennialism," *The Encyclopaedia Britannica*, Fifteenth Edition (Chicago: Encyclopaedia Britannica, Inc., 1974), pp. 12, 201.

77. Adolph Harnack, "Millennium," *The Encyclopaedia Britannica*, Ninth Edition (New York: Charles Scribner's Sons, 1883), XVI, p. 316.

78. Ibid.

79. Philip Schaff, *History of the Christian Church*, Vol. II (Grand Rapids: Wm. B. Eerdmans Publishing Company, 1973), p. 791.

80. Ibid., p. 792.

81. Ibid., pp. 618-619.

82. Harnack, "Millennium," XVI, p. 316.

83. Ibid.

84. Ibid.

85. Ibid.

86. Ibid.

87. Ibid.

88. Ibid.

89. Adolph Harnack, "Millennium," *The Encyclopaedia Britannica*, Ninth Edition (New York: Charles Scribner's Sons, 1883), XVI, p. 317.

90. Ibid.

91. Ibid.

92. Ibid.

93. Ibid.

94. Ibid.

95. Ibid.

96. Ibid.

97. Augustine, *The City of God*, Book XX, chap. 9, trans. by Marcus Dods (New York: Random House, Inc., 1950), p. 725.

98. Ibid., pp. 725-726.

99. Ernest R. Sandeen, "Millennialism," *The Encyclopaedia Britannica*, Fifteenth Edition (Chicago: Encyclopaedia Britannica, Inc., 1974), pp. 12, 202.

100. Ibid.

101. Ibid.

102. Augustine, *The City of God*, Book XX, chap. 7, p. 719.

103. Ibid., p. 720.

104. Ibid.

105. Ibid., Book XX, chap. 8, p. 722.

106. Ibid., p. 723.

107. Ibid., Book XX, chap. 6, p. 717.

108. Sandeen, "Millennialism," pp. 12, 202.

109. Harnack, "Millennium," XVI, p. 317.

110. Ibid.

111. Ibid., p. 319

112. Ibid.

113. Ernest R. Sandeen, "Millennialism," *The Encyclopaedia Britannica*, Fifth Edition (Chicago: Encyclopaedia Britannica, Inc., 1974), pp. 12, 202.

114. Ibid.

115. Ibid.

116. Ibid.

117. George N. H. Peters, *The Theocratic Kingdom*, Vol. 1 (Grand Rapids: Kregel Publications, 1957), p. 538.

118. Ibid.

119. Sandeen, "Millennialism," pp. 12, 202.

120. Ibid.

121. Ibid.

122. John F. Walvoord, *The Millennial Kingdom* (Findlay Ohio: Dunham Publishing Company, 1959), p. 22.

123. Ibid.

124. Sandeen, "Millennialism," pp. 12, 202.

125. Walvoord, *The Millennial Kingdom*, pp. 7, 23-24, 29, 30-34.

126. Sandeen, "Millennialism," pp. 12, 202; Walvoord, *The Millennial Kingdom*, pp. 24, 31-32.

127. Sandeen, "Millennialism," pp. 12, 202.

128. Ibid., pp. 202-203.

129. Ibid., p. 202.

130. Ibid., p. 203.

131. John F. Walvoord, *The Millennial Kingdom* (Findlay, Ohio: Dunham Publishing Company, 1959), p. 23.

132. Ernest R. Sandeen, "Millennialism," *The Encyclopaedia Britannica*, Fifteenth Edition (Chicago: Encyclopaedia Britannica, Inc., 1974), pp. 12, 203.

133. Walvoord, *The Millennial Kingdom*, p. 23.

134. Ibid., p. 24; Earle E. Cairns, *Christianity Through The Centuries* (Grand Rapids: Zondervan Publishing House, 1954), p. 463; Elgin Moyer and Earle E. Cairns, *Wycliffe Biographical Dictionary of the Church* (Chicago: Moody Press, 1982), p. 79.

135. "Our Fair Lady: The Statue of Liberty," *Reader's Digest*, July, 1986, pp. 53, 193-194, 197, 203.

136. John F. Walvoord, *The Millennial Kingdom* (Findlay, Ohio: Dunham Publishing Company, 1959), p. 18.

137. Ernest R. Sandeen, "Millennialism," *The Encyclopaedia Britannica*, Fifteenth Edition (Chicago: Encyclopaedia Britannica, Inc., 1974), pp. 12, 203.

138. John F. Walvoord, *The Millennial Kingdom*, p. 30.

139. Mark Hitchcock, *Blood Moons Rising: Bible Prophecy, Israel, and the Four Blood Moons*, Tyndale House Publishers, Inc., 2014.

140. Book review posted by Joan Nienhuis at http://bookwomanjoan.blogspot. com/2014/04/blood-moons-rising-by-mark-hitchcock.html.

141. Dr. Thomas O. Figart; ©2011, http://www.jashow.org/wiki/index.php/ In_the_Fulness_of_Time/Part_143.

142. Dr. Thomas O. Figart, What Does the Bible Say About.../Part 14 article: http://www.jashow.org/wiki/index.php/What_Does_the_Bible_Say_ About.../Part_14 - Why_did_Jesus_talk_to_Moses_and_Elijah.3F.E2.80.9D _.28Matthew_17:1-13..29.

143. Dr. Erwin Lutzer, *What Will Happen to you One Minute After You Die?*. DVD available at http://www.jashow.org/resources/what-happens-one-minute-after-you-die.html.

144. Gleason L. Archer, Jr. (Tr.). *Jerome's Commentary on Daniel*. Grand Rapids, MI: Baker, 1977. p. 97.

145. Harold W. Hoehner. *Chronological Aspects of the Life of Christ*. Grand Rapids, MI: Zondervan/Academie, 1977. p. 136.

146. Ibid., pp. 138-139.

About the Authors

Dr. John Ankerberg, host of the award-winning John Ankerberg Show, has three earned degrees: an MA in church history and the philosophy of Christian thought, an MDiv from Trinity Evangelical Divinity School, and a DMin from Luther Rice Seminary. He has authored, co-authored and/or edited **155 books and study guides in 20 languages, his writings have sold more than 3 million copies and reach millions of readers each year online.**

Dr. Renald E. Showers is widely recognized as one of the most distinguished theologians in America today. He holds degrees from Wheaton College, Dallas Theological Seminary, and Grace Theological Seminary. He has served on the faculties of Lancaster Bible College, Moody Bible Institute, and Philadelphia College of the Bible. He is a the author of many books, including The coming Apocalypse and The Most High God.

Cathy Sims is director of international outreach for The John Ankerberg Show and previously worked for nearly a decade in the international ministry department of Precept Ministries. Cathy has also taught Bible studies for many years, including numerous aspects of biblical prophecy that have helped many to better know and apply God's Word.

How to Begin a Personal Relationship with God

If you would like to begin a personal relationship with God that promises joy, forgiveness, and eternal life, you can do so right now by doing the following:

- Believe that God exists and that he sent his Son Jesus Christ in human form to Earth (John 3:16; Romans 10:9).

- Accept God's free gift of new life through the death and resurrection of God's only son, Jesus Christ, that he offers you (Ephesians 2:8-9).

- Commit to following God's plan for your life (1 Peter 1:21-23; Ephesians 2:1-7).

- Determine to make Jesus Christ the ultimate Leader and final Authority of your life (Matthew 7:21-27; 1 John 4:15).

There is no magic formula or special prayer to begin your relationship with God. However, the following prayer is one that can be used to accept God's free gift of salvation through Jesus Christ by faith:

"Dear Lord Jesus, I admit that I have sinned. I know I cannot save myself. Thank You for dying on the cross and taking my place. I believe that Your death was for me and receive Your sacrifice on my behalf. I transfer all of my trust from myself and turn all of my desires over to You. I open the door of my life to You and by faith receive You as my Savior and Lord,

making You the ultimate Leader of my life. Thank you for forgiving my
sins and giving me eternal life. Amen."

If you have made this decision, congratulations! You have just made the greatest commitment of your life. As a new follower of Jesus, you will have many questions and we invite you to visit our website at jashow.org to see the many resources we have available or contact us at (423)892-7722. We would love to encourage you and help you as you begin your relationship with Christ.

Other ways you can grow in your new relationship with God include:

- Spending regular time in prayer and Bible reading.

- Finding a Bible teaching church where you can grow with other followers of Christ.

- Seeking opportunities to tell others about Jesus through acts of service and everyday conversations.

For more information on growing in your relationship with God, please visit www.JAshow.org. You can also receive additional materials by contacting us at:

The Ankerberg Theological Research Institute
P.O. Box 8977
Chattanooga, TN 37414
Phone: (423) 892-7722.